Castrum to Castle

Castrum to Castle

Classical to Medieval Fortifications in the Lands of the Western Roman Empire

J.E. Kaufmann and H.W. Kaufmann

Pen & Sword
MILITARY

An imprint of
Pen & Sword Books Ltd
Yorkshire - Philadelphia

Frontispiece: *The Cathar castle of Puylaurens in the Languedoc.*

First published in Great Britain in 2018 by
PEN & SWORD MILITARY
An imprint of
Pen & Sword Books Ltd
Yorkshire - Philadelphia

Copyright © J.E. Kaufmann and H.W. Kaufmann 2018

ISBN 978 1 47389 580 5

The right of J.E. Kaufmann and H.W. Kaufmann to be identified as
Authors of this Work has been asserted by them in accordance
with the Copyright, Designs and Patents Act 1988.

A CIP catalogue record for this book is
available from the British Library

Typeset in Ehrhardt
by Mac Style

Printed and bound in India
by Replika Press Pvt. Ltd.

Pen & Sword Books Limited incorporates the imprints of Atlas,
Archaeology, Aviation, Discovery, Family History, Fiction, History, Maritime, Military,
Military Classics, Politics, Select, Transport,
True Crime, Air World, Frontline Publishing, Leo Cooper,
Remember When, Seaforth Publishing, The Praetorian Press, Wharncliffe Local
History, Wharncliffe Transport,
Wharncliffe True Crime and White Owl.

For a complete list of Pen & Sword titles please contact

PEN & SWORD BOOKS LTD
47 Church Street, Barnsley, South Yorkshire, S70 2AS, England
E-mail: enquiries@pen-and-sword.co.uk
Website: www.pen-and-sword.co.uk

Or

PEN & SWORD BOOKS
1950 Lawrence Rd, Havertown, PA 19083, USA
E-mail: Uspen-and-sword@casematepublishers.com
Website: www.penandswordbooks.com

Contents

Preface

From the Roman Era until the Renaissance, fortifications in Western Europe developed slowly as technological advancements led to architectural innovations. Their strategic role altered based on the size and types of armies prevalent in each era. The Roman army of the Christian Era increased in size to maintain control over the expanding empire and keep in check the massive 'Barbarian' armies that threatened its borders. In an effort to secure their land borders, the Romans built numerous fortifications and created defensive lines requiring a massive military force ready for action year round. Most of Rome's enemies could not maintain large forces over an extended period because they lacked logistical capabilities and, in many cases, they had to attend to their farmlands. The Roman limes across Germania and the Hadrian and Antonine Walls held raiders at bay while castra throughout the empire provided a base for control of key centres. The glue that held all this together for the Romans and allowed for logistical support and reinforcements was the Roman road system. The collapse of the Western Roman Empire in the fifth century changed all this. Huns, Vandals, Goths, Angles, Saxons and others ate away at the empire, finally overrunning large sections of it until even Rome itself was attacked despite its towering Aurelian Walls.

As Western Europe sank into the Dark Ages, new kingdoms appeared in the carcass of the old Western Roman Empire. In most, a feudal system eventually evolved and changed the size of armies and the role of fortifications. The warrior class of the Barbarian tribes evolved into an aristocratic class that relied on serfs to form usually poorly trained and armed militias. The maintenance of the old network of Roman roads and bridges and the upkeep of a standing army eventually became onerous tasks for some monarchs. The nobility often received land grants (fiefs) with resident serfs in exchange for providing military service and soldiers. Some of these kingdoms fared better than others. In the early eighth century, the Franks founded their own empire after the Visigothic kingdom in Iberia collapsed in the face of an Islamic invasion. The Frankish Empire fragmented as Viking raiders targeted their lands in the latter part of the Dark Ages. The Anglo-Saxons, who had replaced the Romans in England during the fifth century, also suffered attacks from these Norsemen. The Celtic people of Ireland built tall stone towers as refuges from the Viking attacks while the kingdoms of England relied on largely earthen and timber forts or castles.

By the tenth century, as the Dark Ages waned, the Franks resorted to building stone castles. In general, however, during the Dark Ages and the remainder of the Middle Ages, lines of fortifications became as impractical as large armies had been. Hundreds of castles of various sizes made of wood or stone cropped up in Europe; most were small and sheltered a single noble family and its retainers.

There is no consensus among historians about the various phases of the medieval era. In simple terms, the first half of the period from the fall of the Western Roman Empire until about 1000 AD has been called the Dark Ages. It is followed by the High Middle Ages, which has two classical ending dates of 1453 and 1492, but actually overlaps with the Renaissance. Many historians further divide this last half into the High Middle Ages ending at the beginning of the fourteenth century followed by the Late Middle Ages that gives way to the Renaissance. This volume covers the history of the fortifications in the lands that were part of the Western Roman Empire and its successors from the first century to the fourteenth century. It concentrates mostly on England and France. The next volume will cover the Iberian Peninsula and the Reconquista, the eastern frontiers of France, the Hundred Years War and changes brought by the appearance of cannons and the development of fortifications during the Renaissance.

This work includes historical background associated with the fortifications in addition to their descriptions. For a more detailed description of the medieval fortifications and a general survey that covers all of Europe we recommend our earlier publication titled *Medieval Fortress* and Sidney Toy's *Castles* and E.E. Viollet-le-Duc's *Military Architecture*.

Acknowledgements

We would like to thank the following people and organizations for their assistance in preparing this project: Miguel Andújar (photo of model), Stephen and Lucy Dawson (photos), Pierre Etcheto (photos and data), Martyn Gregg (photos), Rupert Harding (photos), Gabriella and Lorenzo Mundo (photos), Bernard Lowery (photos and data), Wojtech Ostrowski (illustrations), Colonel Adrian Traas (photos and documents) and Lee Unterborn (data).

Also, thanks to Dr Ann Welton, Hon. Curator at the Old Bell Museum, Montgomery, Wales, for permission to use photograph of a model of Norman motte and bailey at Hen Domen made by Peter Scholefield, and to Mark Hartwell and the Stafford Borough Council in Wales for permission to use drawings of Stafford Castle.

Chapter One

The Roman Era

From Fortified Camp to Fortified Frontier

In the fourth century BC, Ancient Rome, like most other city-states, was protected by walls to ward off its enemies. Built early in that century, the Servian Walls, built of tufa – a soft limestone common in Italy – surrounded the City on Seven Hills. Like those of other cities, they included a ditch on the outside and probably an earthen backing that provided additional support for the masonry and a wall walk. Late in the late third century BC, these walls warded off Hannibal's army during the Second Punic War. However, before the war, the Romans had not been greatly concerned in building fortifications since they had focused on expansion. Their main military weapon for offense and defence became well-built roads that allowed their legions to move quickly to any threatened spot and prepare for offensive operations, react to an invasion and dominate land trade. During the Civil War in the first century BC, the old walls of Rome were reinforced and modernized. According to nineteenth-century historian Theodor Mommsen, after Julius Caesar conquered Gaul the Romans adopted a policy of 'aggressive defence', which was implemented mainly under Caesar's successor, Augustus. It consisted of maintaining positions along the frontier, which incorporated rivers and man-made ramparts. In addition, the Romans founded colonies in the conquered territories and formed alliances with the neighbouring tribes, which served as buffers against other tribes located beyond them. Sometimes, these colonies were established in or near fortifications built by the Roman legions. This policy allowed the Romans time to 'civilize' and acculturate the conquered territories.

Well before the first century AD, the Romans had become skilled builders and used field fortifications like no others before them. Their work, however, was not totally original for they borrowed their construction methods from the Greeks and other peoples of the Hellenistic Age[1] and improved upon them. When a Roman legion advanced into hostile territory, each night it stopped it built a fortified encampment, which was a virtual fort or even a fortress considering the number of men (5,000 or more) it held. During each day the unit remained at the same location, the troops continued to strengthen the position with turf and timber[2] until it became a veritable 'legionary fortress' in our modern terminology. This, however, did not happen very often until the first century AD.

The Roman Empire occupied most of Western Europe, including modern day France, Spain, Portugal and England before the end of the first century AD. Its tentacles reached into what are now the Low Countries, parts of Germany along the Rhine and much of Britain where border walls were built after the first century AD. At the same time, Rome concentrated on holding the Rhine and the area between the Rhine and Danube rivers along the frontier with the hostile Germanic tribes. The Danube formed a frontier for the Roman Empire in Eastern Europe. In all cases, the Romans depended on fortifications to protect the territories they held. The defences from the Netherlands along the Rhine to Switzerland eventually formed the boundary between Germanic and Latinized Europe not only during

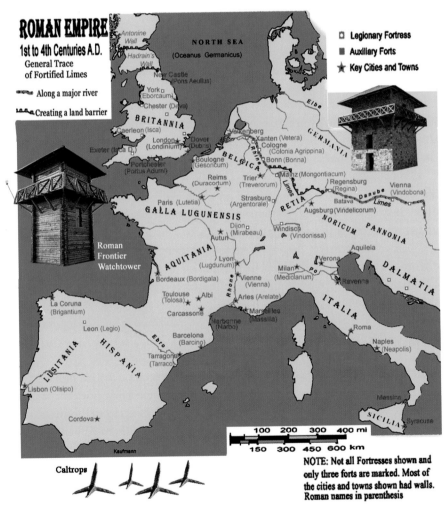

Map of the Roman Limes. Modified by Kaufmann from the 1911 atlas by Shepard. Photos of reconstructed watchtowers: wooden tower near Utrecht by Niels Bosboom, and stone tower near Kastell Zugmantel by Oliver Abels. (From Wikimedia)

the Roman Era, but well into the Middle Ages. This region was first fortified with the Roman limes and eventually became the home of the French Maginot Line and German West Wall, becoming the most heavily fortified area in Europe. Due to the development of feudalism, which resulted in a different type of warfare, this area had no defensive lines during the medieval period.

During the first two centuries AD, especially after the destruction of three legions of Emperor Augustus in the Teutoburg Forest (in modern day Germany) in AD 9, the Romans launched another campaign against the barbarians. It ended in AD 17 when Emperor Tiberius ordered his legions to withdraw behind the Rhine in Lower Germania. Next, Rome tried to consolidate its borders by establishing a fixed frontier and fortifying it. The Romans referred to the frontier as the 'limes' or limits. As these borders were fortified, the term 'limes' eventually came to mean fortified line.[3] Mommsen discovered that the frontier was marked by an Imperial frontier road and an adjacent ditch that resulted from excavating the soil to form an agger or road embankment or rampart.[4] Roman colonies sprouted around the forts built along the Rhine and Danube barriers. An actual defensive line connected the two rivers in the region known as Raetia.[5] The legions struck at the barbarians on the other side of the frontier from their fortified camp whenever they appeared to threaten the empire's security. The section of the limes along the Rhine and the Danube relied mostly on water barriers. The Rhine positions spanned a total length of about 568km (353 miles) and over time it came to include over fifty forts and hundreds of watchtowers.

Defence of the Lower Rhine: The Batavian Revolt of AD 69–70

The death of Nero in AD 68 triggered a far-reaching civil war. As a result, AD 69 became the 'Year of Four Emperors', the third of whom was Vitellius. The seven legions in upper and lower Germania proclaimed him emperor in January 69. That same month, the Praetorian Guard in Rome eliminated Galba and installed Otho as emperor. Vitellius marched on Rome and defeated Otho's army near Cremona at the Battle of Bedriacum in mid-April. Otho committed suicide. In July, with Vitellius still in power, the eastern legions proclaimed Vespasian as emperor during the Jewish War. In October 69, Vespasian's troops defeated Vitellius' legions at the Second Battle of Bedriacum in late December, fought their way into Rome and killed Vitellius. Vespasian did not reach Rome from Egypt until the summer of 70.

The civil war encouraged Julius Civilis, a Batavian auxiliary commander, to lead a revolt in Batavia. In addition to locals, he recruited five cohorts (about 480 men each) of Batavians at Mogontiacum (Mainz). En route, he notified the commander of I Legion at Bonna (Bonn) that he only wanted to pass through without fighting. However, 3,000 legionaries and some auxiliaries came out of the fortress to stop him. Eventually, the Romans broke and retreated to the ditch and gates of the fortress where they took heavy losses. The defeated I Legion 'Germanica' at Bonna surrendered and the fortress was destroyed. The Batavians moved on, avoiding Cologne.

In the autumn of AD 69, the Batavians had the advantage, according to Tacitus. Three legions deserted and joined the rebels. Civilis defeated the Roman V and XV Legions near Noviomagus (Nijmegen). The defeated legionaries retreated to the fortress of Vetera (Xanten). According to Tacitus, the remnants of this force, which included about 5,000 men and a large number of camp followers, took refuge in the fortress, which was well stocked with everything except food. Further up the Rhine another earth-and-timber fortress at Novaesium (Neuss), was destroyed by the rebels and the remnant of its XVI Legion made their way to Vetera. When the revolt had begun in the autumn of AD 69, a coastal tribe supporting the Batavians had launched a surprise attack on the Valkenburg fort, which stood near the mouth of the Rhine protected by the river and was surrounded by three water ditches and destroyed it. Smaller Roman forts in the region had been evacuated and burned while a naval flotilla was lost to the rebels. The Batavians outnumbered the Roman forces including those at the fortress of Mogontiacum (Mainz). The only remaining major force was the XXI Legion in Upper Germania at the fortresses of Vindonissa (Windisch).

The Roman commanders at Vetera had strengthened the ramparts and walls and removed the nearby buildings of a small town. They ordered the legionaries to loot the area to supplement their meagre food supply. The fortress, observed Tacitus, stood partially on the gentle slope of a hill and partially on level ground, a situation that was not ideal for defence.

The rebels opened their attack on the fortress with a hail of missiles from a distance, failing to cause any damage while the defenders pelted them with stones, inflicting casualties. The Batavians next 'charged with a wild shout and surged up to the rampart, some using scaling ladders, others climbing over their comrades who formed a "tortoise". No sooner did some of them scale the wall, however, than the besieged repelled them with swords and shields and buried them under a cloud of stakes and javelins.'

The Batavians resorted to siege engines, with which they were quite unfamiliar. Deserters and prisoners had to show them how to build a sort of bridge or platform of timber on which they fitted wheels to roll it forward. Some of the men stood on this platform and fought as though they stood on a mound, while others, concealed inside, tried to undermine the walls. The defenders, however, destroyed this rude contraption with stones hurled from catapults. Next, the Batavians readied hurdles and mantlets, but the besieged set them ablaze with flaming spears shot from engines and even targeted the assailants themselves with fire-darts.[6]

These setbacks did not end Civilis' efforts to take the fortress by storm. According to Tacitus, his men clamoured for a fight and fought with 'blind fury', so he sent them once again to destroy the rampart. They were beaten back again, suffering losses that mattered little because there were so numerous. During the night, they lit huge fires around the ramparts and sat there drinking wine. They hurled their missiles against the defenders who riposted with great effect. Since the rebels' bright ornaments reflected in the fire making them easy targets, Civilis ordered his men to douse the fires. The Romans stayed on watch the whole night. At the merest sound of rebels climbing the walls or setting a scaling ladder against it, they stood ready to push them back from the battlements with their shields and swords and shower them with javelins. After sunrise, the Batavians appeared with a two-storey wooden tower, which they proceeded to haul up to one of the gates. The legionaries, wrote Tacitus, 'by using strong poles and hurling wooden beams, soon battered it to pieces, with great loss of life'. The weapon that terrified the rebels the most, he observed, was a crane with a movable arm that hung above the enemy below the walls. This arm suddenly dropped and snatched one or more warriors, swung around and tossed them into the middle of the camp.

At this point, Civilis concluded that the fortress had limited provisions and decided to wait the defenders out by continuing the siege. His overconfident German troops, he concluded, lacked the means and skill to succeed in this type of warfare. He launched a surprise attack against the Romans on 1 December at Krefeld and lost in a Pyrrhic victory for the Romans. At this point, he gave up the siege of Vetera and advanced on Mogontiacum. The Romans sent a relief expedition to Vetera, resupplied the fort and strengthened it defences. However, since Mogontiacum was threatened, the Roman force withdrew taking 1,000 of Vetera's defenders with it. As the Romans moved to protect the Mogontiacum fortress, Civilis broke off his siege there and returned to besiege Vetera. In March AD 70, their supplies exhausted, the Romans surrendered Vetera on condition their two legions would be allowed retreat behind Roman lines. The rebels broke their pledge and attacked and destroyed the two legions shortly after they left their fort, despite Civilis' efforts to stop them.

Vespasian's response was to send eight legions to put down the rebellion. A treaty was signed in AD 70. A legion was sent to build a new fortress at Noviomagus in order to strengthen control of the area. Other legions replaced the destroyed fortresses at Bonna, Vetera and Novaesium with stone ones. The fortress at Novaesium remained in service for only a few decades and was replaced with a fort. The Roman defences along the fortified limes of the first century and even the second century were strong despite the events of the Batavian Revolt.

Roman expansion ended early in the second century AD when Emperor Trajan conquered Dacia. He also completed and strengthened the Limes Germanicus begun by Augustus. Lewis Sergeant, another nineteenth-century historian, wrote,

> Starting on the Main and nearly bisecting the great curve of that river already mentioned, it ran northwards, about half-way between the modern Frankfort and Karlstadt; then, taking a wide sweep over hill and valley and morass, amongst the sources of many northward and southward streams, climbing the crests of the Taunus and the northern limits of the Rheingau, it approached the Rhine opposite to Vosolvia (Ober-Wesel). Hence it ran parallel to the stream, across the Lahn, over against Confluentes (Coblenz), at the embouchure of the Mosella and past the modern Ehrenbreitstein, ending in what is now called the Westerwald, a little above the town of Bonn and the tributary Sieg.
>
> The Limes ended at Rigomagus (Remagen) on the Rhine and thence, along the left bank, ran a line of Roman forts, the chief of which were Bonna (Bonn), Colonia Agrippina (Cologne), Durnomagus (Dormagen), Novæsium (Neuss), Gelduba (Gellep), Asciburgum (Asburg), Vetera Castra (Birten), Colonia Trajana, Burginatium (Schenkenschanz) and Noviomagus Batavorum (Nimeguen). From Remagen to Nimeguen is a distance of about 105 miles in a straight line. Near some of these towns there would be permanent Roman camps, whilst some of them were Roman colonies …[7]

In Britannia, Emperor Hadrian, Trajan's successor, ordered the construction of the wall that bears his name across the island to keep the northern tribes at bay. Emperor Antoninus Pius, who succeeded Hadrian, advanced the position northward, creating a new wall that was later abandoned. These walls were different than those on the land frontiers of Europe.[8]

The Romans marked their limes with a vallum (a defensive wall or rampart),[9] which may have been merely an earthen rampart that served as a boundary marker not always intended as a fortification. The fortified limes consisted of a vallum made of the materials from the excavation of the defensive ditch or fossa, usually V-shaped, in front of it. The work was done by Roman troops who often added a wooden palisade to the rampart. Wooden watchtowers, garrisoned by about eight men,[10] served as signal stations between forts and were positioned at regular intervals on the frontier. Some had a surrounding wall and ditch.[11]

Auxiliary forts and legion fortresses, often associated with a Roman colony, occupied key locations on or behind the limes. They usually stood on high ground or at river crossings and some blocked mountain passes. The size and shape of the fortifications varied, but they generally followed a standard pattern. The forts were smaller than a legionary fortress (see sidebar for terminology).

They were built by Roman auxiliary units that usually consisted of non-Romans who were promised citizenship after about twenty-five years of service. The auxiliary units received assistance from engineer specialists from a nearby Roman legion. The shapes and components of both types of fortification were more or less standardized. They were usually square or rectangular, but some conformed to the terrain. Rounded corners were standard. All work was done by legionaries and auxiliary troops in the same way as the entrenched camps during a campaign. The auxiliary forts varied in size from large enough for self-sufficiency to smaller ones that had no headquarters and were probably detached from another position. The smaller positions usually had a single entrance and have been referred to as fortlets. Size also depended on the type of unit (infantry or cavalry) that occupied it, but in the centuries AD the units on the frontier included a cavalry element. Standard features for most forts were similar to those of a legionary fortress. They included barracks, whose number depended on the size and type of detachment it held, a residence for the commander and a centrally-located headquarters. Large forts usually included a granary and most had additional buildings. With few exceptions, the entrances of the fort were situated at or near the centre of each of its four sides. In the later part of the third century, under Diocletian, the number of entrances was reduced as was the size of forts, which were built with higher walls twice as thick as earlier works and no longer used earthen backing. These new forts were meant for smaller garrisons since before the end of the third century a large fort held housed a 500-man cohort and a legionary fortress, a legion of 5,000 to 6,000 men. This reduced size became standard to match the smaller size of the legions, which now numbered as few as 1,000 to 2,000 men. Auxiliary units were reduced to 25 per cent of their original strength. When they had to renovate older positions during this period, the troops rebuilt the walls to enclose a smaller area, but left the old surrounding fossa and added new ones between them and the new walls thus creating three to five ditches.

The Romans also fortified landing sites on the Rhine and Danube because the navy could resupply forts more efficiently by water than by road since ships had a larger cargo capacity than wagons. A fortification was often built on the enemy side of the river, opposite a fort or fortress, to protect the ships while they were unloading. It seems that most of these sites were built during the reign of Constantine and Valentinian.

Fortresses and Forts

One of the first features created for a fortress or fort was the fossa or ditch. The excavated dirt formed the earthen vallum or rampart. This ditch was usually up to 2m (6.5ft) deep and 6m (19.6ft) wide.[12] Many forts had two V-shaped fossae that included obstacles such as an abatis. In front to many of the ditches there were 'Caesar's Lilies', a Roman equivalent of a minefield. These were pits about 1m (3.3ft) deep containing a sharpened stake usually camouflaged with a covering of vegetation. Caltrops may have served as obstacles as well, but evidence of their use is limited.

The earthen rampart or vallum, was 2m (6.5ft) or more in width and about 3m (9.8ft) high.[13] It was covered with slabs of sod (turves) to hold the soil in place and prevent it from washing away into the ditch. The vallum was topped by either wooden palisades or stone walls depending on the era and location. For much of the first century AD the rampart was made only of earth. After AD 50 it appears that the ramparts received a stone face if it was not already made of stone or brick as the fortifications took on a more permanent nature. Some researchers have determined that a well-built earthen fortification could last many years before it needed restoration. However, if they were occupied for a few years or decades, it is only logical that the garrison

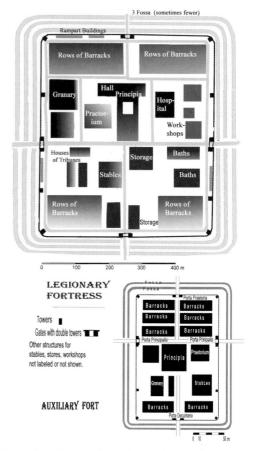

Examples of Roman forts. Top: Legionary fortress. Bottom: Auxiliary fort.

performed maintenance as needed and probably had to clear the fossa often to maintain its V shape. The Romans certainly did not consider the turf-and-timber structures as temporary since they maintained some of them for decades. Sometimes, stone was used to replace wooden features during the repair phase not only of the walls and towers but also of the interior buildings. Stone walls, like the wooden ones, had crenellations. Wooden walls were as thick as the timbers used and placed upon the earthen rampart, which usually had a firm foundation. When stone walls replaced the wooden ones, the soldiers had to cut back part of the front of the earthen rampart to allow for space for the new wall unless it was a new fortification built from scratch. On the sites rebuilt in stone, the earthen rampart remained behind the stone wall as reinforcement unless buildings were later added. Historians seldom agree on the thickness of the stone walls since few examples remain and those that still survive vary in width. When a stone wall was built it often consisted of a core of rubble instead of actual blocks of stone and its thickness varied, averaging 3m (9.8ft). In contrast, stone walls built into the rampart to replace wooden ones were 1m to 1.5m (3.3ft to 4.9ft) thick. The height of the walls is difficult to determine, but most sources give an average of 4m (13.1ft).[14] According to M.C. Bishop, the walls of the fortress of Albing, located in Austria at the confluence of the Danube and the Enns, ranged from 1.8m to 3.5m (5.9ft to 11.4ft) in thickness and up to 5m (16.4ft) in height at the level of the wall-walk.[15]

The gates and towers were distinctive features of Roman legionary fortresses and auxiliary forts. Gates were flanked by a tower on each side. Towers also stood at each of the rounded corners and between the corner tower and entrance gate there were one or more intermediate towers depending on the size of the site. Some forts had neither intermediate towers nor a tower at every corner. Wooden towers supposedly could mount the Roman artillery (ballista), but stone towers offered more defensive benefits. Wooden towers were relatively simple while the stone ones often included arched windows with shutters and, in the case of those adjacent to the gate, a tiled roof. Wooden towers were usually square; the stone ones also tended to be square in the beginning, but later acquired a 'U' or 'D' shape whose rounded section projected beyond the fort's walls thus covering the walls and the entrance.

The area enclosed by the walls varied in size. Early in the first century AD, the army created double legionary fortresses that held two legions. A regular fortress for a single legion could reach up to 500m (547 yds) in length and occupy up to 25 ha (62.5 acres), making it virtually a small town. By the second century, its size shrank to 10 to 15 ha (25 to 37.5 acres). The auxiliary forts occupied a smaller area since they were often intended only for a cohort of about 500 men. Fort Valkenburg, a typical square fort measured about 120m x 120m (131.2 yds x 131.2 yds) and occupied 1.4 ha (3.5 acres). Some of the larger auxiliary forts covered 4 to 6 ha (16 to 30 acres). Auxiliary forts had a number of common features, but they did not include all the facilities found in a legionary fortress. Some of these forts were so small that archaeologists have called them fortlets because they lacked a principia (headquarters facility) and held less than a cohort. There was also a smaller type of fortress of intermediate size between auxiliary forts and legionary fortresses. They were called vexillation fortresses because they housed a detachment from a legion. The *Concise Oxford Dictionary of Archaeology* defines them as temporary bases for detachments (vexillatio) of 2,500 to 4,000 troops from a Roman legion and occupying an area of 6.4 ha to 12.0 ha.[16]

Comparison of First-Century Legionary Fortresses to Eighteenth- and Nineteenth-Century Forts

Fort or Fortress	Shape & Length of sides	Area occupied	Estimated Garrison
First century Roman:			
Vetera (double legionary)	Rectangle 600 x 800m	56.0 ha	10,000
A typical legionary fortress	Square 400 x 400m	16.0 ha	5,000
Eighteenth-century forts in America:			
British Ft. George (near Pensacola)	Square 73 x 73m	.53 ha	1,100
Castillo San Marcos (St. Augustine)	Square 41 x 41m (plus bastions)	.47 ha ?	
Nineteenth-century forts in America:			
Ft. Sumter (Charleston)	Polygon 61 x 92m	.9 ha	650
Ft. Morgan (Mobile)	Polygon 100m each	1.5 ha (not incl. bastions)	600
Ft. Pulaski (Georgia)	Polygon 165m sides & 201m side	3.6 ha.	400

Fortification Terminology of the Roman Empire

The distinction between fort and fortress has never been easy to make. Duncan Campbell, author of *Roman Auxiliary Forts*, points out that early archaeologists used the Latin terms 'castra' for Roman fortresses and the term 'castellum' for forts. The latter generally applied to sites built for auxiliary units, but not always. According to modern terminology, the Roman fortress was greater in size and strength than the auxiliary fort and was even, in some cases, a fortified city. It included most of the amenities of a Roman town. During the reign of Augustus and later, the founding of Roman towns and colonies, mainly by veterans, was part of the Roman strategy of establishing a hold on conquered lands.

Terms associated with parts of Roman fortifications include vallum, porta, praetorium, principia, barracks and balneum. They are found in *De munitionibus castrorum*, the work of a little-known Roman writer of the late second century AD and contemporary of Trajan called Hyginus Gromaticus or Pseudo-Hyginus. According to Hyginus, the entrenched camp of Gelligaer covered up to 40.5 ha (100 acres) and was capable of holding 30,000 men. However, John Ward, author of *The Roman Fort of Gellygaer*, points out that there is no evidence that this particular site was as large as Hyginus claimed.

Another contemporary source of information about the Roman military and its fortified camps was the fourth century AD writer Publius Flavius Vegetius Renatus. The only other description of a Roman entrenched camp is to be found in *The Histories* of the Greek Polybius who composed his work about three centuries earlier during the second century BC. Some illustrations of the Roman fortifications are found on Trajan's Column in Rome. The *Notitia Dignitatum* (The List of Offices) from the late fourth century listed commanders, their units and the places where they were stationed. Otherwise, information from ancient sources is rather scant.

Agger – raised work including an earthen embankment or rampart with no revetment.

Armamentarium – armoury.

Auxilia – usually foreign troops from around the empire hired to serve as light troops. They often included such specialists as archers, slingers, light cavalry, etc.

Balneum – bath.

Basilica – the cross-hall in the principia with an oblong shape, colonnaded and semicircular apse used for trials or assemblies.

Burgus (p. burgi) – small town, military tower or castellum.

Canaba (pl. canabae) – hut, the plural term refers to a group of huts i.e. the civilian settlement adjacent to a fort.

Campus – training area or field.

Castellum – small military camps or civilian community.

Castrum (pl. castra) – military camp of any size. There were no Latin terms, except for castellum, to distinguish these fortifications by size or to indicate whether they were temporary or permanent (field camps, forts or fortresses).

Castra hiberna or **Castra stativa** – winter camps or forts that were permanent.

Castra aestival – temporary summer camps built during the campaigning season in enemy territory.

Castra stativa – permanent or static camp.

Centuria – barrack block.

Civitas (pl. civitates) – planned town founded by Roman officials.

Cohort – a force of about 500 men. Usually ten cohorts to a legion, the first being larger than the others

Colonia (pl. coloniae) – Roman settlements (colonies) in occupied territory. During the first century AD they were formed from retired veterans. They included Arles, Narbonne, Colchester, Lincoln, York and Merida and many others. Arles and Merida were founded in the first century AD.

Fabrica – workshop.

Fossa – the defensive ditch, usually V-shaped.

Groma – survey instrument used for laying out the camp or fort.

Horrea – storage building, including granaries.

Intervallum – space between the walls and buildings inside the fortification.

Porta – door or gate.

Porta decumana – rear gate.

Porta praetoriana – main gate.

Praetorium – commanding officer's quarters, usually adjacent to the headquarters.

Principia – headquarters.

Thermae – (thermal) baths.

Turris (pl. turres) – watchtower or turret.

Valetudinarium – hospital.

Vallum – walls or ramparts of a fortification. Some authors use this term instead of fossa.

Via decumana – road leading to the rear entrance (porta decumana) of the fort.

Via praetoriana – main road leading to main entrance (porta praetoriana).

Via principalis – main road that runs between the two side entrances – porta principalis sinistra (left) and porta principalis destra (right).

Vicus – settlement, they usually appeared near forts and fortresses. See civitates.

The principia or headquarters was the heart of all fortifications. It was generally located in a central position at the intersection of main road or via praetoriana and a lateral road running between the two side gates. When the fortification was built of stone or was converted to stone, the principia was built like a forum with a peristyle courtyard that included in many cases a number of rooms, a hall with columns and a basilica. The hall and the basilica were reserved for official functions. Several of the rooms served as offices. A shrine included a place for the unit's standards and a subterranean vault where money and other valuables were kept. Some of the rooms were used as an armoury.

The commander and his officers had their own quarters. The commander's, located next to the principia, was called the praetorium. In a legionary fortress, it was large and included lodgings for the commander's family and servants. It included an interior courtyard, a dining room, a kitchen, a bath and a toilet. In some cases, it comprised stables for his horses. The tribunes' houses were similar but smaller. In newly-built or timber fortifications these structures may have been much simpler than in the stone ones.

Hospitals were found in fortresses, but they were not a common feature in forts because auxiliary units lacked the specialized personnel. Baths, on the other hand, were considered necessary for hygiene. However, they were often outside the ramparts because their heating system could be a fire hazard, especially when most of the structures were wooden. The baths included a changing room like a modern-day locker room in a gym. From there the men entered a series of warmer rooms with baths that became progressively hotter. One of the rooms was a steam room heated by hot air circulating beneath the floor and produced by heat from a furnace room. The hottest room was like a sauna. After cleaning their bodies with scrapers and even oils, they entered a cold bath. The private bath in the commander's quarters had fewer features. To supply the baths, water was diverted from a nearby source (stream, river, etc.) and, if necessary, carried by an aqueduct to the fort entering near one of the gates to keep it under observation. It filled a large reservoir from which pipes, often made of lead, carried it underground to various points in the fort including the baths, the latrines and even smaller tanks the troops used for washing and cooking. The communal latrines were located against the ramparts, with the cooking ovens. Like those provided for the officers, they had running water that kept the sewage flowing out of the fort through a sewer system. Running water and other sanitary facilities would not be found in fortifications or most cities in the West for centuries (more than a millennium) after the fall of Rome.

The troops were quartered in barrack blocks that usually housed eighty men[17] of a century per barracks. The centurion had separate quarters that included a bedroom and living room. Each contubernium or group of eight men was allotted one bedroom in the back and one storage room in front for equipment, personal effects and cooking facilities. The barracks and the other structures in the fortress had two levels at times. In some masonry forts, the foundation of the buildings or part of the walls were made of stones and the rest of the structure was made of timber. The granaries had raised floors and ventilation slits below to keep vermin out and to prevent the stored grain from rotting and possibly spontaneously combusting. Granaries may have been the first structures to be converted into stone. A fortress often had other storage facilities as well as workshops that produced a variety of items from bricks to weapons. Some fortresses and forts included stables. The buildings were either of wood, brick, stone or a combination of these materials. They usually and had tile roofs.

Outside the walls of a fortress, there often was a training or parade ground, an amphitheatre, a bathhouse and even burial grounds. Settlements often grew nearby and some fortresses even became the centre of a new colony.

During the reign of Augustus in the first century AD, marching camps became permanent and their tents were replaced with wooden structures. More sophisticated features, like plumbing and bathhouses, were added.[18] By mid-century, Rome's strategy led to gradually changing from walls of timber and turf to stone. Specialists often were brought from a nearby legion to direct construction of some parts of the forts. Although the Roman fortresses and forts tended to follow a standard pattern, each one was also unique when it came to the actual details of the layout. The size and character of these Roman fortifications changed during the last five centuries of the empire in the West. Their ruins are not as intact as those of many medieval castles and post-medieval fortifications. Most of the information we have about them comes from the limited ancient sources mentioned and from archaeological excavations. As a result, there has been a great deal of speculation about them. However, these Roman fortifications greatly resemble the European castles of the High Middle Ages, whose non-defensive features within the walls generally lack the sophistication of the Roman amenities.

Another key feature and trademark of the Roman Empire was its road network which was used for political, economic and military purposes. The Roman forts and fortresses were linked to this system, which extended right into the fortifications. The street grid was similar in both forts and fortresses. In addition to the via praetoriana and the via decumana, there was a road that ran around the base of the ramparts giving quick access to threatened areas. Some forts did not have four gates. The troops employed standard road building methods within the fortress. The roads inside and outside the fortifications were metalled (cobles covered with a surface layer of small or crushed stone) and included a drainage system. D-shaped tower and towers projecting beyond the walls were not incorporated in Roman defences until the Late Roman Empire.

The Legionary Fortress

In general, the legionary fortress served as the base for a legion that controlled a province. In provinces with internal strife, more than one legion and fortress were needed. In some cases, when a detachment (vexillatio) was needed in a certain area, the smaller vexillation fortress was built. Auxiliary units and their forts were also deployed where necessary. The greatest concentration of legionary fortresses and auxiliary forts was along the Limes of Europe from the Rhine to the Danube and in northern Britain.[19] Legions were not supposed to be quartered in Rome, but the Praetorian Guard, created by Augustus, had the equivalent of a legionary fortress on the outskirts of Rome, which later became incorporated into the Aurelian Walls.

Although legionary fortresses and the auxiliary forts had many features in common, no two forts nor two fortresses were identical. The size, shape, style and even the location of interior buildings varied. One reason for this was that, as far as we know, there were no standardized blueprints for the construction of these positions. In addition, legions or auxiliary cohorts seldom had the opportunity to build such permanent positions even though they had experience in building marching camps, which were rather standardized. A permanent position required other considerations based on the location and resources needed and available. As a result, the main features of each fortified site were typical, but their execution varied from place to place.

The Roman legionary fortress at Bonn typifies the evolution of a Roman fortress during the four centuries of the empire. The ramparts almost formed a square 524m by 528m (573 yds by 577 yds), covering 27.8 ha (69.5 acres). Its original entrances were centrally located in each wall. The first fortress was built of timber and turf by I Legion Germanica between the reigns of Caligula and Nero. Sometime between the reign of Vespasian in the first century and the mid-fourth century, it was rebuilt in stone by I Legion Minerva, which adds to the difficulty in dating the ruins that were occupied for so many centuries. Not all historians and archaeologists are in agreement. According to one source, I Legion built the camp with earthen ramparts in AD 43 and replaced the wooden buildings with stone ones in AD 52. More recent archaeological work indicates the first stone work was begun after AD 71. The fort was rebuilt once more in the 230s and major internal changes were made in the mid-second century and under Constantine's reign in the fourth century. The Franks destroyed the fortress about ten years after Constantine's reign. Roman troops reoccupied the abandoned site and rebuilt the fortress with some changes in AD 360. Stephen Johnson contends that these last renovations occurred before the Constantine era.[20] However, his research was done before the 1980s when no distinction was made. According to Johnson, the Bonn fortress had a typical playing-card shape, common before the fourth century, and was surrounded by double ditches.[21] The first stone walls of an unspecified date were relatively thin and lacked the backing of an earthen rampart. They included non-projecting rectangular towers for the gates and intervals along with masonry structures on the interior of the walls to support a wall-walk. The main street between two entrances passed by the principia and praetorium. Communal latrines were located along the inside of the western wall: the officers had private latrines in their quarters. Ten barracks buildings were located adjacent to the road that went around the ramparts and gave access to the wall walk. Stables were located next to the two main roads that ran across the fort from the four entrances. The compound included a military hospital and the baths, which was unusual since it was customary to place the baths about 100m (109 yds) or more outside the walls. Several farm buildings occupied positions between barracks. The tribunes' quarters were near the principia and praetorium. The officers had their own facilities, including private latrines. The immunes (legionnaire specialists such as carpenters, engineers, artillerymen, medical personnel, etc.) also had their own quarters.

The fortress at Bonn was contemporaneous with other Rhine fortresses such as Cologne, Remagen, Koblenz, Boppard and Bingen, which stood about 20km (12.4 miles) apart. According to John Breeze, it belonged to the same system of forts that protected permanent bridges, were supposedly 'built with thick walls, bastions, two single-portal gates protected by projecting towers', and included about sixteen buildings, mostly barracks.[22] Bonn, however, does not seem to exhibit all the characteristics of these Constantine-era forts. It must be said, however, that it may be difficult to ascertain the changes it underwent from the extant remains. The fortress at Cologne, on the other hand, presented all of the features mentioned above and has only two single-portal entrances, which replaced twin-portal entrances. It also had two rows of eight rectangular long buildings none of which appeared to be the traditional praetorium or principia. Instead of towers, these newer fortresses had circular bastions (towers), but the gates were still flanked by D-shaped towers. As Johnson points out, there was no earthen backing for the new, thick walls. During the Late Empire, when the castra were rebuilt, their gates were often blocked up leaving only two gates. In addition, posterns (a small entrance) for sorties were placed next to some of the towers. Breeze attributes the D-shaped towers to Diocletian. He also points out that an increasing number of new forts had irregular oval or triangular shapes and that barracks were built along the walls making 'these forts more like medieval castles than earlier Roman forts'.[23]

Roman Strategy and the Army

Every century or so significant transformations affected strategy and the role of fortifications in the Roman army. The first centuries of the Republic saw the evolution of the formidable Roman legions. The most significant change took place in 107 BC when Marius turned the citizen army into a professional one. In times of war, the soldiers were no longer drawn from the property-owning class. Instead, the poor could enlist for periods of about sixteen years, later raised to twenty-five years, and the government provided their weapons. On completion of their service they received land in conquered territories to help establish colonies in the empire. The new system created a better trained and more effective military force as Rome expanded across the Mediterranean world. One drawback of the professional army was that the legionaries often demonstrated more loyalty to their generals and paymasters than to their government. The result was civil wars, one of which led to the creation of an empire and others that weakened it in the face of the barbarian threat.

Until the time of Augustus and even later, the overarching strategy was one of conquest. The legions' primary tactical actions were offensive rather than defensive. The defeat in the Teutoburg Forest in AD 9 forced the Romans to pull back from Germania and create defensive positions. Expansion of the empire ended early in the second century AD with Trajan's conquest of Romania. Fortifications became necessary as the empire went on the defensive. This was followed by Hadrian pulling the army back from Scotland and creating his wall. The next emperor, Antoninus Pius, advanced further north creating his own wall, which the Romans held for a short time before they pulled back to Hadrian's Wall after they restored it. Thus, in the second century AD, the Roman army was largely on the defensive in Europe, attempting to fortify and hold a line that ran from the Rhine to a section between the upper Rhine and upper Danube and then along the Danube. Early in that century, the Romans established their limes east of the Rhine, but later in the century, tribal movements in Europe put pressure on this part of the frontier and even along the Danube. During the same period, devastating raids resulted in Roman defences built on the Rhaetian frontier. In Britain problems appeared along Hadrian's Wall while on the coast Germanic barbarians launched sea raids. Furthermore, North Africans attacked Spain.

The death of Marcus Aurelius and the ascension in 180 of his maniacal son, Commodus, marked the beginning of a period of political instability for Rome. In the far north, the Caledonians penetrated the Antonine Wall and continued to advance while a new guerrilla war broke out in Spain. After the murder of Commodus in 193 a succession of emperors began with mostly short reigns and violent deaths. In 193 Septimus Severus' (193–211) legions made him the fourth emperor that year. Moving across the empire to put down revolts and invasions he brought some stability. He created a strategic reserve of five legions and improved conditions for soldiers. He had existing forts repaired and strengthened but his death brought instability back with his sons. Strategic policy was to hold the frontier with legions stationed in fortresses, continue to build new fortifications in stone and replace those of wood, from which they were to block enemy penetrations of the limes. By the 230s the Alamanni destroyed many forts on the Rhaetian frontier and other Germanic groups penetrated the Limes further north. The rapid succession of new emperors made the situation worse. One of these, Valerian, became the first emperor to be captured when the Persians defeated him. Valerian's son, Gallienus, attempted to restore the situation in the late 250s along the Rhine and Danube, defeating an invasion of the Juthungi[24] at Milan in 259, while the Alamanni went on a rampage through Gaul and also threatened Italy. The situation continued to deteriorate when Postumus, the governor of Lower Germany, revolted and created a Gallic empire that included Lugdunensis, Aquitania and Narbonensis (most of modern-day France and the Low Countries).

Postumus' Gallic Empire was a 'Roman Empire' that included all of Iberia, all the provinces in Gaul to the Rhine River and Britannia. This empire's capital was in Trier, in Belgica, and remained there for fifteen years. Since he had other threats to deal with, Gallienus failed to recover the breakaway Gallic Empire during his reign, which ended in 268. Meanwhile, Postumus rebuilt Trier, restored the Rhine frontier and checked the barbarian invaders. He also built smaller fortifications along the road network to prevent the barbarians that penetrated the frontier from using it. Gallienus attempt to defeat Postumus in 265 failed and soon he had to deal with a Persian invasion in the East. In 268 he stopped a major invasion the Balkans as the Goths broke through the Danube barrier. Next he put down a revolt in Italy. Meanwhile, Postumus had to crush a revolt in Upper Germany in 269 where he defeated the rebellious governor at Mainz, but was murdered by his own troops for not allowing them to pillage the city. His successor lasted two days. One of his generals, Victorinus, took power late in the summer, but the Iberian provinces did not recognize him and Emperor Claudius II (268–70), who replaced Gallienus, sent troops to the peninsula and also took back the lands east of the Rhône. This led to a revolt in central Gaul in 270, which he ended by taking the city of Autun after a seven-month siege. At the beginning of 271, Victorinus was murdered for having seduced one too many his men's wives.

In 270 Rome had two more emperors after the death of Claudius II. When Aurelian took over he engaged the Germanic invaders of the Italian peninsula and decided to fortify Rome. His Aurelian Walls became the city's first new walls since the Servian Walls of the fourth century BC. Work began and continued on the walls as he continued to engage and repel Roman's enemies. In 274 he defeated the Gallic Empire and restored its lands to Rome. He continued fighting the enemies of Rome, only to be murdered in 276. Several more emperors followed with more invasions and rebellions to contend with until the early 280s. The Aurelian Walls of Rome were completed before 282.

Stability returned when Diocletian, commander of the cavalry of the imperial bodyguard, ascended to the throne in 284. He quickly reorganized the empire so that he was able to handle both external and internal problems more effectively. He established the Tetrarchy, dividing the empire into four parts with two Augusti and two junior partners (Caesars) ruling each of the sections. Diocletian took control in the East and he put Maximian in charge of the West. The power of Rome and its Senate waned and four new capitals appeared, one for each section of the empire: Trier, Milan, Thessalonica and Nicomedia. Diocletian also reformed the military and the imperial administration system.[25] Constantine, who had served under Diocletian, took power in 307, eliminated competition and became sole ruler in 325. He also became the first Christian emperor.

Some time early in the fourth century a major change took place in the organization of the army. This included the formation of frontier troops called limitanei, a second-rate force that manned fortifications and were not expected to engage the enemy beyond them. They also acted as a police force and a customs service. The ripenes or river guards patrolled the Rhine and Danube and maintained a flotilla based at river forts. The first-rate troops were the comitatenses or mobile field army, which moved to threatened areas as needed. The comitatenses consisted of legions, auxilia and cavalry vexillationes. Ideally, the infantry units numbered about 1,200 men like modern-day regiments. The comitatenses came to rely heavily on Germanic auxiliaries.

Zosimus was very critical of Constantine I's border policies. 'Constantine I adopted a measure that gave the Barbarians free access into the Roman dominions. For the Roman empire, as I have related, was, by the care of Diocletian, protected on its remote frontiers by towns and fortresses, in which soldiers were placed; it was consequently impossible for the Barbarians to pass them, there being always a sufficient force to oppose their inroads.' But Constantine destroyed that 'security by removing the greater part of the soldiers from those barriers of the frontiers and placing them in towns that had no need of defenders; thus depriving those who were exposed to the Barbarians of all defence'. Zosimus blamed Constantine I for allowing the empire to degenerate into a 'miserable state'.[26] By the fourth century, the Roman army had abandoned all territory beyond the Rhine and the Danube, which became again the frontier of the empire.

In 364 the empire split again with Valentinian I (until 375) ruling the Western Empire and Valens (until 378) the Eastern. According to Ammianus Marcellinus, who lived in the last half of the fourth century, Valentinian, the last major builder of fortifications in the West, fortified the Gallic banks of the Rhine from its headwaters in the Tyrol to the sea with 'lofty castles and fortresses and a perfect range of towers in every suitable place, so as to protect the whole of Gaul'.[27] According to Hugh Elton, he issued orders to build towers annually and both he and Julian (361–3) before him erected new forts and repaired old ones when they were not campaigning.[28] Valentinian defeated the Alamanni after they penetrated the Rhine barrier and captured the fortress at Moguntiacum (Mainz). Next, he moved his headquarters at Lutetia (Paris), engaged in campaigns against the Picts and fought back Saxon incursions into Britain in 367. Afterwards, he crossed the Rhine and advanced up the Neckar valley where he built new fortifications east of the Rhine including a fort at Basilia (Basel). In 374, some barbarians broke through the Raetian frontier and others crossed the Danube. Valentinian died the next year and it was not long before the Romans lost control of the Rhine barrier. Construction of fortifications declined in the West, but it continued along the Danube under the aegis of the Eastern Empire.

After Valens was defeated and killed at the Battle of Adrianople in 378, Theodosius I (379–95) took the throne and fought the barbarians until they cried peace in 382. He allowed the Visigoths to settle in Thrace, which had far-reaching consequences since they moved west into Italy under Alaric in 401. Theodosius also allowed many non-Romans to serve in the army thus sowing the seeds of eventual disaster. According to Ammianus, he restored cities and fortresses and created outposts on the frontiers to recover lost territory. He invaded Italy and removed a usurper, eventually taking control of both empires. On his death, the empire was again divided. Theodosius' 12-year-old son Honorius (395–423) was put on the throne of the West and Flavius Stilicho, his mixed-race guardian (half Vandal and half Roman), assumed the regency. The Western Empire was on its last legs, the frontier was no longer secure and only a Roman Army heavily dependent on non-Roman – mostly Germanic – elements stood between the Germanic invaders and the fortified cities that served as the last protection for the Latin Romans.

Roman Emperors

The term 'emperor' derives from the Latin word 'imperare', which means 'to command'. Thus, an 'imperator' was a man commanding a military unit. Augustus and his successors adopted the title and gradually expanded its meaning to mean the political and military leader of the Roman Republic, which, in turn, became an 'Imperium' or Empire. Eventually, the term 'imperator' acquired the meaning of a hereditary monarchic title, the meaning we ascribe to it today.

The Julio-Claudian Dynasty
27 BC–AD 14	Caesar Augustus (Gaius Octavius).
14–37	Tiberius Claudius Nero.
37–41	Caligula (Gaius Julius Caesar Germanicus).
41–54	Tiberius Claudius Drusus Nero Germanicus – forts built on Rhine and Upper Danube and the gap between the rivers in Raetia.
54–68	Nero Claudius Caesar Augustus Germanicus.

The Year of Four Emperors (AD 69) and beginning of the Flavian Dynasty
68–9	Servius Sulpicius Galba, Marcus Salvius Otho and Allus Vitellius.
69–79	Titus Flavius Vespasianus.
79–81	Titus Flavius Sabinus Vespasianus.
8 –96	Titus Flavius Domitianus.

The Five Good Emperors and Adoptive Emperors
96–8	Marcus Cocceius Nerva.
98–117	Marcius Ulpius Trajanus.
117–38	Publius Aelius Hadrianus – Hadrian's Wall.
138–61	Titus Aurelius Fulvus Boionius Antoninus Pius – Antonine Wall

161–81	Marcus Aurelius (Marcus Annius Verus) – Antonine Wall abandoned.
180–92	Lucius Aurelius Commodus.
193–7	Four additional emperors

The Severan Dynasty

193–211	Lucius Septimus Severus.
211–17	Caracalla (Julius Bassianus).
217–22	Two additional emperors.
222–35	Severus Alexander (Marcus Julius Gessius Alexianus).
235–85	Barracks Emperors.
235–53	Ten additional emperors.
253–60	Publius Licinius Valerianus.
253–68	Gallienus (Publius Licinius Egnatius).

Emperors of independent Gallic Empire 259–273

| 259–68 | Postumus (Marcus Cassianius Latinius). |
| 268–75 | Three additional emperors – Forts east of Rhine and north of Danube abandoned. |

Barracks Emperors (continued)

268–70	Marcus Aurelius Valerius Claudius II.
270–5	Lucius Domitius Aurelianus – Aurelian Walls of Rome begun. Forts in Dacia abandoned.
275–6	Marcus Claudius Tacitus.
276–82	Probus (Marcus Aurelius Equitius) – Completed Aurelian Walls in 280.
282–5	Three additional emperors, including Diocletian in 284.

The Tetrarchy – Empire divided into two Western and two Eastern parts.

East –	284–305	Diocletian (Gaius Aurelius Valerius).
West –	286–305	Maximian (assumed the name Marcus Aurelius Valerius).
West –	305–37	Three additional emperors.
East –	305–24	Two additional emperors.

Constantine Dynasty

| 307–37 | Constantine The Great (Flavius Valerius Constantinus) – sole emperor in 323. |
| 337–64 | Six additional emperors. |

Dynasties of Valentinian and Theodosius

West – 364–75	Flavius Valentinianus I	East – 364–78	Flavius Julius Valens
West – 375–94	Four more emperors	East – 379–95	Flavius Theodosius I
394–5	Theodosius I, The Great – sole emperor		
West – 395–423	Honorius	East – 395–527	seven additional emperors
424–74	Ten more emperors		
West – 475–6	Romulus Augustulus	East – 527–65	Justinian I

Romulus Augustulus was the last Latin emperor of the Western Roman Empire. He did not achieve much and was forced to abdicate at the age of 16. He was replaced by Odoacer, a Germanic mercenary, who took the title of King of Italy. For historians, this marked the end of the Western Roman Empire and is used as a convenient point to mark the beginning of the Dark Ages, which were actually well under way.

Chapter Two

Fall of the Western Roman Empire

The First Battles for Britain

Julius Caesar landed on the island of Britain on 26 August 55 BC. He had embarked at Boulogne with two legions. The Britons followed his fleet as he looked for a place to land, probably near Deal. His troops stormed ashore, driving the Britons back, and a few days later met them again in battle. The wretched weather damaged his fleet and kept his army close to shore. Caesar retreated with his troops and returned a year later with five legions. This time, he penetrated further inland, but after several engagements he left once again and no Romans returned to the British Isles until the next century.

Emperor Claudius landed with four legions and an equal number of auxiliary troops to take part in a campaign to conquer Britain in AD 43. He stayed for only a fortnight but his legions conquered much of England as far north as York and Chester and towards Cornwall and Wales in the west during the following decade. In AD 60, Queen Boudicca led her Iceni tribe in a revolt involving up to 100,000 Britons. Her troops destroyed London and St. Albans killing thousands of Romans. Her army was finally defeated at the Battle of Watling Street. In AD 78, Julius Agricola, took over as governor and led his legions into Caledonia (Scotland). In AD 84, he won a major victory at Mons Graupius (exact location unknown). He started a line of forts covering the Scottish Highland passes, but he was replaced before they were completed. The Romans slowly fell back into present day England where legionary fortresses had been established at York[1] and Chester.[2]

Before he was recalled, Agricola selected a site north of Perth to build a legionary fortress named Inchtuthil that was to support his planned forts for the Highland passes. Work began on a low plateau between AD 83 and 86, but it was never completed even though it was partially converted to stone. Its earthen ramparts were covered in stone and its baths, built outside the perimeter, were also done in stone. Its size, 465m x 440m (508.5 yds x 508.5 yds)and covering 20.5 ha (51.2 acres), was comparable to that of the fortresses at York and Chester. What is unusual about this incomplete and apparently dismantled fort are the remains of a construction camp and a nearby fortified compound. This indicates that the fortresses may have had additional construction crews to support the legionaries who laboured on the fortifications.

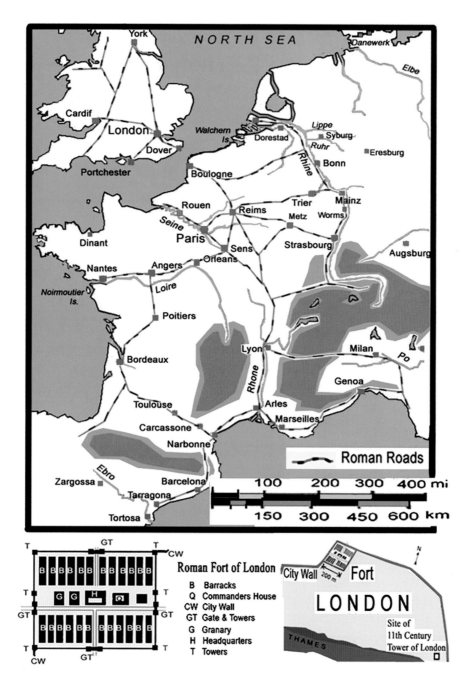

Roman roads, London, Roman fort.

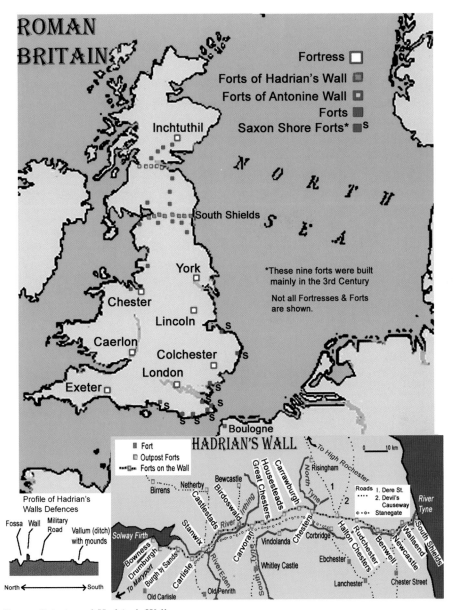

Roman Britain and Hadrian's Wall.

In AD 122 Emperor Hadrian (117–38) began the border wall named for him. This may be considered the beginning of the fortified Limes Britannicus. He was also the emperor credited with creating the fortified limes on the frontier of Germania (Limes Germanicus) including a timber palisade across the Raetia frontier covering 550km (350 miles). Thus, Hadrian may deserve the credit for fortifying the frontiers of the empire in Europe and moving toward a defensive posture even though his successor, Antonius, attempted to expand the European borders once again. However, he too continued to secure them with new defences. According to historian Henry M.D. Parker. 'Hadrian put into effect a definite system of frontier defence and for this purpose the legions were, as far as possible, kept in their own provinces',[3] which made it possible to recruit from local sources. In Britain, the Romans adopted the policy 'of employing the auxilia as the first line of defence and keeping the legions in garrisons behind the front, but connected with it by good roads'. Parker also suggested that this policy was extended to other Roman frontiers. The three legions in Britain – probably assisted by auxiliary cohorts – set to work on the wall, which ran for over 117km (73 miles) across the island.[4] The wall did not rely on a river for defence. Instead, it crossed the Tyne and Irthing with bridges connecting the wall on each bank of those rivers.

Hadrian's Wall was a stone wall up to 3m (9.9ft) wide at the base and about 3m (10ft) to 4.4m (14.5ft) high for two-thirds of its length between Newcastle and the River Irthing. The remaining third was made of turf with a base of 5.9m (19.3ft), to which a stone facing was later added.[5] During the first two years of construction, changes were made which account for the change in thickness of the wall. Archaeologists assume the wall's rampart walk served only for patrolling and observation since it was too narrow for a fighting platform. About every mile (Roman mile) or so, there were milecastles with turrets (watchtowers) in between. Detachments from three legions directed and completed most of the construction, which, according to some estimates, took three to six years. During the winter months, the legions and auxiliary cohorts did little if any construction work, but they had other duties to perform. Archaeologists assume that the milecastles, actually fortlets, which were built into the wall, had an entrance that allowed access through the wall and were surmounted by a tower. There was also another gate on the opposite (south) wall. Each milecastle included two-room barracks sufficient for a sixteen-man garrison although some may have had quarters for up to sixty-four men. Usually, two turrets (watchtowers) occupied the interval between the milecastles. They were probably over 9m (29.6ft) high and held an eight-man garrison. The lower level included a hearth for cooking. The troops that were posted here from a nearby fort were the equivalent patrols or were considered to be occupying an outpost. The turrets were generally built of stone, except for those along the turf section of wall, which were first made of turf and timber.

A V-shaped ditch ran in front of the curtain wall between towers to which it was connected. A berm in the form of a level strip of land between the wall and the ditch served two purposes.[6] In the first place, it allowed the troops on the ramparts a good line of sight for hurling javelins on attackers attempting to negotiate the steep sided fossa. In the second place, it allowed the troops enough room to surge out of the milecastles and forts and deal with assailants who managed to reach the berm. The milecastles, like the forts, opened onto a crossing point.

South Shield (Fort Arbeia) on mouth of River Tyne - Hadrian's Wall

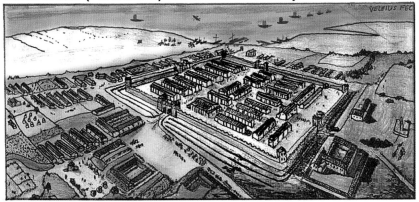

Fortlet similar to Milecastles of turf & timber

1. Barracks (12 - each for
        80 men)
2. Headquarters
3. Commanders House
4. Granary
5. Stables
6. Hospital

**Auxiliary Fort
for 1000 men**

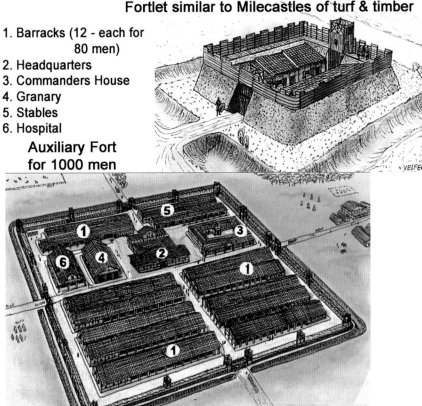

Drawings by *Veleius*

Roman Forts. Drawings by Veleius of South Shields, fortlet, and auxiliary fort of Hadrian's Wall.

After construction of the wall was well underway, someone in authority decided to add forts to the wall.[7] In some cases, the troops had to rebuild milecastles under construction or nearing completion. Years earlier, several forts were built along Agricola's Stanegate (Stone Road) close to the wall between Carlisle and

Cordbridge. The Stanegate, constructed decades earlier, became the main supply route until it was replaced with a military road that actually followed the wall and passed through the east-west entrances of the forts on the wall. Although there is disagreement about which forts actually formed part of Hadrian's Wall, it is generally agreed that it included seventeen forts. South Shields on the east end and Cordbridge, like several other forts, were not connected to the wall. Archaeological evidence seems to suggest that most of these fortifications were actually supply forts. All the forts belonged to the standard auxiliary type with the four entrances (some had two additional small ones), towers (corner, interval and gate), fossa, headquarters, commander's house, barracks (and often stables), workshops and granaries. Many of the larger ones had hospitals. Some forts were larger than others. Almost all had similar playing-card shapes and layouts and their stone curtain walls were backed by an earthen rampart. Since most are in ruins, the data varies on the thickness of the stone part of the walls and even the earthen backing. For example, the walls at the fort at Housesteads identified are recorded as being 1.3m (4.3ft) thick, at Chesters, they are 1.5m (4.9ft) thick and at Carrawburgh, 1.7m (5.6ft).[8] In most forts, a third or more of the walls projected beyond the line of Hadrian's Wall, but there were many exceptions. For instance, at Housesteads, the northern wall was flush with Hadrian's due to the steep terrain below it. At times, on the west side where the wall was made of turf, one-third of the forts' area projected beyond the main wall, but when the turf wall was replaced with a stone one, their northern walls was made flush with the new wall. When a third of the fort projected beyond the wall, like at Halton Chesters, there was one main entrance leading to the ditch crossing and an entrance on each side leading to the flat berm between the wall and the ditch.

The South Shields (Arbeia) fort, built ca AD 129 on the south bank of the Tyne, protected the port and the town. It was not linked to the wall because the river formed a barrier. Hadrian's Wall ended near the fort of Wallsend (Walls End, Roman Segedunum) on the north side of the Tyne, less than 100m (109 yds) from the south-east corner of this outpost. The section between Newcastle (Pons Aelius) and Wallsend, which was a late addition, is considered narrow since it was only 2.3m (7.7ft) thick, while most of the wall was thicker. Wallsend, unlike most forts on the wall, had only one entrance behind the wall. It was typical of many of the auxiliary forts on the wall with a rectangular shape of about 120m x 138m (131 yds x 150 yds). It had a tower at each rounded corner, four gates with a pair of flanking towers each and interval towers between each gate and the corner tower, except on the northern sectors of the east and west walls. The number and location of towers varied from fort to fort. The headquarters was in the standard central position, with the commander's house on one side and a granary on the other. Segedunum was large and important enough to have a hospital located between the granary and the west wall. On the north and south side of the fort, there were barrack blocks for eighty men each with the standard two rooms for

B - Barracks for troops with Centurians quarters on one end
C - Commanders quarters
G - Granary
H - Hospital
HQ - Headquarters with offices, shrine, hall, and courtyard.
 L- Latrines

**Housesteads Fort
2nd Century**

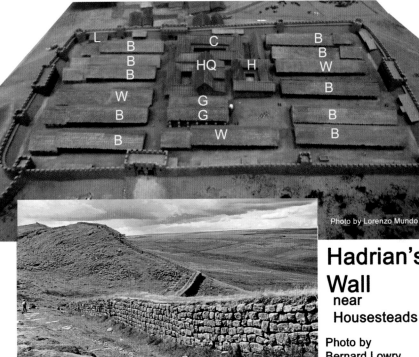

**Hadrian's
Wall**
near
Housesteads

Photo by
Bernard Lowry

Hadrian's Wall and Housesteads. Top: Model of Housesteads. Centre: Remains of Hadrian's Wall. Bottom: Sections of frieze on Trajan's Column with lower part showing lookout signal posts, next section a Roman fortified camp with tents of the headquarters, and section above that the construction of a fortified camp.

each eight-man unit. There may have been six to ten of these barracks some of which may have actually been workshops. In the second century, the garrison consisted of a mixed cavalry and infantry unit of 600 men (120 cavalry).

The Housesteads (Vercovicium) fort, near the centre of the line, occupied a position along a ridge and required fewer interval towers on its north side. Due to its location, it did not protrude beyond the wall. It was rectangular and measured 180m x 110m (197 yds x 120 yds). One of the long sides that formed the north end of the wall was 1.3m (4.3ft) thick and was backed by an earthen rampart, which was common in most of the forts. It is estimated that the walls were a little over 4m (13ft) high. The garrison might have numbered between 800 and 1,000 men.[9]

A Roman bridge with stone piers crossed the North Tyne linking two parts of the wall a short distance from the Chesters fort. Another key bridge, which was part of the wall, crossed the River Irthing east of Birdoswald at Willowford. The rivers did not add to the defences, except in a few cases when they passed behind the forts and served as an obstacle to an enemy who breached the wall.

Fort location (Roman Name)	Approx. size*	Approx. unit size**	Notes
South Shields (Arbeia)	188m x 98m 2.1 ha	500 men (cavalry)	4 entrances. Not connected to the Wall
Wallsend (Segedunum)	138m x 120m 1.7 ha	500 men (cav/inf)	½ projected beyond wall. 4 entrances (one behind wall)
New Castle (Pons Aelius)	? 2.3 ha	500 men	A castle was built on site so data limited
Benwell (Condercum)	170m x 120m 2.0 ha	1,000 men (cav/inf)	⅓ projected beyond the Wall. Type A and B
Rudchester (Vindobala)	157m x 117m 1.8 ha	500 men	⅓ projected beyond the Wall. Type A and B
Halton Chesters (Onnum)	134m x 122m 1.6 ha	500 men (cav/inf)	4 entrances with only one inside wall
Chesters (Cilurnum)	177m x 132m 2.3 ha	500 men (cavalry)	⅓ projected beyond Wall. Type A and B
Carrawburgh (Brocolitia)	140m x 109m 1.5 ha	500 men	Type C ?
Housesteads (Verovicium)	180m x 115m 2.0 ha	800 to 1,000 men	Type C
Great Chesters (Aesica)	128m x 108m 1.4 ha	500 men	4 entrances Type C
Carvoran (Magnae)	134m x 110m 1.5 ha	500 men	Type D (220m south of wall and 160m south of Vallum)

Fort location (Roman Name)	Approx. size*	Approx. unit size**	Notes
Birdoswald (Banna)***	158m x 121m 2.1 ha	800 to 1,000 men	Type A(before wall changed to stone, 1/3 projected out)
Castlesteads (Camboglana)***	114m x 114m 1.5 ha	500 men	4 entrances ?
Stanwix (Petriana or Uxelodunum)	213m x 183m 3.8 ha	1,000 men (cavalry)	Type C
Burgh by Sands (Aballava)	145m x 137m 2.0 ha	500 men (cav/inf)	Type A and Type B. Fort enlarged twice
Drumburgh (Coggabata)	96m x 82m 0.8 ha	Less than 500 men	
Bowness (Mais)	220m x 130m 2.8 ha	1,000 men	

Type A: Six gates of which two are small. Type B: Three gates open outside Hadrian's Wall (one on each of three sides projecting beyond the wall) Type C: Fort did not project beyond Hadrian's Wall. Type D: Fort located behind Hadrian's Wall.
*Number vary by sources and some forts were enlarged over the years.
**Usually infantry auxiliary cohorts.
***Most agree these two names were in error in the original Roman documents and reversed and that Banna is Birdoswald, not Camboglana.
1 ha (hectare) = 2.5 acres

Like the forts, the ditch to the south of the line was a late addition. Called the 'Vallum' (not to be confused with the standard usage of the term vallum meaning wall), it consisted of a wide flat-bottomed ditch, a mound running along each side high and stone crossing points at gateways. It was located about 60m (65 yds) south of the wall and was about 6m (20ft) wide and 3m (10ft) deep. It was apparently designed to isolate the battle area in the event of an enemy penetration.

Several forts were built north of the line to serve as outposts. They also blocked North-South roads. Some of these forts were built long before the wall between AD 85 and 90 under Emperor Domitian but after Governor Agricola campaigned in Caledonia and defeated the tribes at Mons Graupius and was recalled in AD 85. Birrens, Nethery and Bewcastle were founded on the western side of the wall at the time it was being built while several forts on the Dere Street[10] were abandoned in AD 180. Hadrian's Wall remained in use until about AD 142 because Rome was on the move again.

Emperor Antoninus Pius, who succeeded Hadrian in AD 138, ruled from Rome during a largely peaceful period and depended on capable military commanders because he was not a military man himself. His governor in Britain, Lollius Urbicus, had to put down an uprising. The governor was a capable general and proceeded to secure the region and deal with problems created by the Brigantes and other tribes north of Hadrian's Wall. In AD 139, he planned an attack from the fort at Cordbridge for the following year. He assembled all three of his legions stationed at Chester, York and Caerleon and auxiliary units, advanced along Dere Street, using its forts for support, into the Scottish Lowlands and crushed all resistance by AD 142. Soon, possibly in AD 142, he ordered work to begin on the Antonine Wall.[11] Hadrian's Wall was largely abandoned. An estimated 7,000 men, elements of all three legions, took part in the construction of the new wall. According to some sources, It took them only one to two years to finish the task; according to others, it took them as much as six years.

The Antonine Wall was built of turf, timber and stone and spanned the 55 to 60km (35 to 38 miles) between rivers flowing into to the Firth of Clyde and the Firth of Forth. Its stone base supported a line of earthen ramparts covered with sections of turves. Timber was the standard building material for the forts, fortlets, gates, battlements and interior structures. However, some of the main buildings like the headquarters, commanders' homes and baths, were mostly made of stone or a combination of wood and stone. The rampart reached an estimated height of 3m (10ft) and was crowned by the wooden parapet. A ditch in front of the wall is estimated to have been at 12m (40ft) wide and up to 4m (13ft) deep in parts. A berm between the ditch and the rampart was about 6m (20ft) wide.[12] As in the case of Hadrian's Wall, a metalled military road ran parallel to the wall. Unlike Hadrian's Wall, the Antonine Wall did not include a vallum behind it.

Soon after construction on six forts began, changes in planning led to the building at least ten additional forts similar to the milecastles of Hadrian's Wall to replace the fortlets. As a result, the new forts ended up only about 2.4 to 4.8km (1.5 to 3 miles) apart. Like the milecastles of Hadrian's Wall, they occupied positions behind the wall and their north side was joined to the rampart. However, there is no evidence of turrets on the wall, but David Breeze points out that if they were built of wood, their remains would be gone.[13] The forts had turf ramparts from 3.7 to 6.1m (12 to 20ft) thick, built on a stone base like those of the wall with the standard four gates, each flanked by two towers. The forts had standard features for an auxiliary fort including corner towers, although they varied in size. Unlike those of Hadrian's Wall, these forts did not project beyond the actual rampart of the wall. About ten fortlets, smaller than most standard structures of this type, remained after the completion of the new forts. Archaeologists have identified several positions that served as signalling platforms. Four forts served as outposts north of the wall. In addition, excavations uncovered the remains of about eighteen camps for the legionaries doing the construction. Such remains rarely appear elsewhere because they were temporary, but the troops needed a protected camp to work from while building defences in Britain or elsewhere when on a frontier.[14]

Up to 7,000 auxiliary troops were required to man the Antonine Wall. A number of these soldiers came from as far away as North Africa and the Middle

East where the climate was much different. The line remained occupied from 143 to 164 AD. Troops removed certain components such as gates from Hadrian's Wall when it was abandoned and the 'Vallum' south of the wall was partially filled in.

The situation changed shortly after the death of Antoninus Pius. Marcus Aurelius took the throne in AD 161 only to find himself engaged in a war with Parthia that lasted several years and was followed by an outbreak of the plague in Rome brought by his returning troops. In AD 166, the Marcomanni and other Germanic groups began a new war and broke through the Danube barrier. By AD 170, Aquileia in Italy was under siege. Marcus Aurelius was continuously engaged on this northern front until his death in AD 180.

There is no consensus regarding events in the province of Britannia during Marcus Aurelius' reign. According to some historians, the wars in other parts of the empire forced him to give up Rome's frontier in the lowlands of Scotland. Others claim that in 155 or 158 troops abandoned the Antonine Wall, removing what they could and burning the rest, but returned shortly after that. This was also a time when Emperor Antoninus' generals moved the frontier about 30km (19 miles) into Germanic lands and might have needed to move the troops stationed in Britannia for reinforcement.[15] By AD 164, during the reign of Marcus Aurelius, the Romans abandoned the wall and restored Hadrian's Wall. In AD 180, when Commodus succeeded his father Marcus Aurelius, the tribes north of the Wall rose up and broke through the wall leaving a path of destruction. Near Dere Street, Forts Rudchester, Halton, Chesters and Cordbridge and to the west, Fort Birdoswald, many milecastles and turrets were destroyed. The Romans soon reclaimed them and repaired the damaged fortifications. According to David Breeze, the troops removed numerous crossings that had been added to the Vallum south of the line when they had abandoned it for the Antonine Line. However, despite the restorations, it was eventually taken out of service. In addition, points out Breeze, the causeway crossings of the ditch on the north side of the milecastles were removed. At this time, a military way was built along the wall, but no attempt was made to fill the gaps between the forts or to use a density similar to the Antonine Wall.

Another civil war broke out and the unstable Commodus was strangled in late AD 192. After his successor was assassinated, there was a scramble for power. Among the various pretenders to the throne was Clodius Albinus, governor of Britain, who sailed from the island with his three legions and some auxiliary units, leaving the province and Hadrian's Wall lightly held. He was defeated in 197 at Lyons by Septimus Severus, who had ascended the throne in the spring of 193.[16] In 208, Severus and his son Caracalla arrived in Britain to put an end to Rome's problems with the tribes of Caledonia (Scotland). Septimus Severus led the army north from Hadrian's Wall and reoccupied and repaired the Antonine Wall. Before completing the conquest of the north, the 65-year-old Severus died at York in 211. His sons made peace with the northern tribes and departed Britain with Caracalla and his brother as co-emperors. Later, Caracalla did away with his brother.

The next major crisis in Britain took place in AD 287. Almost twelve years after the elimination of Postumus' 'Gallic Empire', Marcus Aurelius Musaeus Carausius, commander of the North Sea fleet based at Boulogne, invaded Britain and proclaimed his own empire. He used his troops to garrison the coastal forts and repair Hadrian's Wall while he negotiated a peace with the Picts. Many of the coastal forts dated from earlier in the century and later became part of command known as the Saxon Shore Forts. Carausius was assassinated in 293 and his successor, Constantius I, invaded Britain in 296 and suppressed the revolt. Constantius ordered the restoration of some of the forts on Hadrian's Wall, including the now-famous Housesteads.

Roman Britain remained largely at peace until about AD 343, when more problems flared up in the north. In 367, some of the tribes in Caledonia united and overran the defences almost driving the Romans off the island. Valentinian I (364–75), Emperor of the West, who was involved with fighting the Alamanni on the Rhine at the time, was appraised of the situation in Britain. He left Gaul to engage the northern tribes on the island, but also had to deal with invading Saxons on the coast. In 368, he appointed Flavius Theodosius, father of the future emperor Theodosius, Comes Britanniarum (Count of Britain), which made him the island's military commander. Valentinian returned to Gaul to take on the Alamanni who were on the move again. Theodosius drove the invaders back across Hadrian's Wall in 369 and restored the wall.

Valentinian I died in 375 while defending his European borders and his sons Gratian and four-year-old Valentinian II became co-emperors. Magnus Maximus, who succeeded Theodosius as military commander of Britannia, continued the fight against the northern tribes. When the army became dissatisfied with Gratian's leadership, Magnus Maximus took the opportunity to declare himself emperor in 383. He crossed into Gaul taking most of the island's garrison with him, leaving Britain vulnerable once again.[17]

Most of the Roman troops in Britain departed during the first decade of the fifth century after Flavius Claudius Constantinus led a revolt in AD 407 and declared himself Emperor Constantine III in Britain and Gaul. In 408, while Constantine III took most of his army into Gaul and moved south to Arles where he set up his capital, the Picts and the Scots fought the Saxons who took advantage of the situation to cross the Channel. Constantine III re-established the frontier on the Rhine. In 409, as the Visigoths threatened Italy, Honorius, who became Western Roman Emperor at the age of 10 in 393, had no choice but to recognize Constantine III until he died in 411.

Meanwhile, the Saxons continued their invasion of Britain and in 411, Honorius was only able to order the citizenry to take up arms and defend the island. The Governor of Britain built the Saxon Shore forts to check the Germanic sea invaders since the Roman navy had lost control of the sea in the late third century. The coastal forts included Portchester (Portus Adurni), Pevensey (Anderitum), Lympne (Portus Lemanis), Dover (Dubris), Richborough (Rutupiae), Recuvler (Regulbium), Bradwell (Othona), Burgh (Gariannonum) and Brancaster (Branodunum). Most of these forts had thicker and higher walls than other Roman forts and fortresses. Portchester's walls were 6.1m (20ft) high and Pevensey's were 8m (26ft). Portchester was square with projecting towers

Roman fort of Portchester 1. 12th Century Keep 2. Bailey 3. Moat
4. Gatehouse 5. Palace 6. Water Gate 7. Early 12th Century Church

Saxon Shore Forts from the Notita Dignitatium *('List of Offices'). View and plan of the Roman wall of Portchester and the twelfth-century Norman keep in one corner of the Roman fort.*

Map of Barbarian raids and the Gallic Empire. Modified by Kaufmann from the 1911 atlas by Shepard.

about every 30m (65.6ft) and a gate on each side. Pevensey was an oval shape with projecting D-shaped towers at irregular intervals. Recuvler was once located on a promontory on the mouth of the Thames (the terrain has changed and half of the fort has washed into the sea). Square shaped, it included a pair of defensive ditches on the landward sides in front of its 3m (10ft) wide and 6m (20ft) high wall (thinner near the top), which was backed by an earthen rampart. The fort may have held 500 men and included the standard features of auxiliary forts: headquarters, commanders' house, barracks and bathhouse. It also served as a signal station. These shore forts had concrete walls like most other stone forts and occupied key coastal locations. Most of these forts included thicker walls than auxiliary forts and projecting D-shaped towers, although some like Richborough had projecting rectangular towers. Although most are third century forts, a few, like Dover – a second-century fort – occupied older sites. Few other coastal forts on Britain or in Gaul across the Channel were similar to these in overall strength. They all remained in use for centuries after the Saxons, Angles and Jutes overran England.

The Walls of Rome

During the early years of the Pax Romana, except for those near the frontier, few Roman cities in the empire had new encircling walls. The city walls of Rome built by Aurelian in the third century exhibited many of the features, both old and new, that would appear in other fortifications, including those built for other cities. The growing threat of the Germanic tribes from the North Sea to the Black Sea, especially after the death of Marcus Aurelius, left cities beyond the frontier vulnerable to raids and even invasions. The third century proved to be a turbulent period that threatened to tear the empire asunder. Emperor Aurelian (270–5) took part in restoring stability and earned the title of Restitutor Orbis (Restorer of the World), which appeared on many of his coins.[18] He first set out against the Juthungi who had breached the Alpine barrier at the Brenner Pass and invaded the peninsula. Aurelian chased them back to the Danube. Soon after, he had to deal with the Vandals, the Marcomanni and others. Despite suffering a serious reverse when his legions were ambushed, leading to riots in Rome, he finally turned back the invaders at the River Metaurus in central Italy and then turned his attention to the East shortly after that. However, the barbarians had penetrated so deep into the Italian Peninsula that they came close to threating Rome where the Servian Walls, over 600 years old, had deteriorated so much that they no longer provided adequate protection. In 271, Marcus Aurelius ordered the construction of new walls, the Aurelian Walls, which would be finished later in the decade.[19] According to Zosimus, Emperor Probus finished them six years later while another ancient source claims that they were completed sooner, which seems unlikely. Improvements and modifications on the walls continued through the centuries until the post-medieval era when accommodations were made for cannons.

The old Servian Walls were up to 10m (32.8ft) high and about 3.6m (12ft) wide, even 13.5m (45ft) thick in one section according to William Burr. Its circuit was 11km (7 miles) in length. Its fossa was 29.6m (95ft) wide and 9m (30ft) deep with a berm 7m (23ft) wide between it and the ditch. The ditch was updated a few centuries later when Rome was threatened. The wall consisted of large tufa blocks held together with cement mortar and resting on a foundation of concrete. The estimated sixteen gateways were rather simple and were protected by towers inside the wall. The walls had no projecting towers. There were arched openings of over 3.2m (11ft) for catapults.[20] Even by the first century AD these walls were

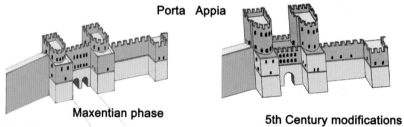

Gates of Rome's Aurelian Walls. (Photos of Port Apia by Lorenzo Mundo. Drawings by W. Ostrowski)

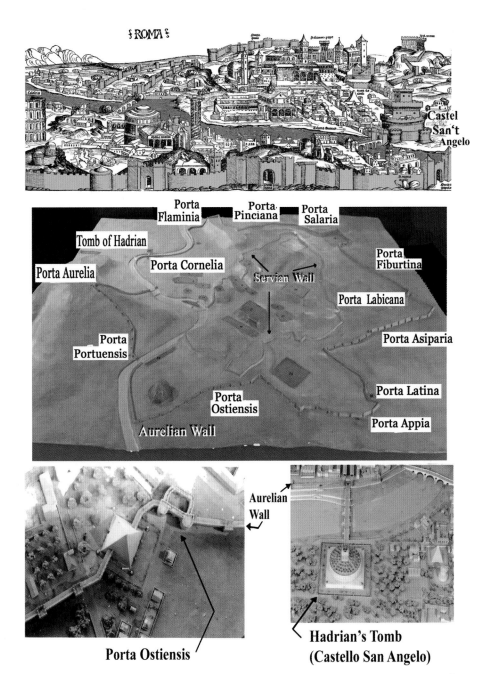

The Aurelian Walls. Top: 1493 woodcut from Hartman Schele's Welchronike Roma *(from Wikipedia) showing walls added to right Bank and enclosing the Vatican. Middle: Model of the Aurelian Walls.* (Photo by Lorenzo Mundo) *Bottom: Model showing Porta Osteinsis and Hadrian's Tomb.*

no longer adequate since the city had grown significantly, just as the walls had deteriorated.

Aurelian's assassination during a campaign in AD 275 did not stop work on his new walls. His 75-year-old successor, Marcus Claudius Tacitus, continued the campaign in Asia Minor, but he succumbed either to another assassin or to disease in the spring of 276. The Praetorian commander, Marcus Annius Florianus (supposedly his half-brother), replaced him and continued the campaign. Before long, the legions of the Middle Eastern provinces proclaimed Marcus Aurelius Probus emperor. Probus convinced Florianus' troops to murder him. This, in September 276, the usurper Probus was officially the new emperor. He completed Rome's new walls while he engaged the enemies of Rome until his troops murdered him in September 282.[21] Although Aurelian and his successors mostly proved to be successful generals, their short reigns and political instability exposed Rome to serious danger at a time when its new defences were still incomplete.

When it was finally completed, Rome's new enceinte of was 18km (11 miles) long. The walls were about 4m (13ft) thick and up to 20m (65ft) high in some places. Roman engineers had not been involved in this type of major project for centuries. The legionaries and even the auxiliary troops were involved in camp and fort construction. Permanent forts that were not made of timber and turf required the skills and experience only found in the legions. However, a 6,000-man legion could easily tackle the building a fortress that might include 1.6km (1 mile) of stone walls and several towers and gates, but would be taxed by a project involving an 18km (11.2-mile) circuit built in and around a city instead of open ground. Hadrian's Wall was more than six times the length of Rome's and had required troops from three legions as well as auxiliaries and possibly up to six years to build. However, its stone walls and even those of many of its fortresses were not as wide or as high as most city walls.[22] The emperor could not spare any legions to build the wall, so the government conscripted members of the citizenry from local guilds, but military engineers most likely directed the work. This may account for the irregularities in the quality of the work and explain why it took most of a decade to complete.

A Roman defensive wall included a foundation, the wall standing upon it from the ground to the battlements, galleried sections in some sectors, battlements, towers and gates. Construction crews had to clear a path through the outskirts of Rome, which included some built up areas, in order to lay the foundations. In some cases, the engineers found it expedient to incorporate existing structures into the wall rather than destroy or remove them. Thus, the Praetorian camp – a fortress built by Tiberius – the pyramid of Caius Cestus,[23] the Castrense Amphitheatre and several sections of an apartment complex were amalgamated into the city walls. Ian Richmond estimates that between one-tenth and one-sixth of Rome's wall consisted of these and other pre-existing structures.

Construction of the wall proceeded in a systematic way. First, a 4m (13ft) wide trench was excavated. Next it was lined with wooden slats and filled with the concrete to form the foundation. Where sections of this foundation protruded above ground level, cut blocks of tufa served as facing.[24] The concrete wall consisted of an aggregate of tufa and travertine mixed with quick-drying cement made of lime and pozzolana ash.[25] The surface of the wall was covered with tiles or bricks. Most of the tiles came from older buildings. A concrete mixture bonded this exterior covering to the walls. In many sections, probably due to the inexperience of the civilian work force, this outer face was not properly prepared

Assyrian Siege Warfare 9th Century B.C. Similiar Methods and Weapons in use for almost 2000 years

British Museum, photos
by Lorenzo Mundo

Assyrian siege warfare from the British Museum. 1. Siege tower with ram. 2. and 3. Mining and destroying the walls. (Photos by Lorenzo Mundo)

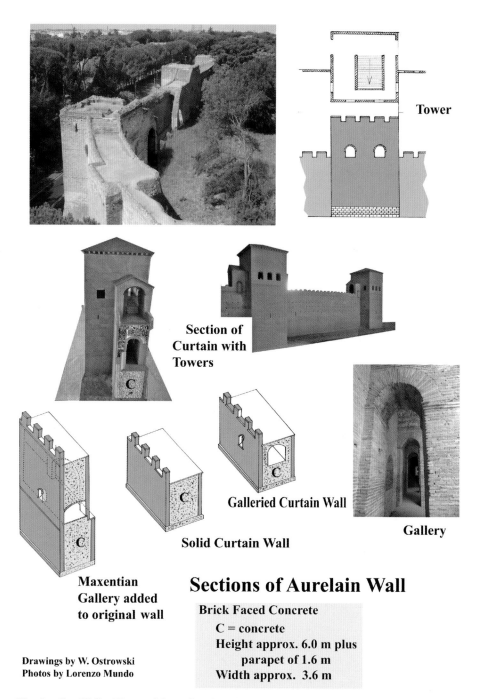

Tower

Section of Curtain with Towers

Galleried Curtain Wall

Solid Curtain Wall

Gallery

Maxentian Gallery added to original wall

Sections of Aurelain Wall

Brick Faced Concrete
C = concrete
Height approx. 6.0 m plus parapet of 1.6 m
Width approx. 3.6 m

Drawings by W. Ostrowski
Photos by Lorenzo Mundo

The Aurelian Walls: Photos of the wall and model by Lorenzo Mundo. Drawings of three sections of the wall by W. Ostrowski.

and eventually fell away from the wall.[26] The wall averaged about 8m (26ft) in height in most places, which included 6m (19ft) above the foundation, the rampart walk and battlements. The wall, which tapered off from the foundation, was 3.6m (12ft) thick at its top. In some parts of the wall, it was not solid, but included a barrel-vaulted gallery above 3m (10ft) of the solid wall. This gallery opened in arcade style to the rear and had narrow arrow loopholes along the front of the wall.

Rome's enceinte included eighteen gates each flanked by a pair of towers and five posterns.[27] At about every 30m (98ft) was one of 381 projecting towers built into the walls, except along the Tiber where the planners thought a major assault would be more difficult. Except for the flanking towers of gates, the wall towers were of the older rectangular design, about 7.6m (25ft) long and rose 4.5m (14.7ft) above the wall. The towers protruded 3.35m (11ft) beyond the wall, were solid up to the level of the wall gallery and had a facing like the walls. There were chambers in the towers at the level of the wall ramparts that had large shuttered arched windows on each side and two on the front to accommodate a couple of ballistae that could be turned to the three openings. To equip all the towers would have required over 700 bolt-firing ballistae, but it is doubtful that such a number was available. It is more likely that a small number remained in storage until needed.[28] Later, the ballista chambers were converted into positions for archers. A stairway gave access from the ballista chamber to battlements on the roof of the tower. The gates, many of which had two arched portals, were flanked with towers. The original towers and gates built in the 270s were less impressive than their later replacements. In *The City Wall of Imperial Rome*, Ian Richmond points out that the wall could not stop an army with the proper siege engines. Rome's Praetorian Guard and other organizations in the city such as the urban cohorts (a sort of police force) and the vigiles (for police and fire duties) could not properly defend the wall.[29] The first major challenge came when Diocletian and Maximian of the Tetrarchy abdicated in 305. Maxentius (306–12), disappointed at not being made an Augustus, took the title of emperor with the support of the Rome's citizenry and Praetorian Guard.[30] Other members of the Tetrarchy declared him a public enemy. In 307, Severus, whose capital was at Milan, led an invasion of Italy supported by Galerius in the east. Since the Roman legions knew how to conduct a siege and build the necessary machinery, Maxentius' position became vulnerable. He bribed Severus' army when it reached Rome and forced Severus to flee and he had him killed later. This close call caused Maxentius to restore the walls and begin a new building phase. However, in 310, when Constantine I, the Great (306–37), descended on Rome the work was still incomplete. The towers were mostly unfinished and the fossa was still at the initial stages of excavation. Thus, Maxentius decided to fight outside the walls only to be defeated and die at the Battle of the Milvian Bridge.

Constantine allowed the work to continue and the results were the impressive gates, some of which still stand today. The gates, first built in the 270s, had flanking gate towers with windows on the second level, like the wall towers. The section of curtain above the gate linking the towers also had arched windows. The gates had a single or double archway entrance depending on the importance of the roads that passed through them. The Maxentian improvements increased the towers from two storey structures to four with heights of up to 34m (111.5ft). The new work added two levels to the gate towers and curtains with windows in the chambers and galleries. The upper level of the towers was above the rampart walk. Further changes came in the fifth century during the reign of Honorius (395–423) when the double-archway entrances were converted into single archways which included a portcullis and the mechanism to operate it in the curtain wall above. These changes varied from gateway to gateway. After a serious earthquake in 442, most of the walls held up well, but a number of buildings including the Coliseum and the gateway at Porta Apia were damaged. The gate required major repairs, which resulted in the addition of another level to the towers. The foundation of the walls, according to Ian Richmond, was inadequate for the increased height of the walls of the Maxentian phase.

One interesting feature of the Aurelian Walls was the inclusion of garderobes that emptied over the walls, somewhat like those of castles centuries later. This type of crude sanitation in built up areas is generally not associated with the Romans and even their permanent fortifications had latrines with running water. The garderobes may well have been a late addition to the walls and since it was a long distance from the ramparts to public latrines in the city, they may have been needed.

Thus, the Aurelian Walls underwent several phases of construction between the 270s and the early fifth century, which are reflected in the various styles of curtain wall sections. In general, the walls of the 270s were about 6.1m (20ft) high and 3.66m (12ft) wide. The battlements were 1.07m (3.5ft) to 1.4m (4.5ft), giving a total height of about 7.5m (25ft). During the next phase of construction – Maxentian's improvements – the walls rose to 18.3m (60ft) in many sections and a new gallery was placed over the old rampart walk. In *Ancient and Medieval Siege Weapons*, Konstantin Nossov pointed out that scaling ladders over 10m (32.8ft) in length were too unwieldy and impractical for a successful assault by escalade. A 12m (39.4ft) long scaling ladder was required to reach a 10m (33ft) high wall. Thus, the original 8m (26ft) high Aurelian wall was vulnerable. The increased height changed the situation. Ian Richmond suggests that the original wall was only a barrier that, at best, could intimidate barbarians untrained or ill equipped for siege warfare. The Maxentian improvements, when they were completed in 404, changed the situation. In addition, the higher walls required fewer troops to defend them, especially with the type of weapons available in the era of the late Roman Empire.

Rome, the Army and the Fall

The empire began its decline soon after its creation. In the third century AD civil wars and invasions kept Rome largely on the defensive. Diocletian brought back some political stability with his Tetrarchy and built a number of forts in an attempt to secure the borders. However, peace did not last past his retirement in 305. Constantine the Great restored the situation in 311. By then, Rome had become little more than a symbol as other cities, like Constantinople, replaced it in political importance and the empire became permanently divided into two parts. Constantine reduced the size of the legions to as few as a thousand men and disbanded the old Praetorian Guard replacing it with special imperial guards often recruited from Germanic groups to form 400-man regiments. Cavalry contingents became an integral part of the smaller legions. Constantine pulled troops back from the frontier into the interior where they were not needed. On the one hand, he is credited with creating a large mobile reserve to meet external threats; on the other hand, he is blamed for weakening the military by softening them through the policy of 'bread and circuses' and generating problems with the locals in the towns and cities where they were stationed. The limitanei declined into second-rate units with reduced ability to hold the frontier. Thus, by the end of the next century, they largely devolved into peasant militias. The legions, whose mobility increased, spent the last half of the fourth century engaged in campaigns against Persia and the Germanic tribes.

Later in the fourth century, Emperor Valentinian I (364–75) ruled the Western Empire and his brother, Valens, the Eastern. His capital was the city of Trier rather than Rome. From there, he held the Alamanni on the Rhine, but he also had to ward off the northern tribes at Hadrian's Wall. He died of a heart attack in 375 while holding the Danube barrier. In 378, his brother Valens was overwhelmed by the Visigoths at Adrianople, leaving both empires in grave danger from other Germanic tribes on the Rhine and the Angles, the Saxons and the Jutes in Britannia.

Theodosius I (379–95) took over in the East and helped turn it into a greater military power than the West. He allowed the Visigoths to settle within the empire and become his allies, including 20,000 of them serving in his army by 394. This decision is sometimes referred to as the beginning of the barbarization of the Roman army, which soon became a problem for the Western Empire. Theodosius also marched on Rome to remove the pretender Maximus Magnus in 388. When Theodosius died in 395 his pre-adolescent son Honorius became Emperor of the West (395–423). Alaric, King of the Visigoths, rose against him, but was defeated in the Balkans by Honorius' general Stilicho, a man of mixed Roman–Vandal ancestry. Relations between the two empires deteriorated. The Goths continued to threaten both and, in 401, Stilicho was forced to pull troops out of Britain and Gaul to meet the Vandals as they breached the frontier. Alaric took advantage of the situation to invade northern Italy and was stopped at the walls of Milan where Stilicho beat him again in 402. Although Alaric retreated, Honorius moved his capital from Milan to Ravenna, which was more easily defended. Alaric made one more attempt in 402 and was defeated at Verona. However, in 405, the Ostrogoths invaded Italy, ravaging the region for months until Stilicho vanquished them in 406 with the help of Alans and Huns. Stilicho was done in by court intrigues instigated by Romans who feared leaders with mixed blood. In 407, the Vandals, Alans and Suevi crossed the Rhine and plundered Gaul. When Alaric turned up again in 408, 10,000 German auxiliaries, resentful of the execution of Stilicho, defected to him. With Honorius trapped in Ravenna, Alaric marched on Rome. Fortunately for the Romans, his troops lacked the means and skill to attack the walled city. After a long siege, the senate bought him off in 409. Alaric then returned to Ravenna, but he was back at Rome's gates 410. The city was at the point of starvation, when someone opened the Salarian Gate on 24 August 410 allowing the Visigoths to pour into the city. For the first time in over 800 years, Rome had fallen to an enemy. Alaric died while he was preparing for an invasion of Africa. The year of 410 began with six men claiming the throne while Honorius was under siege.[31] The Western Empire was now ripe for destruction.

Honorius died in 423 to be replaced by a usurper until the Eastern Emperor sent his forces to help install Valentinian III (425–55). Flavius Aetius, his general, who was of Germanic blood, became Rome's last great military leader. In 428, he defeated the Franks in Gaul. In 432, Aetius was defeated in battle by a faction supporting Valentinian's regent, but he was allowed to return in 433.[32] The empire continued to fracture, but in 435 he destroyed the Burgundian kingdom and pushed them into the region of Savoy. Next, he struck at the Goths who had Narbonne under siege and took their capital of Toulouse. In 442, he recognized Vandal control of North Africa. In 449, the Huns, many of whom were Aetius' allies, were allowed to settle in Pannonia.

Many Roman and barbarian campaigns involved sieges. In 450, Attila led the Huns into Gaul, taking one fortified city after another, but failed at Paris and moved on to Orleans. Here, according to Gregory of Tours, he launched a fierce assault with battering rams that sent the walls rocking and on the verge of collapse. Aetius arrived in the nick of time to save the city and break the siege. In 451, he defeated Attila at Chalons in Rome's last great battle in the West.[33] After this, his forces were too depleted to stop Attila from marching on Rome. In 452, the Huns, decimated by disease, failed to take Rome and were neutralized. Aetius' reward was his execution at Ravenna as a result of court intrigue. Shortly after this, the Vandals crossed over from Africa and took Rome in May 455. Flavius Ricimer, a German, became the Master of Soldiers in 456. He exercised control over the last emperors and took Rome in 472, but died shortly afterward. In 476, Flavius Odovacer, a Germanic leader in Roman service, removed Romulus Augustulus, the last Latin Emperor of the West, at Ravenna and Aetius proclaimed himself king.

Walled cities of the Roman Empire from the first to the fourth centuries AD. Map modified by Kaufmann from the 1911 Atlas by Shepard. Photo: the large Porta Nigra of Trier (one of four gates on the north side of the city) built of grey sandstone in the late second century AD. Originally two four-storeyed towers. (Photo by Berthold Werner from Wikipedia)

The Growth of Urban Fortifications

Until the third century, like Rome, few cities and towns in the Roman Empire were defended by circuits of walls. At that point, the West suffered greatly from barbarian raids and failure to stop them caused cities to restore old or build new enceintes. The first Roman effort at creating walled towns in the western part of the empire began with Augustus and continued through the first century. In some places, rectangular plans similar to a legionary camp were adopted. This was the case at Aosta, Turin, Ljubljana and Barcelona. In other places, such as Fréjus, Lyon, Orange, Nimes, Cologne, Trier, Avenches (Switzerland) and Vienne irregular enceintes covering up to 200 ha (500 acres) were favoured. The towers were relatively simple, rectangular or circular in shape. Gate towers flanking the entrances were D-shaped, rectangular or square. For a while during the second century, the Romans ceased building city walls, possibly because of the cost and because they relied on secure frontiers. Later in that century and during the next, Trier, Xanten (Netherlands), Tongres (Belgium) and Augst (Switzerland) received defences. In Britain, a large number of towns including London, Exeter and Leicester were fortified and the old legion fortresses at Colchester, Gloucester and Lincoln were converted into settlements during the first century. At York, which also began as a first-century fortress, parts of the walls were incorporated into new ones. In the early fourth century, a ten-sided 9.1m (30ft) high tower was added. The poorly maintained walls remained standing through the Dark Ages until the Danish Vikings occupied the city and restored them in 867, extending them with timber and turf. They destroyed all seven Roman towers leaving only the multi-angular tower standing. The walls of many other Roman cities survived through the Dark Ages in various conditions.

The city walls continued to follow the pattern set at the time of Augustus with thicknesses between 1 to 3m (3.3 to 9.8ft), square or round towers and walls with earthen backing. Often, the gates had large double portal entrances and flanking towers. However, there were no innovations until work began on the Aurelian Walls of Rome. The procedure for building new walls was quite standardized. Usually, a trench was excavated and filled with materials to create a stable foundation, which was covered with a layer of mortar. Next, construction began on a concrete core that received a facing of stone, bricks and/or tiles. In the last centuries, with space at a premium, the Romans stopped using an earthen back and made freestanding walls.[34] Before the end of the Western Roman Empire, the land between the Rhine and Pyrenees including all of Gaul numbered over fifty-five walled cities and many walled towns.

In the third century in Gaul, Aurelian repaired the damage the barbarian raiders had wrought. He rebuilt the walls of Dijon and fortified other sites. According to Stephen Johnson, the city walls of this era reached a high level of sophistication. The towers protruded beyond the walls, allowing enfilading fire from archers and ballistae. The fortified towns and cities of this period included

Bonn (Bonna), Mainz (Mognontiacum), Strasbourg (Argentorate) and the provincial capital of Cologne (Colonia Agrippina) near the Rhine frontier.[35] Within the empire, Reims (Durcortum), Lyon (Lugdunum), Narbonne (Narbo), Toulouse (Tolosa), Marseilles (Massilia) and Paris received fortifications. Postumus is credited with building the walls of Mainz in 259 and linking them to the fortress, but by 451 the city had already been sacked several times by barbarians. In Iberia, Leon (Legio), Tarragona (Tarraco), Merida (Emerita Augusta), Cordoba, Lugo and others received defences. The walls of Lugo were about 2.1km (1.3 miles) long, 4.2m (13.8ft) thick, 8 to 12m (26 to 39ft) tall and enclosed an area of over 34 ha (85 acres). They included an impressive number of towers: about ninety rectangular and D-shaped two-storey towers with five gates flanked by towers. The Gallic city of Autun had walls from the Augustan era, but new ones built in the third century after barbarian raids

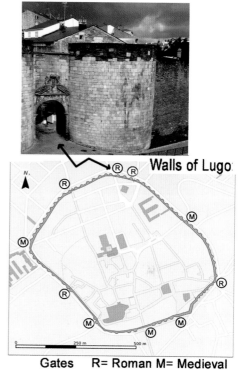

Roman and medieval walls of Lugo. (Wikipedia)

had reduced populations led to a new smaller circuit that only enclosed 10 ha (25 acres) of the original 200 ha (500 acres) of the old wall. Other cities suffered similarly from the raids. Trier, founded by Augustus, served as a capital and before the end of the second century had its impressive and massive Black Gate (Porta Niagra) added to the city walls. This did not keep the Germanic tribes out in 256. The city was besieged unsuccessfully by the usurper Magnus Magnentius in 353 and sacked by the barbarians in 360 and four more times in the first half of the fifth century. It fell to the Huns in 451. Amazingly a Roman army skilled in siege warfare was unable to take the city, whereas the barbarians had no difficulty. Walls without good troops simply could not save the empire.

While Rome's Aurelian Wall was free standing, in most of the other cities, the walls were not as thick and an earthen backing was necessary at the time they were built. Many walled towns began as legionary fortresses. Such was the case of Chester where the fortress walls and towers were changed from turf and timber to stone (sandstone) backed by an earthen rampart at the end of the first century AD. The work came to a halt, not to restart until early in the next century.

The most important city walls in England were those of London (Londinium), which became the administrative capital. A small fort on the north-west side of the city served units that moved in and out of the city for administrative purposes. The city walls, built probably early in the third century and the fort from the previous century (circa AD 110) were on the north side of the Thames. The wall was over 3.2km (2 miles) long and enclosed 130 ha (325 acres). Its width varied from 2m to 3m (6.6ft. to 9.8ft) and its height reached up to 5.8m (19ft). It had a concrete core made of rubble – mostly Kentish ragstone – and cement and its

Reconstruction of Roman lines of circumvallation similar to those at Alesia. Bottom left: scattered caltrops served like a minefield to prevent men and animal from advancing.

exterior face was covered with squared ragstone blocks. A standard 2m (6.5ft) deep ditch ran in front of it. Towers were added to the wall in the fourth century. Saxon sea raids forced the Romans to build a wall along the Thames around AD 280. The city was abandoned after 410 and was not reoccupied until the end of the Dark Ages.

In Gaul, the town of Lutetia (Paris) located mainly on an island (Ile de la Cité) in the Seine, did not receive stone walls until the fourth century as it developed into a transportation hub. No accurate estimates are available from the ruins, but the walls extended around the banks of the island for about 1.2km (0.75 miles). They were 2 to 3m (6.6 to 9.8ft) thick and 2.3 to 3.2m (7.5 to 10.5ft) high, which was not impressive although some estimates are as high as 9m (29.5ft). In 451, after overcoming the walls of Mainz, Cologne, Trier, Metz, Reims and Amiens and sacking those cities,[36] Attila tried to take Paris and failed. He moved on to Orleans where he failed again before being defeated at the Battle of Chalons. In 476, Odoacer removed the last Roman emperor and, with the approval of the meek senators of Rome, took control of Italy while the remainder of the empire broke up into barbarian-held kingdoms and Europe slipped into the Dark Ages.

Ditch Defences

A defensive ditch, with or without obstacles in it or in front of it, was common in all Roman fortifications. Often, two and sometimes three ditches encircled a fort. Roger Wilson in *Roman Forts* cites Nod Hill in Dorset (England) as an example. The earthen fort was surrounded by three ditches. The two closest to the rampart were V-shaped ditches about 1.5m (5ft) deep. There was a similar ditch, known as a 'Punic' ditch, about 16.8m (55ft) away. All three ditches were steep on the outer side. The Punic ditch was the easiest to breach, but at about 27.4m (90ft) from the rampart, the attackers were within range of hand-thrown projectiles. The level stretch of about 16.8m (55.1ft) may have included various types of obstacles like 'lilies', caltrops and the like. The next ditch was more difficult to get out of since both of its sides were steep. The final ditch was actually less steep on the side facing the wall and angled enough to allow the defender on the rampart a clear view. Here, the attackers could use their shields for protection as they tried to climb out under the defenders' fire. When they failed to breach the wall and tried to retreat, they had to renegotiate the steep sides of both ditches, the open area and the Punic ditch, which was easy to get into but difficult to exit. Apparently, the Romans realized that during most battles of their times, the greatest number of casualties were not inflicted when both sides engaged in combat, but when one side fled the battlefield. The Punic ditch gave the Romans more time to strike at an enemy in retreat.

The ditches of earthen and stone fortifications were of little value unless they were constantly maintained. The bottom section of the ditch had a slot called the 'ankle breaker'. M.C. Bishop suggests that this feature was the result of cleaning the ditch because it was the width of a shovel blade. The garrison had to remove debris and the sides had to be maintained so they did not erode into the ditch. This type of work may have been only just better than latrine duty. These ditches were the fort's first line of defence and their only weak points existed where the roads leading into the fort crossed them.

Carcassonne

Bayonne

Roman Walls and Towers

Autun

Barcelona

Photos by Pierre Etcheto

Examples of Roman walls and towers. (Photos by Pierre Etcheto)

Chapter Three

The Dark Ages in the West Part I

Collapse of the West and Rise of the East

As the power of the Western Roman Empire waned in the fifth century, the Germanic barbarians ascended in the West. The Franks eventually ruled most of Gaul and the lands east of the Rhine, the Visigoths took control of Iberia, the Ostrogoths took over the Italian Peninsula, and the Angles, Saxons and Jutes overran England. Thus, as the Dark Ages set in, Germanic groups controlled the once Latin-dominated lands of the West. However, large elements of the native Gallic populations remained.

As the Roman Empire in the West stopped providing security, in many places including Britain, the region around the Rhine and any area suffering from raids, the Romans – probably the local militia forces – began building hilltop forts as refuges. These turf and timber structures were often erected on old Iron Age hillforts. Many of these old sites, such as Maiden Castle in England, still had impressive earthworks consisting of large ditches backed by banks. Some of Britain's Celtic groups had used them as protection from the Romans when they first invaded the island. In the fifth century, however, many of these sites were too large for the local population. As a result, only a small portion of the old sites was fortified.

Only in Britain did the locals put up stiff resistance. In other parts of Europe, the Celtic-Romanized populations became pawns in contests between Germanic groups. However, the Britons eventually fell under the domination of the invaders while the Celtic populations of modern-day Wales and Scotland held them off. Before the last Britons of England finally surrendered, they held a number of Roman fortified sites such as York and Chester and forts in Hadrian's Wall like Birdoswald and restored and modified some Iron Age hillforts, few of which were located in the south-east due to the terrain. It is this struggle that was immortalized in the legend of King Arthur.

Circa 500,[1] a chieftain of the Britons, possibly the legendary Arthur, defeated the Saxon invaders at the Battle of Mount Badon leading to a relatively peaceful period until mid-century. The precise location of this battle is unknown and the details about it vary from version to version of the legend. It can be concluded, however, that some petty warlords who dominated Britain came together in this battle to stop the tide of Saxon conquest. The descriptions of the battle site allude to a hillfort, but no version of the story tells us whether it was the Britons

Maiden Castle. Top: Aerial photo by Major George Allen 1935. Bottom: Ground view.

or the Saxons who held it. According to Geoffrey of Monmouth,[2] the Britons charged the Saxons holding the hilltop fort and took the site after three attempts. It is more likely, however, that the Britons held the fort and broke the Saxon siege since most of the Germanic groups had little interest in defending fortifications during the fifth and sixth centuries.

Two sites, South Cadbury and Tintagel (the monastery under the castle), have links to the Arthurian legend. South Cadbury was one of the largest and most impressive hilltop forts. Archaeology has revealed that it had a drystone wall built on the last bank. An earthen rampart backed that wall and its wooden crenellations. The entrances were wooden gate towers. The internal buildings were typical wooden structures with thatched roofs similar to those found in towns. Most of the Briton sites were probably similar and had no resemblance to the stone castles depicted in Arthurian legend. The Saxons defeated most of the remaining tribes of Britons in England and pushed into Wales before the end of the seventh century. From this point on, England became Anglo-Saxon. The ninth century gave rise to Anglo-Saxon fortifications built to stave off the assaults of the Norsemen.

On the Continent, the Vandals left the European scene as they crossed the straits to North Africa, subdued that region and even attacked and sacked Rome in 455. The Vandal king, Genseric, landed his army at Portus, the seaport of Rome across the Tiber from Ostia and marched on Rome, which was ruled by Emperor Petronius Maximus at the time. Petronius was killed by the fleeing mob after only about seventy days in power. When Genseric reached the gates of Rome, Pope Leo I came out and offered him the city and all he could plunder as long as he promised not to harm the Roman citizens. The Vandals spent a fortnight plundering the city, leaving the citizens unharmed and only taking a number of slaves back to Carthage with them. The Visigoths strove to consolidate their position in Iberia and Aquitania, while the Franks, Burgundians and other Germanic tribes did the same in the remains of the Western Empire. The Frankish kingdoms, usually at each other's throats, finally united before dividing again due to inheritance. The objective for the barbarian leaders in Iberia, Gaul and the Rhine area was to take key cities, which, in most cases, still had their Roman fortifications. The barbarian armies had little skill in siege warfare and preferred to meet the enemy in the open field. It is unknown how long and in what condition the Roman-era walls remained. If they were built of concrete with stone and brick facing, they should have lasted for centuries, but their battlements would probably have required some maintenance. If they were of stone or had a non-concrete core, their lifespan was shorter because people stripped the stonework for their own private use or officials used it to build public structures and churches. The Franks, the most powerful and lasting of the Germanic groups, seemed skilled enough to build impressive churches and palaces, but their fortifications were few and less impressive. As a matter of fact, neither the Franks nor any of the other groups maintained most Roman facilities, especially those related to sanitation, which fell into disuse. The Romans' well-built roads and bridges, on the other hand, endured for centuries, no thanks to their new owners. During the eighth century, the Germanic kingdoms faced both the Islamic invaders and the Saxons. Charlemagne engaged the rebellious Saxons for years after he invaded their lands in 772. He defeated them at Sigiburg in 775. He then left garrisons at fortified camps at Sigiburg and Eresburg. According to contemporary descriptions, Eresburg was apparently an Iron Age hill-top fort more heavily fortified than most. When the Saxons revolted in 776, they destroyed the fort at Eresburg.[3] After he defeated them again in 777, Charlemagne built a new camp at Karlstadt. During the next century, the Franks used the old defences of Paris and built new but not impressive ones to stop the Vikings.

In the Italian peninsula, fortifications continued to play a key role for a number of years, especially in the sixth century when Emperor Justinian of Byzantium attempted to conquer Italy.

The Byzantine Empire Invades Italy

Odovacar made himself King of Italy after removing the last Latin emperor in the West. His rule lasted less than two decades as the Eastern Roman Emperor convinced Theodoric, leader of the Ostrogoths, to remove him. In 489, the Ostrogoth army passed through the Julian Alps into Italy where it met and defeated Odovacar's troops in battle. Odovacar withdrew into his fortress at Ravenna while Theodoric took Verona and Milan. Theodoric then began a three-year siege of Ravenna. His efforts were diverted when Gundobad, king of the Burgundians, invaded the Italian Peninsula followed by the Rugians. Theodoric drove both of them back and returned to the siege, which lasted from July 491 to February 493. However, he was unable to breach what Charles Oman called the city's 'impregnable walls'.[4] Finally, famine forced Odovacar to yield.[5]

Ravenna's first walls were not as impressive as those of other Roman fortified cities of the third and fourth centuries and they enclosed a town of only about 33 ha (82.5 acres). The Romans built new walls around many of the cities in northern Italy such Bologna, Parma, Mantua, Brescia and Pisa, and increased the thickness of the walls at Rimini. In other places, such as Florence and Lucca, the city walls remained unchanged. The emperors picked Ravenna for their capital because in addition to its walls, the city was surrounded with marshes and lakes, which offered additional protection. This well-sited city on the Adriatic was linked to waterways that reduced an eight-day trip to Milan by land to about four. By the beginning of the fifth century, its two suburbs of Caesera and Classe (about 4km [2.4 miles] south of the city) extended south along the Adriatic with lakes and marshes on the west. Honorius and Valentinian III extended Ravenna's walls and Odovacar completed them, enclosing 166 ha (415 acres). In the Late Middle Ages, many of the walls and circular gate towers were destroyed.[6]

Rome remained the largest city on the peninsula and the residence of the Pope who influenced most of the Christians of Western Europe. Ravenna never replaced it as the spiritual centre of the West, but it was sacked twice in the fifth century even though no great battle took place in either case. In 410, the gates were opened to the Visigoths after three sieges. In 455, the Vandals made an agreement that allowed them in without even a serious siege. Emperor Justinian of Byzantium sent Flavius Belisarius to reconquer the lost lands of the Western Empire. Undoubtedly one of the greatest generals in history, Belisarius won fame in 531 by defeating the Persians with the odds against him. In 532, he saved Justinian's throne by crushing the Nike Riots in Constantinople. In 533, he launched his mission in the West. After landing an army in North Africa in 534, he defeated Gelimer, the Vandal king, outside Carthage and later that year, he forced him to surrender. Next, Justinian sent him in to Italy to destroy the kingdom of the Ostrogoths. After taking Sicily and putting down a revolt in North Africa, he embarked for the mainland at the end of 536.[7]

The first major city Belisarius laid siege to was Naples whose city walls, which dated from the period of Greek settlement in Magna Graecia, were not much of an obstacle by this time. There is no good description of them. Belisarius isolated Naples with his army and navy, keeping the ships out of range of the artillery mounted on the city walls. After taking a fort in a suburb, he tried to negotiate the surrender of the city. The Neapolitans, convinced by their leaders that the Goths could hold the walls, decided to resist. According to the medieval scholar Procopius (Prokopios), the Byzantine army was repulsed many times and incurred heavy losses assaulting the walls. The seaside of the wall was not accessible and the remainder required moving through difficult terrain and steeply sloping ground. Even cutting the aqueduct did not help since the city had sufficient wells.

As with Rome, the Gothic king Theodahad refused to help Naples because he was too afraid to act. The Gothic chiefs held a council near Rome and elected a new king, the famous but elderly Witigis. On hearing the news, Theodahad fled to his fortress of Ravenna but was assassinated in December 536. The siege continued and Belisarius prepared to abandon the effort and march on Rome in December before winter set in. However, just before Belisarius' forces set out, one of his men, who was investigating the aqueduct, discovered that it was blocked only by a boulder at the point where it entered the city. Several Isaurians[8] were sent to break up the obstacle in secret. Once the work was done, Belisarius sent in 400 men and two trumpeters at night. Some of the men panicked and turned back, so he dispatched additional troops. Meanwhile, the general ordered some of his men to taunt the Goths and engage in a shouting match with them from below the tower nearest to the aqueduct to divert their attention and thus keep the element of surprise. Meanwhile, the men moving through the aqueduct followed it deep into the city until they reached an opening from which they could climb out. At this point, the aqueduct was above ground level. The assailants dropped to the ground, rushed to the nearest wall and took the Goths on two towers of the northern wall by surprise. The troops waiting below this section of the wall with scaling ladders advanced when the trumpets sounded from inside the city. Since none of their ladders was tall enough to reach the top of the walls, they had to bind two ladders together. Instead of Goths, the soldiers who attacked the wall on the seaward side faced Jews who fought stubbornly until daybreak when they were taken from behind and had to flee. On the east side, other Byzantine troops, without ladders, set fire to the gates, which were not even guarded. The sack of the city began after its surrender, but Belisarius ordered the plundering to cease and released the captives. The twenty-day siege was over and over 800 Goths were captured. Belisarius left 300 men in Naples, sent a garrison to Cumae, the only other stronghold in Campania and marched on Rome.

Witigis, the new king of the Goths, decided to go to Ravenna since he did not think Rome had been sufficiently prepared for defence. As Belisarius approached with only 5,000 men, he left a garrison of 4,000 men in Rome urging the Romans to remain loyal to him. The Byzantine troops entered the city through the Asinaria gate (on the south-east side) as the Goths departed through the Flaminia Gate (on the north side) on 9 December 536. Rome had once again fallen, this time without much of a fight and the city was not sacked.

Belisarius began repairing parts of the crumbling Aurelian Walls. According to Procopius, he modified the merlons by adding a wing forming a sort of flanking wall on the left side to protect his men from missiles shot by troops storming the wall on their left. He had a deep moat dug and strengthened the walls up to the Tiber. He had the granaries filled with wheat from Sicily and ordered the citizens to bring in provisions from the countryside.

Meanwhile, he sent his army northward as far as Tuscany and installed garrisons in a number of towns; the most important being stationed at Spoleto and Perugia between Rome and Ravenna. Both towns were linked to the Via Flaminia, which ran from Rome to Rimini. Witigis had not realized that Belisarius' army was so small or he would not have abandoned Rome. Even so, the Byzantines inflicted more defeats on him in the north. Finally, Witigis marched on Rome in March and Belisarius pulled back most of his army to Rome, only holding on to Perugia and Spoleto. Witigis ignored those two cities concentrating his main effort against Belisarius' army at Rome. Belisarius built a gate tower at the Milvian Bridge, about 3km (2 miles) north of Rome to delay the enemy from crossing the Tiber, but when its garrison saw the size of the Goth army, it fled during the night. Unaware of the situation, Belisarius arrived with a thousand cavalry and was attacked by Witigis who targeted him hoping that his defeat would wipe out the Byzantines. The Goths' cavalry was defeated, but the opportune arrival of their infantry forced the Byzantines to retreat to the city as more Goth cavalry arrived. The citizenry closed the Salarian gate fearing that if the Goths entered with the fleeing Byzantines there would be a slaughter. They thought that Belisarius was dead, but he was among the troops trapped between the wall and the moat. It was dark and with no other alternative, the general ordered a counter-attack. The Goths fled, convinced that the troops had come from inside Rome. Thus Belisarius was finally able to bring his men into Rome.

Witigis prepared for a siege in February 537. His army – which was massive according to Procopius – possibly numbered as few as 20,000 and could not surround the entire city.[9] Witigis deployed them in six fortified camps, five of which covered five of the fourteen main gates between the Via Flaminia and the Via Praenestina on the left bank of the Tiber on the north and east sides of Rome. The sixth camp was placed on the right bank was near the Vatican and covered the area between Hadrian's Tomb and the Aurelian gate. The Goths' camps were built on the same pattern as those of the old Roman legions.

The Goths proceeded to block all fourteen aqueducts then set to work on building siege machines and even digging mines. Belisarius, on the other hand, posted his best officers at the Flaminia and Praenestina gates and positioned himself between them, near the Pincana and Salaria gates from where he could lead a counter-attack. He ordered his lieutenants to build stone walls inside the gates to prevent any traitors from opening them. Remembering his own surprise attack at Naples, he told his men to seal the aqueducts. As the water supply was thus cut off, the flourmills fell idle. To remedy the problem, Belisarius anchored a pair of barges with a waterwheel jury-rigged between them in the rapidly-flowing water passing beneath the Aelian Bridge (Pons Aelius) on the Tiber next to Hadrian's Tomb. The Goths floated trees and debris down the river and broke the mechanism. Belisarius then had chains stretched across the opening under the bridge to catch the flotsam the Goths sent against his barges.

The siege of Rome lasted one year and nine days. Belisarius had only 5,000 men left to hold the city. According to Procopius, the city had suffered from famine and disease since spring. The Goths launched an attack on the eighteenth day advancing to the northern parts of the wall with oxen pulling huge siege towers the height of the walls and battering rams mounted on four wheels. They did not attack the Flaminia gate due to the steep terrain. However, between that gate and the small Pinciana gate there was a section of wall known as the 'Broken Wall' that had probably split more than a century before. The locals did not let Belisarius rebuild it, claiming that St. Peter protected this sector. Strangely enough, the Goths never launched an attack against it. As the Goths approached the Salarian gate, volleys of arrows from the walls felled the oxen pulling the siege machines before they came within reach of the walls. Witigis shifted the assault toward the Praenestine gate, where the scene was repeated. The Goths' advance slowed when an iron bolt from a ballista killed one of their leaders who was shooting arrows from up a tree. Belisarius arrived to find the enemy inside a section of the outer wall, which had been in poor condition even before Witigis' men dug a mine beneath it. Behind this section of wall there was a short length of wall the Romans had built as an animal enclosure for the arena. The Goths broke in, but Belisarius counter-attacked and slaughtered hundreds of Goths. Belisarius ordered the gate opened and chased the fleeing Goths only stopping to set their siege engines on fire. North of the Tiber, the Goths attacked Hadrian's Tomb, which had been converted into a fort and the Aurelian gate. However, they had only scaling ladders and no siege engines. Relying on the river for protection, Belisarius had not expected an assault and had stationed only a few troops there. As the Goths were about to make a breach, the desperate defenders started hurling pieces of the marble statues at them. Procopius estimated that 30,000 Goths died, a number larger than that of the Byzantine army.

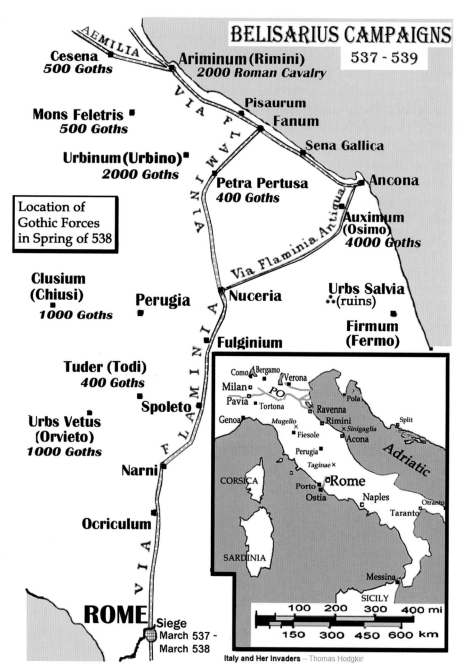

Belisarius' Italian campaign. Modified from Thomas Hodgkin's Italy and Her Invaders.

Before the assault, Witigis had tried to convince Belisarius to surrender honourably. After he halted the assaults, he tried to starve him into submission. Belisarius rationed food and sent out the women, children and slaves through the Appian gate and by boat to Naples while the Goths licked their wounds and looked on. The emperor did not dispatch reinforcements until December, but bad weather forced them to turn back.

The two aqueducts that follow the Via Appia and the Via Latina meet and cross each other's path near the city. The Goths took two sections where they cross and walled up the lower arches with stone and mud to form a fortress. From there, they could maintain a post with a few hundred men (Procopius claims 7,000 men) to block the Byzantines' attempts to bring in supplies or reinforcements. Finally, as rations and hopes of resupply dwindled, Belisarius' men insisted on attacking one of the Gothic camps. The general acquiesced, but the battle was a resounding defeat and they had to race back into the city. After that, he continued with the tactics of skirmish with mounted archers. Reinforcements finally arrived at Ostia in the autumn; a three-month truce was signed in December and about 1,600 troops reached Rome in early 538.

The truce did not last long as Witigis' plans fizzled out after he made one more attempt to bribe a couple of Roman defenders and launched an attack with scaling ladders. Belisarius sent mounted archers to shower the enemy with arrows and then ride back through the gates. In early 538, after Ioannes (John), known as John the Sanguinary, his bravest and cruellest lieutenant, arrived with supplies and troops from Naples, he sent him north to plunder Gothic territory with 2,000 cavalry. Ioannes ravaged the area, but when he came up to the fortresses between Rome and Rimini, he declared most of them impregnable and moved on. Witigis' uncle met him in battle and he was killed. Ioannes was thus able to advance to Rimini and take it. Meanwhile, pestilence swept through Witigis' forces besieging Rome and morale declined. News of Ioannes' advance convinced Witigis to lift the siege in March 538. He burned his camps as he left pursued by Belisarius who killed hundreds of his men near the Milvian Bridge.

Belisarius' campaign in Italy was mostly marked by fortress warfare rather than great battles like Hannibal's Cannae. The peninsula was dotted with fortified sites, many of which were simple hilltop towns easily protected by natural features and the occasional older Roman fortification. The major cities had walls. After taking Sicily and advancing through the South, Belisarius had been forced to either take or bypass 'fortresses'. Neither he nor Witigis could afford to take their entire army on their operations and they had to leave garrisons in fortified positions to their rear. The siege of a major city like Rome required a large force; its defence also needed thousands of men. Mass movements of troops at the time often resulted in losses for other reasons than battle. Since communications were slow, fortress garrisons often had to await orders that could arrive too late. The mountainous terrain of most of the Italian peninsula favoured fortress warfare and forced the leaders to decide what to hold and what to abandon with the limited forces at their disposal.

Gothic Siege Engines

Although the Germanic people knew little about siege engines, many Goths and other groups who were hired by the Romans before the fall of the Western Empire apparently learned siege craft from their employers. They built siege engines similar to those of the Romans, although they were not as expert in their use. According to Procopius, during the siege of Rome, Witigis instructed his men to build

> wooden towers equal in height to the enemy's walls and he hit on their true height by making many calculations based upon the courses of the stone. Wheels were attached to the base of these towers under each corner, which were intended, as they turned, to move the towers to any point the attacking army wished at a given time and the towers were drawn by oxen yoked together. After this he prepared many ladders that would reach up to the parapet and four engines called rams. This engine is of the following sort. Four upright wooden beams, equal in length, are set up opposite one another. To these beams they fit eight horizontal timbers, four above and an equal number at the base, binding them together. After they have made the frame of a four-sided building, they surround it on all sides not with walls but with a covering of hides, in order that the engine may be light for those who pull it and that those within may be safe from being shot by their opponents. On the inside they hang another horizontal beam from the top by means of chains that swing free and they keep it at about the middle of the interior. They then sharpen the end of this beam and cover it with a large iron head, precisely as they cover the point of an arrow or they sometimes make the iron head square like an anvil. And the whole structure is raised upon four wheels, one being attached to each upright beam and no fewer than fifty men move it from inside. When they bring it up to the wall, they draw back the beam that I just mentioned by turning a mechanism and then they let it swing forward with great momentum against the wall. This beam by frequent blows is able quite easily to batter down and tear open a wall wherever it strikes and that is where the engine gets its name, because the striking end of the beam, projecting as it does, butts against whatever it may encounter, as do male sheep. Such, then, are the rams used by the assailants of a wall. The Goths were also holding in readiness a vast amount of kindle-wood, consisting of wood and reeds, in order that by throwing them into the moat, they might make the ground level and their engines might not be prevented from crossing it.

These heavy siege engines were pulled across the fields to the walls by teams of oxen. Some of the warriors carried ladders to scale the walls. The defenders used bows and arrows to prevent the assailants from reaching the walls and spears to repel those that came at a closer range with the height of the walls giving them an advantage. The ballista represented the heavy artillery of this time. Procopius explained:

> Now these engines have the form of a bow but on the underside of them a grooved wooden shaft projects, which is loosely attached and rests upon an iron rod. So when men wish to shoot at the enemy with it, they make the parts of the bow, which form the ends, bend toward one another by means of a short rope fastened to them and they place in the grooved shaft the arrow, which is about one-half the length of the ordinary arrows that they shoot from bows, but about four times as thick. However, it does not have feathers of the usual sort attached to it but, by inserting thin pieces of wood in place of feathers, they give it in all respects the form of an arrow, making the point which they put on very large and proportionate to its thickness. The men who stand on either side wind it up tight by means of certain devices and then the grooved shaft shoots forward and stops, but the missile is discharged from the shaft with such force that it attains the distance of not less than two bow shots; when it hits a tree or rock, it pierces it easily.[10]

An additional siege technique was mining, which was used to bring down the walls since catapults and other types of tension and torsion artillery were not very effective. However, the defender's heavy weapons could inflict significant damage on the attackers' siege engines.

When Witigis extracted his army from the siege of Rome and raced towards Ravenna, he left garrisons at certain fortified cities to hinder the Byzantine conquest of Italy. Thus, he stationed a thousand men at Chiusi and a similar number at Orvieto and 400 men each at Todi and the key mountain crossing of Petra. He defended Osimo with 4,000 and Urbino with 2,000 troops. At Cesena and Mons Feletris (Monteferetra) he left garrisons of 500 men. Witigis next advanced at a slow pace, avoiding the Byzantine-held fortified cities of Narni, Spoleto and Perugia on his way to Rimini. Belisarius ordered Ioannes to withdraw his cavalry from Rimini and replace it with an infantry garrison taken from the fortress of Ancona before Witigis' arrival.

Belisarius set out from Rome preceded by a small force that was to relieve the troops at Rimini. Taking the shortest route, they reached the Passo del Furlo on the Via Flaminia which had been fortified at both ends by the Goths. At the narrowest part of this gorge with mountain towering on either side, the emperor Vespasian had built a 38m (124.6ft) tunnel known as the fortress of Petra Pertusa ('Tunnelled Rock'). The force of 1,000 Byzantine cavalry hardly made a dent in the defences with its bow and arrows, but it held the attention of the defenders, keeping them hiding in their small fortifications. In the meantime, Isaurian mountaineers climbed the steep sides of the mountain and once they reached the top, they rolled rocks onto the defenders below. The Goths could not reach the safety of the tunnels as pieces of masonry, including their tower, began to break off. Demoralized they quickly surrendered.

Meanwhile, Witigis, who was not moving with much speed, reached Rimini where he built another siege tower. This time, he made it higher than the walls and designed it so that his troops could push it under cover since oxen-power had failed at Rome. The tower included a wide winding staircase to allow his warriors to ascend rapidly and pour over the walls. The Byzantine troops probably watched the tower with trepidation, knowing that they might be unable to stop it. However, they were heartened when Ioannes, leaving only a small force behind, led them out that night to dig a ditch and create a vallum in front of the weakest section of the town walls. However, they were discovered at dawn and had to retreat quickly behind the walls. Witigis had the careless guards executed and ordered his men to prepare fascines to breach the ditch. Next, they filled in the section of trench under a hail of arrows and stones aimed at them by the defenders on the walls. The fascines could not bear the weight of the giant tower, which bogged down in the trench. Beyond, the earthen rampart provided a further near-insurmountable obstacle. Thus, the Goths had to pull the tower back to their camp before nightfall in order to save it.

At Rimini, Ioannes sortied against the Goths, leaving a small garrison behind. The Goths suffered heavily in the engagement and made no further attempt to attack the city. Further down the coast, one of Witigis' generals led an assault against Ancona, which, despite the fact that it was dominated by a Roman castellum on a hill, was not easily defended. Conon, an Isaurian general who had recently arrived by sea, was in charge. He created new defences consisting of a trench about a kilometre out of the city on the plain to protect the city below the castellum. When a large force of Goths forced him to retreat to his hilltop fort, the garrison shut the gates before he and his men could reach the safety of the walls. Conon and his troops had to scale the walls with ropes while a small number of defenders fought off the Goths. Conon managed to hold the fort, but Ancona's fate was not so felicitous.

Belisarius advanced along the Flaminian Way, clearing the fortified towns of Todi and Chiusi where the garrisons of 400 and 1,000 respectively surrendered hearing of his approach and the promise that they would be spared. About this time, Narses, a eunuch with a powerful position in the palace and a skilled military leader, arrived at the head of 5,000 troops and 2,000 Heruli, who were still considered barbarians by the Romans. He received authority from Emperor Justinian to take charge in Italy. Ioannes, still under siege at Rimini, was still considering surrendering and evacuating in a week if no relief materialized. Belisarius dispatched 1,000 men to the coast to block the Gothic detachment at Osimo while the bulk of his troops sailed to Rimini by boat and the remainder of his force advanced along the coast passing through Fanum (Fano) and Pisaurum (Pesaro). Belisarius and Narses led a cavalry group well ahead of the army through Fermo and the ruins of Urbs Salvia (destroyed in the previous century by Alaric) and moved deeper into the Apennines advancing quickly towards Rimini. Fleeing Goths warned Witigis that Belisarius was on the way and sowed panic throughout the camp. Thus, when the fleet appeared, the Goths broke camp and fled to Ravenna. Ioannes was unable to pursue them with his demoralized garrison. The relief force destroyed the enemy camp. Ioannes was not pleased with the belated victory but gave Narses the credit for the rescue.

Narses overruled Belisarius' plan for a two-pronged effort that called for one force to relieve the besieged garrison at Milan and the other to eliminate the fortress of Orvieto. He moved against the stronghold of Urbino instead. However, since the Goths refused to surrender, Belisarius was forced to besiege the city with part of the army while Narses and Ioannes forged on toward the next objective, Cesena. Unlike Ioannes, Belisarius did not believe that Urbino was impregnable. Although located atop a round and very high hill that was steep, but it was not an impossible climb, and a level approach existed on the north side. He ordered his men to build a large battering ram to push up to the walls. Instead of resisting, the Goths quickly capitulated in December 538 because the spring providing them with water had dried up. Meanwhile, Ioannes tried to storm Cesena by escalade, but the scaling ladders were insufficient and his force suffered significant losses, so he declared this was another impregnable site and marched off.

Belisarius decided to take his part of the army to Orvieto where the Gothic garrison had been under siege for several months. Located on a hill, Orvieto was a natural fortress with no walls and appeared almost unassailable. The starving garrison surrendered as soon as Belisarius arrived in 539. In the Po valley, the situation deteriorated for the Goths with the loss of Milan. In 558, a 1,000-man expedition dispatched from Porto by Belisarius disembarked at Genoa and marched inland, brushing aside Gothic troops that fled to the safety of the walls of Pavia, which held Witigis' treasury and arsenal. The Byzantine troops merely bypassed Pavia and marched on Milan where they were warmly welcomed by the citizenry. Leaving only 300 men to hold Milan, the Byzantine army went on to occupy Bergamo, Como and Novara. As Belisarius' army took one stronghold after another between Rome and Rimini, Witigis sent a large force to retake Milan. A Frankish army from across the Alps had already laid siege to the city and cut off the food supply. Since the defenders did not have enough soldiers to man the walls, the citizens pitched in. In spite of this, the Byzantine commander was forced to surrender in early 539 and he was offered honourable treatment. However, the terms of the truce did not apply to the citizens who were slaughtered as their city was razed.

In 539, after he recalled Narses, Belisarius concentrated his efforts on the two fortresses between Ravenna and Rome remaining in Gothic hands: Faesulae (Fiesole) near Florence and Osimo. Witigis had sent some of his best troops to Osimo while he held Ravenna with – according to Procopius' estimates – up to 40,000 Goths. Since Fiesole stood on a hill that the Byzantines considered unassailable, they decided to blockade it. Uraisis, a nephew of Witigis, led a relief army that crossed the Po at Pavia. His path south was blocked by a Byzantine army encamped at the un-walled town of Tortona. The two forces established defensive positions and waited. More Franks poured through the Alpine barrier, but the Goths soon found out that they were not allies when the Franks attacked them. Uraisis' troops fled back to Ravenna. The Byzantine troops opposite them thought Belisarius had sent a relief force until the Franks assaulted them as well. They too fled, many of them joining the troops besieging Fiesole. Some of the troops went all the way to Osimo to warn Belisarius of the new threat.

Probably in May 539, Osimo, which stands 280m (900ft) above the valley, was put under siege by Belisarius' force estimated to number 11,000 men. The Goths came out to strike at his camp, but were driven back as the seven-month siege began. The Goths sallied out of the fortress to forage, which led to minor engagements. Belisarius ordered his troops to destroy the Goths' cistern, which filled from a spring on the north side of the town just outside the walls. This operation resulted in a major clash in which Belisarius himself had to intervene and at the end of which the water supply was not destroyed.[11] The only good news for the Byzantines was that Fiesole had surrendered, probably in November or December 539. When the soldiers and their prisoners reached Belisarius' camp, the worried defenders of Osimo sent messengers to Witigis asking him for relief and supplies. However, he was too preoccupied with the threat from a hostile Frankish army in the Po Valley to come to their aid. As a result, the garrison of Osimo agreed to surrender on condition it would be allowed return to Ravenna.

Next, Belisarius set out to put Ravenna under siege and sent a blocking force into the Po Valley. This expedition found and destroyed Witigis' supply ships on the Po grounded from a sudden change in the water level. Belisarius opened negotiations with the Franks. Meanwhile, a fire of unknown cause destroyed many supply magazines in Ravenna. When a 4,000-man relief forced failed to rescue the city, the Goths tied to buy off Belisarius with many strange offers, including making him Emperor of the West. In the spring, the Goths finally opened the city gates to him. However, he did not accept the title of emperor nor plunder the city, but he sent Witigis to Constantinople. With the exception of Pavia and Verona, most of the remaining Goth strongholds in Italy, including

Cesena, surrendered. Justinian recalled Belisarius and most of his troops to deal with a new conflict with the Persians.

Belisarius' great victory in the Italian campaign was short-lived for by 542, a new Gothic king, Totila, reconquered most of Italy. He defeated a Byzantine army at the Battle of Mucellis (Mugello) after which the Byzantine troops avoided pitched battle. That summer, he bypassed Rome (held by Ioannes), Ravenna, Spoleto, Florence and Perugia. He took Naples and razed a large section of its walls, but treated the defenders honourably. In 544, as Rome was threatened and Totila besieged the fort at Otranto in Calabria, Justinian sent Belisarius with a small number of troops back to Italy. Belisarius arrived with supplies just in time to save Otranto. Next, he sailed northward to Pola and Ravenna while Totila captured Tivoli when traitors opened a gate for him. The Goths slaughtered the citizens as the Isaurian garrison escaped. As a result, Rome was cut off from supplies from Tuscany via the Tiber. In late 545, Totila laid siege to Rome. The garrison sallied forth to engage the Goths, but ran into a trap and retreated, never to venture out again during the siege. The city was isolated and soon the citizens and troops were ravaged by famine. Belisarius left Ravenna in early 546 and landed at Porto. He wanted the Roman garrison to engage the enemy while he forced his way up the Tiber with protected ships. Bessas, the commander of the garrison, refused. Nonetheless, Belisarius sailed up the Tiber with a flotilla of small ships loaded with supplies and a pair of barges mounting a tower and carrying flammable materials to hurl at the enemy. The Goths had blocked the river with logs, chains and towers on each end, but Belisarius destroyed the enemy positions and breached the chains. Unfortunately, news reached him that the commander of Porto had been captured after a sortie. Afraid that Porto had fallen and concerned for his wife whom he had left there, Belisarius turned back. He fell ill soon after his return.

Once again, Rome was betrayed, this time by Isaurian soldiers who agreed to allow Totila's Goths to climb their portion of the wall near the Asinaria Gate during the night of 17 December 546. Once inside, the Goths went to the gate and opened it to their companions. Bessas and many of the defenders fled the city. Many of the citizens had already left when Bessas had denied them access to food and forced them to buy it from him and his troops. Shortly after he took Rome, Totila prepared to leave the city to deal with Byzantine troops threatening his line of communications. When he learned of this, Belisarius sent him a message pleading with him to spare the buildings of ancient Rome. Totila, who may have believed that he would be able to retake the city, decided to grant his wish. In the spring of 547, Belisarius left a small garrison at Portus and led his army to Rome where he found out that Totila had razed up to a third of the Aurelian Walls and destroyed all the gates. Belisarius ordered his troops to patch them up with the nearby stones without using mortar. His men also dug trenches around the walls. Twenty-five days later, Totila returned after he received notice of the occupation of the city. The Byzantines had not replaced the gates by the time the Goths arrived. Then next day at dawn, Totila's force stormed the walls. In a fierce battle that continued until nightfall, Totila's contingent incurred heavy losses. The garrison placed a large number of caltrops in front of the open gateways. The next day, the Goths launched another assault with similar results. This time, the garrison pursued them until Belisarius brought it back before it could be cut off. A few days later, the battle outside the walls was renewed and the Goths were routed. Totila broke off the siege and destroyed all the bridges, except the Milvian, which was too close to the city. He retreated to Tivoli where his men rebuilt the fortress he had destroyed. Belisarius replaced the gates of Rome and the year of 546 ended without any further major action. He left 3,000 men under Diogenes, one of his subordinates, in Rome when the emperor recalled him to Constantinople in 548.

Totila reappeared before the walls of Rome in the summer of 549. The Byzantine troops had gone without pay for quite a while and a group of Isaurians guarding the Porta San Paolo were displeased since they were owed several years' salary. Since people who had betrayed Rome to Totila in the past had been well rewarded, the Isaurians decided to strike a bargain as well. On the agreed-upon night, Totila sent trumpeters to the Tiber to blow their horns to draw the defenders to the river wall while the traitors opened the Gate of St. Paul. Many Romans were slaughtered. Diogenes fled for help to Civitavecchia, the only stronghold remaining in central Italy. Paul, one of Diogenes' cavalry officers, gathered 400 horsemen and took over Hadrian's Tomb. Totila attacked the stronghold at dawn, but pulled back after sustaining heavy losses and decided to starve out the defenders. The next day, the Byzantines prepared for a suicidal charge against the Goths, but Totila offered them the choice of returning to Byzantium without weapons or joining him. Except for Paul and one man, they all joined the Goths.

Totila restored the city and reopened the games at the Circus Maximus. However, when his offer of peace to Justinian was rejected, he marched on Civitavecchia and offered the same terms of surrender he had given Paul's men to defenders and citizens alike of the city. Diogenes held out until the spring of 551. Rimini had been betrayed to the Goths and at the end of 550 and Reggio's starving garrison had surrendered. Totila had crossed into Sicily to plunder the island as an act of revenge.

In 551, Narses was sent to reconquer Italy. He spent much of the year preparing an army. Upon hearing this news, Totila pressed on with his siege of Ancona in order to deprive the Byzantines of a base from which to operate in the area between Crotona and Ravenna. He encouraged the Romans to restore their damaged city. He also built the largest fleet the Goths Fleet had in an attempt to challenge Byzantine operations in the Adriatic, especially to relieve Ancona. The Byzantine fleet of fifty ships engaged and defeated the Gothic navy of forty-seven ships at the Battle of Sinigaglia (Sena Gallica), north of Ancona,[12] in the late summer of 551. As a result, the Goths were forced to lift the siege of Ancona and retreat to Osimo. Early in the spring of 552, the siege of Croton was broken and the Gothic garrisons of Tarentum and Acherontia surrendered as morale sank. Totila tried to negotiate with Justinian, but his envoys returned empty handed.

Narses assembled an army at Salona, the site of Diocletian's Palace near modern-day Split in Croatia, and marched around the Adriatic. After a minor encounter with Franks who blocked his path to Ravenna, he moved along the coast using the fleet to cross the river deltas thus outflanking the Franks who had barred his way. In the meantime, Narses, after resting in Ravenna for one week, headed southward to Rome. He had to bypass the fortified Petra position and find another route to the Via Flaminia. The anxious Totila set out of Rome and the two armies clashed at Taginae in the Apennines. The Gothic army numbered up to 20,000 men and the Byzantine contingent 25,000 or more.[13] The only major battle of the war resulted in the death of Totila. The Gothic forces surrendered or fled. Fortified towns like Narni, Spoleto and Perugia quickly opened their gates to the victors. Tarentum's (Taranto) governor was not ready to surrender and the Byzantine forces had to move against it. Meanwhile, Narses proceed to Rome. The Gothic troops left behind concentrated at Hadrian's Tomb. Narses could not cover Rome's entire enceinte, nor could the Goths defend it. After Narses attacked at three points and failed, a group of soldiers with scaling ladders found an unguarded section, made it over the wall and rushed to open the gates. As the Goths fled, some of them took positions at Hadrian's Tomb and others at Porto. The troops at the tomb quickly surrendered in exchange for their lives; Porto and Civitavecchia capitulated shortly after that. Totila's general Teias took over his title and gathered the remnants of the Gothic army near Naples. He tried to break the siege of Cumae where Totila's brother held out with most of the Goths' treasure, but the Byzantine forces trapped him near Mount Vesuvius. However, since he held a strong position, he managed hold them at bay. Finally, he decided to attack only to meet defeat and die in battle in March 553, thus ending the war and the rule of the Ostrogoths in Italy. Aligern surrendered a year later and joined the emperor's army. The Ostrogothic army marched north disappearing into the mists of history, while the cities they had held surrendered one by one. Some of the Goths integrated into the imperial army, like Aligern; others simply mingled with and became part of the local population; others still may have submitted to or joined Frankish or Alemanni raiding parties.

After the final battles, Narses' army was too weakened to check the Franks and Alamans who raided the peninsula. The best it could do was to take and hold cities, until he finally engaged the Franks and Alemanni with a force of about 18,000 men against almost twice that number at the Volturno River. He defeated them at Casilinum (Capua) in 554, forcing them to leave the peninsula. By 556 most of the cities held by the Franks and the Goths in the north were cleared. In

569, the Longobards (Lombards) appeared in northern Italy to fill the vacuum left by the Ostrogoths.

The Gothic Wars represent a major phase in the military developments in Western Europe during the Dark Ages. The Visigoths had established themselves in the Iberian Peninsula after the Franks took their fortified capital at Toulouse and drove them from Aquitaine. The Angles and the Saxons were overrunning the Britons who were already unable to put the old Roman defences to good use. However, the battles were mostly small scale. The Franks under the Merovingians, like many of the other Germanic tribes, were moving towards feudalism. However, they were not able to muster massive armies and continue to engage in large-scale battles until the eighth century. Fortifications played only a small role during this period even though the Romans had left behind hundreds of fortified towns and cities. When Justinian launched his campaigns in the West and engaged in the Gothic Wars, he was fighting on other fronts including in Iberia against the Visigoths. Like in Italy, fortified ports and cities played a major role as the Visigothic armies began to shrink. The forces the Byzantines fielded were never as large as in the glory days of Rome.

The trend was for smaller armies, which resulted in fewer major battles and more sieges. However, these smaller armies could barely conduct a successful siege, which meant that most of the time the attackers ended up trying to starve the besieged into surrender. At the beginning of the Dark Ages, the Germanic groups lacked the sophistication needed for siege warfare, but by the sixth century they used the old Roman stone and masonry fortifications that were still reasonably intact. They even built their own, made mostly of wood and turf and of simpler design. Some, like the Alemanni, built hilltop forts often made of dry stone. Most of the Germanic groups used spears and javelins as missile weapons, but some of them also employed the bow and arrow. Storming walls by escalade usually required huge numbers of men to overwhelm the defenders and the most common siege machine was the battering ram. The Germanic groups did not like to attack or even defend walls. For instance, the Ostrogothic commander of Ariminum challenged Narses to battle in the open and 'fight like men', but Narses ignored him and bypassed the city. Usdrila, on the other hand, met him in battle and lost as Narses continued his march to meet Totila at the battle of Taginae. The Byzantine army held the edge thanks to its better generals, equipment and horse archers who devastated enemy formations. Naturally, the situation was completely different on Byzantium's front with Persia and the Balkans.

An additional factor in the warfare of this period was the leader. The loss of someone like Belisarius, Totila or any other successful commander as well as some distinguished warrior could bring about defeat on the battlefield. That is why early in the battle for Rome the Ostrogoths targeted Belisarius, resulting in his men having to rescue him. This situation continued throughout the medieval era.

Terrain also played a key factor. In the plains of Gaul, large armies continued to clash until the eight century, while in Iberia, Italy and Britain, most activity revolved around the defence of towns and cities. In Italy and in Iberia, most urban centres relied on natural features such as hills and mountains for their defence, which allowed many of them to act almost independently of an overlord like the Holy Roman Empire. City-states like Genoa and Venice emerged from the Dark Ages largely unburdened by feudalism and able to amass wealth through trade and the might of their navies. Both Venice and Genoa were protected not only by their man-made defences, but also by their geographical locations. Venice stood on a group of islands in a lagoon and steep mountains surrounded Genoa.

The Kingdom of the Franks and the Role of Fortifications

The Franks, who established themselves between the Bay of Biscay and the Rhine, both hurt and helped Rome. The greatest change took place when King Clovis converted to Christianity. His Merovingian dynasty fought to dominate the lands of Gaul and the bordering regions. The Merovingians used and maintained Roman roads and fortifications and adopted Roman military methods. They depended on Roman fortified cities and forts to deal with rebellious dukes and to expand their territories. However, the greatest threat materialized in the eighth century with the spread of Islam. Conducting a successful siege required a massive force and well-organized logistical support to maintain so many troops. As a result, the Franks favoured open battle, but since the Romans left behind so many 'fortress' cities,[14] they often had no choice if the enemy hid behind the walls.

On the death of his father in 482, Clovis ascended to the throne of the Salian Franks to rule one of three Frankish kingdoms. In 486, Clovis defeated the last Roman forces in Gaul and before long only the Ripuarian and Salian Frankish kingdoms remained. He established his capital in Paris, probably due to its Roman walls and because of its location. In 500, Clovis allied himself with the Ostrogoths to attack Dijon, the capital of the Burgundian kingdom. The city included a Roman castrum. According to Gregory of Tours, Aurelian had rebuilt the walls with large squared stones for the first 6m (20ft) and smaller stones further up, bringing it to a height of 9m (30ft) and a width of 4.5m (15ft).[15] The city enceinte included four well-defended gates and thirty-three towers and was almost square, but rounded at the corners. It was most likely part of the original legionary camp. The condition of the walls at the time is unclear; however, King Gundobad of Burgundy preferred to fight outside of them. His brother, Godigisel, who apparently instigated the war with Clovis, changed sides during this battle, which led to Gundobad's defeat at Dijon. Gundobad fled to the fortress of Avignon where Clovis, unable to engage him in open battle, laid a long siege. His siege arsenal probably consisted only of rams, which explains why the Franks concentrated on smashing gates and used escalade against the walls wherever possible. Gundobad convinced Clovis that the defences were too strong and surrendered, agreeing to pay tribute to end the siege. Soon Gundobad rebuilt his forces and went after his brother. He besieged Godigisel at Vienne, a walled city the Romans had rebuilt in the first century and improved over the years with a smaller but more complex system. The Romans had reduced the original 7km (4.4-mile) circuit of the walls to 2km (1.2 miles) to accommodate a smaller population in the third century. Gundobad took the city the same way Belisarius later took Naples by removing a boulder that blocked the aqueduct where it entered the walls. His men moved into the city taking their opponents by surprise. They sounded the trumpets while the troops outside rammed through the gates and poured into the city. Godigisel took refuge in an Arian[16] church where he was slain.

Meanwhile, Clovis forged an alliance with the Ostrogoth Theodoric the Great and attacked the Visigothic Kingdom of Alaric II in Aquitaine. After he defeated the Visigoths at Vouille near Poitiers in 507, he wintered at Bordeaux. Next, according to Gregory of Tours, he took Angouleme where 'the Lord showed him such favour that the city walls collapsed of their own weight as he looked at them'. Obviously, no one had maintained the city walls, making them vulnerable. Clovis drove the Visigoths from the city and took control of Aquitaine. The Ostrogoths advanced through Septimania and put Carcassonne (Carcaso) under siege in 508.[17]

The Visigothic king, Theodoric II, who occupied Carcassonne in 453, is said to have improved its Roman walls.[18] Carcassonne, located between the Cévennes and the Pyrenees Mountains, sat on the main trading route between Bordeaux and Imperial Rome. More importantly, it was the direct link between Toulouse and Narbonne and occupied a key location on this passage between the mountains. It was first fortified by the Gauls. Later, Roman veterans formed a settlement here and built an impressive set of walls around the city during the fourth and fifth centuries. They quarried the sandstone for the walls from the edge of the plateau overlooking the Aude River where the city stands. About one-third of the original Roman wall remains in the form of the inner wall between the Narbonnaise and the Aude Gates. During the reign of the Visigoth Euric[19] between 466 and 484, the name of Carcaso changed to Carcassona. The Visigoths either reinforced the Roman walls or built new ones. After Clovis defeated the Visigoths at Vouille in 507, he took control of Aquitaine. His new ally, King Gundobad of Burgundy, besieged Carcassonne in 508 and tried unsuccessfully to take the walls.

When they lost Toulouse in 507, the Visigoths moved their capital to Barcelona, then Merida and finally to Toledo by mid-century. Toledo stands on a defensible site overlooking the Tagus River occupied since Roman times. The successor of Alaric II held Carcassonne, Narbonne and most of Septimania until 511 when the Franks and the Burgundians briefly took Narbonne. The Visigothic king Leuva, whose capital was at Narbonne, sent his brother Leovigild to rule Spain.

Leovigild became the king of Spain and Septimania in 568 and ruled from Toledo. He supressed the Sueves and took control of most of the peninsula except for the Byzantine province in the south-east. His fame came from founding several cities and running a government that met the needs of his subjects. He also converted to Catholicism. The Merovingian king Guntram of Burgundy invaded Septimania in 586 (584?) with an army of 60,000 men and placed Carcassonne under siege, but failed to take it. King Reccared, son of Leovigild, handed him such a defeat

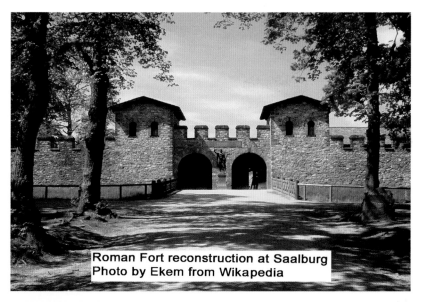

Top: Roman fort reconstruction at Saalburg by Ekem. (Wikipedia)
Bottom: old drawing of the walls of Nîmes.

with his smaller Visigothic army that the Franks never again threatened the Visigothic kingdom. Septimania with its fortress cities remained part of the Visigothic kingdom until the Saracens invaded in the eighth century.

When Wamba inherited the throne of the Visigothic kingdom in 672, Hilderic, governor of Nîmes, tried to unseat him by leading a revolt in Septimania. Wamba sent a Greek named Paul with an army to crush the revolt. When Paul reached Narbonne, his officers and the rebels made him king. His emissaries incited a

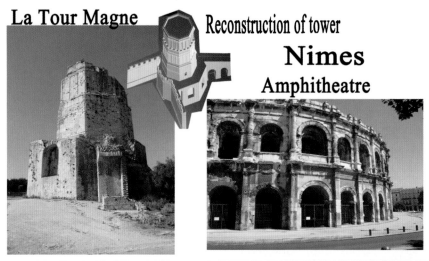

Top: Roman Nîmes, La Tour Magne and amphitheatre. (Photos by Pierre Etcheto)
Bottom: Narbonne's towers. (Photo on left by Pierre Etcheto)

revolt in north-east Spain. Wamba was fighting Basques in the western Pyrenees when news of Paul's treachery reached him. After subjugating the Basques, he put down the insurrection in north-east Spain and marched on Narbonne. Paul panicked and fled to Nîmes before Wamba and his army and a fleet reached Narbonne in August 673. He told the inhabitants that he would be merciful if they surrendered, but they turned him down. His assault breached the old Roman walls. Next, Wamba dispatched an army of 30,000 men against Nîmes, Paul's last refuge. The force arrived that September. After unsuccessfully assaulting the city defences, its commander requested reinforcements. The next day, Wamba arrived with 10,000 additional soldiers and renewed the assault. Paul, who apparently did not believe the city walls would hold, urged his troops to engage in open battle assuring them the enemy's morale was so low that they would flee. His troops,

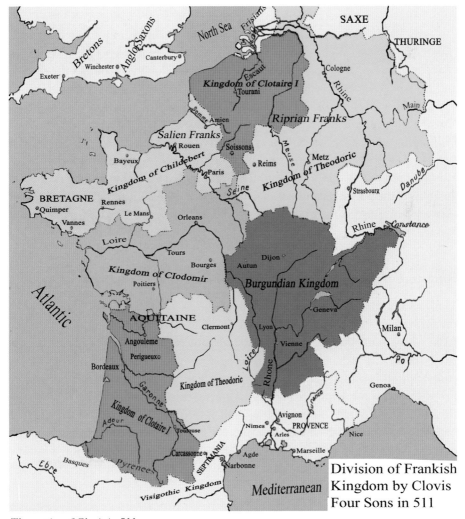

The empire of Clovis in 511.

however, refused. The city walls included about eighty round towers about 7m (22.9ft) high and the Tour Magne (Great Tower), at the highest point in the city, which still stands at 33m (108.2ft) today.[20] There were ten gateways in the first-century walls. Inside this tower is a more ancient one that is 18m (59ft) high. At a length of 6km (3.7 miles), its first-century walls were the longest and the thickest in the province of Narbonne. It is unknown where Wamba directed the attack, but the battle resumed and after five hours of combat, his men forced open one of the gates. Apparently, Wamba employed only rams and possibly ladders. Once they made the breach, the Visigoths swarmed into Nîmes, slaughtering nearly everyone. Meanwhile, Paul fled with the remnants of his army into the Roman amphitheatre with walls 21m (66.8ft) high. His men blocked the arches and converted it into an easily defended citadel. On 3 September 673, the citizens felt resistance hopeless and sent their bishop to plead for mercy. Wamba spared Paul, before he returned to Toledo. The revolt was suppressed.

Clovis died in 511 leaving his empire divided among his sons into four kingdoms (Austrasia, Orleans, Neustria and Soissons), which triggered a period of weakness characterized by intrigues and civil wars. By 613, Clotaire II unified the Franks and his son, Dagobert, helped strengthen the kingdoms in 639. Pippin (Pépin) of Herstal, as Mayor of the Palace (chief administrator) ran all three kingdoms (Austrasia, Neustria and Burgundy) for the 'do-nothing' Merovingian kings by 687 ending more than a century of chaos. With the Frankish kingdom on the rise, the power of the Visigoths began to wane after a period of prosperity under Wamba's reign. For the Franks and the Visigoths, success and control depended on holding the old fortress cities, which was not a problem for the Franks on their frontier with the Saxons where the Romans had left few fortifications east of the Rhine.

Roman Fortifications during the Dark Ages

Many assumptions have been made about the use of Roman fortifications after the formation of Germanic kingdoms on Roman territory during the Dark Ages. Even today, no solid archaeological data supplements the few written records from the era to establish whether these Germanic groups made significant contributions to military engineering or simply used existing works and methods. From Iberia to the Rhine many walled towns existed before the arrival of the Romans. The Romans built new ones and improved the enceintes of many old ones. It is an accepted fact that during the third century and throughout the next century most Gallic cities received 'monumental'-type Roman fortifications similar to the style used with Rome's Aurelian Walls with some impressive gates such as at Trier and Susa.[21]

After the mid-third century, the shapes of enceintes were generally irregular and took advantage of the topography. In some cases, as in Autun and Avignon, the newer wall had a smaller circuit than the older one because of shrinking populations. Most of the Roman-era walls were intact when the Germanic tribes took over, especially since the Romans left garrisons, usually composed of local troops to maintain them. In some instances, the invaders actually destroyed sections of the walls during a siege. It is logical that they would repair the damage using the Roman-trained locals and maintain the defences rather than build new walls. Many Germanic tribesmen had served with the Romans and adopted their methods and technology even though they lacked their masters' sophistication. As a result, rather than innovating and building new fortifications, they concentrated on maintaining and repairing existing fortifications.

From the Dark Ages until the tenth century, the Britons returned to less sophisticated defences. Where possible, they used the remains of Romans walls and old Iron Age hillforts. In the Frankish kingdom, the only new fortifications were largely turf and timber with occasionally a stone base for bridge towers. There is no evidence of additions to the Roman walls that remained in use to hold off the Vikings in the ninth century. In Visigothic Spain, until the eighth century collapse, most fortifications were built during the fourth century by the Romans. This includes Barcelona (Barcino), Pamplona (Pompaelo), Gijón, Zaragoza (Caesaraugusta), León (settlement of Legion VII) and other locations with high walls and projecting D-shaped towers. A new building phase took place late in the fifth century under the Visigoths at Leon, Uxama, Gijón and Tarragona (Tarraco) in Spain and Lisbon in Portugal.

Byzantine troops sent by Justinian reconquered south-eastern Iberia and the Balearic Islands in the sixth century. Some of the forts they erected were simple square enclosures with projecting corner towers. However, according to a few historians, these fortifications may have been built by the Visigoths rather than the Byzantines. The Visigoths might have built fortifications similar to those of the Romans rather than repairing existing ones since the skilled labour force was available, however fighting from behind walls was not a specialty of any of the Germanic groups. The only type of projectiles available, from spears to arrows, had a limited range. When the enemy attempted to scale the walls, the defenders could hurl rocks at them. Except for the bolt-firing ballista and catapults, there was not much else in artillery available at the time.

East of the Visigothic capital of Toledo, was the city of Reccopolis, which overlooked the Tagus River. The Romans are credited with destroying a Celtic fort at the site in 179 BC. Although there are claims that there was a town at the site between AD 350 and 450, there is no proof of its existence during this period beyond a cache of old coins found at the location. The Visigothic king Leovigild, who is said to have built many 'fortresses', established Reccopolis and named it for one of his sons. Between 578 and 582, in addition to a palace and a church, a wall was built that could be attributed to the Visigoths, unless an earlier Roman settlement had actually existed there. The ruins of the wall give it a thickness of

2m (6.5ft) and a height of 7m (22.9ft) making it thinner and lower than most Late Roman-era city walls. It was made of ashlars and included many square towers. Unfortunately, there is little additional information available about the defences of Reccopolis.[22]

Víctor Lluís Pérez García has shown that the Visigoths adopted the Late Roman technique of forming double fortified limes in the Pyrenees.[23] The first line consisted of watchtowers and forts at the base of mountain passes and the second line – about 50km (31 miles) to the rear – comprised fortified towns and small forts. Pérez García points out that the Romans had no reason to fortify this area since it was not a border region for them. Thus, he concludes, the Visigoths must have built it. The Roman walled town of Rose included a seventh-century fort.

As the Byzantines occupied the Iberian Peninsula in the south-east from Cartagena to Seville since the 530s, King Leovigild fortified his southern frontier with double lines between 568 and 586. The Romans had built fortified towns and walled cities of the second line during the third and fourth centuries. The amount of Visigothic additions is a matter of speculation, but it is likely that they are mostly to be found in the first line. Archaeologists have identified a large number of similarities between the Byzantine fortifications and the alleged Visigothic ones, which has led to a great deal of debate on the extent of Byzantium's influence on Visigothic military architecture.

In *Medieval Civilization* Jacques Le Goff suggests that the Germanic groups such as the Franks and the Goths probably did not build any significant fortifications because none of them numbered over 100,000 people when they entered the Roman Empire. This means that they never represented more than 5 per cent of the total population. Thus, these groups, which were mainly composed of warriors, were absorbed by the local populations that supported them. It is likely that their tribal societies lacked skilled professional engineers and that it may have taken generations to develop a base of such specialists.

The Visigoths and Franks from Gaul to Iberia

The history of the Visigoths, Franks and other Germanic groups is far from simple. The Franks migrated into northern Gaul and dominated the area in the fifth century while the Visigoths made their entrance into the empire from the Danube region. The Visigoths defeated Emperor Valens at Adrianople in 378, sacked Rome in 410 and moved into Western Gaul where they established a kingdom at Toulouse. Meanwhile, the Vandals passed through Iberia and moved on to conquer North Africa and the Sueves occupied much of Hispania. King Theodoric II (463–6) invaded Iberia and his Visigoths defeated the Sueves and spread terror throughout the peninsula.

His successor, King Euric (466–84), expanded control in south-west Gaul and pushed his borders west and north to the Rhône and Loire. He drove the Romans from Iberia.

The Franks under Clovis (466–511) became a threat to the Visigoths. Clovis' first major victory was the Battle of Soissons (486) when he eliminated the last bastion of the Western Roman Empire beyond the Alps.[24] He defeated other Frankish kings, except for the Riparian Franks and united his people west of the Maas River. He established his capital in Paris. Next, he subjugated the Burgundian kingdom and turned on the Visigoth Alaric II in a religious war to remove Arian heretics from Gaul. His victory at Vouille in 507 ended Visigothic rule in Aquitaine. Clovis died leaving his four sons to divide his land into four kingdoms. The Franks absorbed the Burgundian kingdom. Finally, internal problems and conflicts left Clotaire in control of all four kingdoms by 558. When Clotaire died in 561, like Clovis, he divided his kingdom among his four sons.

The Visigoths had a similar succession problem when the illegitimate son of Alaric II, Gesalec, took over. Amalaric, the legitimate son and heir, had the support of his grandfather, King Theodoric the Ostrogoth, who intervened and defeated Gesalec near Narbonne with the help of the Burgundians, who were Clovis' allies at the time. Gesalec fled to Barcelona with Theordoric's troops in hot pursuit. From there, he escaped to Africa to seek help from the Vandals, but he was rebuffed. In 510, the Burgundians took Narbonne while the Franks besieged the Ostrogoths at Arles. The Ostrogoth army recovered all the cities of Septimania for Amalaric, but Theodoric wrested Provence from the Franks and kept it for himself while continuing to dominate his Visigothic grandson. When Theodoric died in 526, Amalaric controlled most of Iberia and Septimania, but he died in a war with the Franks in 531. He had lost Narbonne to the Franks and moved his capital into Iberia. Theudis the Ostrogoth, who had been regent for Amalaric during his childhood, ascended to the throne. He drove the Franks back over the Pyrenees after they invaded Navarre and placed Zaragossa under siege for over a month. He was assassinated in Seville in 548 and was succeeded by Theudegesil who suffered the same fate in 549. The latter's son, Agila, took over and tried to subdue independent territories in Iberia until he was defeated at Cordova. Since Agila abused his power, a nobleman named Athanagild sought aid from the Byzantine Emperor Justinian who dispatched 2,000 troops in 554. The Byzantines captured many towns from Valencia to Andalusia and defeated Agila near Seville giving Byzantium a firm hold on southern Spain. In the sixth century, the Byzantines were more skilled at siege warfare than their Germanic antagonists were. Agila retreated to Mérida where he was assassinated by his own men in 554. Athanagild took the crown only to find himself at war with the Byzantines for the thirteen years of his reign. He also had to fight the Franks in Septimania, but despite this strife, his kingdom prospered.

When the Franks divided into four kingdoms at Clotaire's death, kings Sigebert and Chilperic married Athanagild's daughters to form an alliance. Athanagild died in 567 leaving his two sons, Liuwa and Leovigild, in charge, Leovigild, who was campaigning in north-west Spain in 570, moved against the Byzantine forces and took Cordova in 572. Liuwa died in 573 leaving him sole leader. Leovigild and his son Recared put down a revolt first in Toledo and then in Galicia and Andalusia. The Byzantines incited revolts in Narbonne and on the coast between Catalonia and Valencia. Between 578 and 580 Leovigild achieved a short peace, but soon had to contend with another civil war led by his own sons. First, in 581, he crushed a revolt of the Basques in northern Spain. In 583, his son, Hermengild, revolted against him and he drove him back to Seville and paid the Byzantines to break their alliance with his son. The siege of Seville lasted two years after which his son fled to Cordova where he surrendered. Leovigild also destroyed the Sueve kingdom in 583 leaving only two areas in Iberia under Byzantine control. He died in 586 while his son fought the Franks in Septimania.

Before Leovigild's death, Guntram, the Frankish king of Orléans, supported a revolt in Galicia, but the Visigoths sank his fleet and Recared drove the Franks back from Septimania for a second time. Recared converted to Catholicism,[25] signed a treaty with Byzantium and went to war with the Basques. Upon his death, he was succeeded by several kings between 603 and 612, which gave the Basques another opportunity to revolt. After Sisebut ascended to the throne in 612, he suppressed the Basque insurrection and declared war on Byzantium, taking its territory in eastern Iberia and leaving it only one province in the south-west. The death of Sisebut in 621 put his son in power for a few months, but when he died, a general named Swinthila took over. In 629, Swinthila conquered the last Byzantine province in Iberia. In 631, a nobleman named Sisenand, backed by a Frankish army, took Zaragoza and dethroned Swinthila. Sisenand died in 636 and Chintila was elected king. Chindaswinth took power in 642 and his son Receswinth inherited the throne in 653 and kept it for twenty-three years. In 672, Wamba was elected king and he waged war throughout his reign. He put down another Basque revolt and other uprisings that involved the duke of Tarragona, the count of Nimes and the bishop of Narbonne. He bombarded the walls of those cities with catapults and possibly ballista, but there is no record about the success of these weapons. Finally, Muslims invaded near Algeciras, but he defeated them.

Erwig took over from Wamba, the last great Gothic leader, while he was recovering from an attempt to assassinate him with poison in 680. Erwig lasted until 687 when Wamba's nephew, Egica, replaced him. Egica's son Witza came to power in 701. Witza, unlike his predecessors, died a natural death at the end of 708, but not before repelling both a Muslim and a Byzantine invasion. In 710, the nobles challenged his successor Achila and made Roderick, Duke of Baetica, king. Roderick defeated Achila, forcing him to flee to Africa. Then disaster struck when another Islamic invasion brought an end of Visigothic rule on the Iberian Peninsula.

Although fortified cities offered good refuges for both Franks and Visigoths, in the eighth century they still chose to fight in the open rather than engage in a siege. These warriors were renowned for their horsemanship, but cavalry was of little value in siege warfare. By eight century, only the Franks were finally able to mobilize enough men to take on fortified cities. Until then, the Germanic groups lacked enough archers, the best short-range artillery against troops behind walls. The Visigothic army was no match for invading Islamic forces that had already faced Byzantine troops, some of the best in Europe and Asia, including heavy cavalry.

Chapter Four

The Dark Ages in the West Part II

Fortress War in Western Europe

Information about warfare in the Dark Ages, especially during the period between the fall of Rome and the mid-eighth century, is rather murky. Written records are lacking. Frankish military leaders relied on the few military handbooks available, including the work of Vegetius (fourth century) and Emperor Maurice (sixth century). Some historical records written by clerics, like Gregory of Tours, do not shed much light since the authors often attributed the outcome of battles to religion rather than tactics. The account of the ninth-century siege of Paris by the Benedictine monk Abbo of Saint-Germain gives an inadequate description of the defences the Vikings faced. Information compiled in later periods is mostly based on conjecture. More recently, archaeology has shed additional light on this period. Nonetheless, details on battles, especially sieges, are often few and mostly inaccurate.

In his two volumes on Merovingian and Carolingian warfare, historian Bernard S. Bachrach has shed much light on the subject. Hundreds of walled cities, towns and smaller fortified sites remained in the West when the Ostrogoths and other tribes overran the remains of the Western Empire. Most had been built or reinforced by the Romans during the fourth century. Like in Rome, the citizens formed urban militias to maintain the defence of the walls and gates. The Franks continued to rely on these urban militias to maintain the fortifications they were to defend. As a result, one can assume that many of the Roman walls survived until as late as the ninth century, although one cannot ascertain their dimensions after repairs and modifications. Charlemagne and other Franks built palaces and stone churches, but had little interest in building formidable walls. This may be not only due to the expense, but also to the fact that many urban areas still had and maintained their old walls.

Bachrach estimates that attacking a fortified site required an advantage of 4 to 1, even though modern warfare theorists consider a 3 to 1 ratio an adequate advantage against a defender in battle. He reckons that 25 per cent of the assaulting men would be killed or wounded. Both attackers and defenders had light artillery like the 'onager', a torsion catapult that hurled stones, a variety of slings and the ballista, which looked like a giant crossbow, fired bolts at high velocity, but inflicted little damage on walls. In the sixth century, the heavy artillery included catapults that could break up walls. The deadly traction trebuchet was added to the arsenal at a later date.[1] These weapons could be used to hurl flammable material like 'Greek Fire'. The Franks and their Germanic brethren did not use sophisticated siege machines as the Romans did. They depended heavily on ladders, often put together on site with materials carried in the baggage train.[2] This required the army to include specialists, such as carpenters and smiths. The troops required training with the equipment so they could ascend ladders under fire in full gear with weapons and shield. Usually, the ladders had to be over 10m (32.8ft) long to reach the top of most walls. The most common siege engine was the ram, often mounted on a wheeled platform with some type of wicker and/or wood roof to provide cover from enemy missiles. The rams were most effective against wooden gates, but could damage some masonry walls. The Franks also used a similar wheeled contraption called a tortoise,[3] which was pushed up to the wall to provide cover while the attackers used iron tools to undermine the walls. Although Bachrach concludes that the Franks were able to muster massive armies, many other historians believe that their armies could not number more than a few thousand at most. Considering these factors, it is understandable that the Franks and their brethren preferred to starve out the enemy during a siege rather than to launch a costly assault.[4]

The Islamic Invasion of Iberia

After a Saracen raiding force led by Tarik ben Ziyad landed near Gibraltar in April 711. Tarik received the support of Julian, the Visigothic commander of Ceuta,[5] because King Roderick had raped his daughter whom he had sent to court. Before this, Musa ben Noçayr had put Ceuta under siege and negotiated with Julian. Tarik put Julian in charge of an advance force.

Julian transported the Arab force of over 5,000 men to Gibraltar (named for Tarik), while Roderick assembled an army of 100,000 according to an Arab chronicler, but probably closer to 10,000 in reality.[6] While Julian guided the Muslims and sent his spies out, Roderick had to contend with his own subjects' plots against him, which contributed to his defeat at the battle of Guadalete in mid-July. Roderick drowned during the battle.[7] His death sent the Visigothic army fleeing in disarray to the town of Écija where it was defeated once again after a long and bloody engagement with Tarik's forces. The army next took refuge in Toledo. Tarik's raid turned into a march of conquest. Julian advised him to send detachments to Córdoba, Granada and Málaga while he moved against Jaén. On his way to Jaén, Tarik found Toledo abandoned like many other towns. The Roman walls were still intact, but the Visigoths were not ready to defend them. At Córdoba, an Arab detachment was guided by a shepherd who warned them that the walls were strong and high. After they tried to scale the walls, the shepherd led them to a breach that was nonetheless still difficult to climb. The Arab detachment managed to get on the ramparts and raced to open a gate for their comrades. The 400 defenders took refuge in a church and held out for three months. At the town of Orhiheula (north of Cartagena), the Visigothic leader came out to meet the Arabs and was defeated in another bloody battle. The leader, the few survivors and the women of the town did their best to defend the walls, but they were eventually forced to negotiate a surrender. Tarik returned to Toledo in October before advancing northward to Galicia.

Musa ben Noçayr, jealous of Tarik's success, entered Spain with a force of 18,000 Arabs in June 712. With Julian's help, he advanced to Carmona, supposedly the strongest fortress in Spain. Julian's men pretended to seek refuge in the city and then opened the gates for Musa's cavalry that night. After that victory, Musa marched on Seville and took the city after a siege of several months. He marched on Mérida. The Visigoths rode out of the city to attack him but they were decimated in an ambush. The few survivors of the ambush retreated behind the city walls and another months-long siege began. After his forces sustained heavy casualties, Musa decided to use a siege tower to breach the strong walls. His men tried to undermine a tower from the cover of this siege machine, but the defenders killed most of them. After the siege, the Muslims gave this stone tower the name of 'Tower of the Martyrs'.[8] After this unsuccessful attack, Musa offered the citizens of Mérida terms of surrender and they capitulated at the end of June 713.

Sources: Ibn El-Athir and E. Fagnan (trans.), *Annales du Maghreb & de l'Espagne*, 1898 translation; James Murphy, *History of the Mahometan Empire in Spain*, 1816.

Nonetheless, there is circumstantial evidence that the old Roman fortifications remained effective well into the eighth century. Duke Eudo (Odo or Eudes) of Aquitaine relied on them in his campaign against the Muslin invaders and for his resistance to Frankish domination. According to Bachrach, 'For the Aquitanian dukes, these fortress cities [from the Late Roman Empire] remained fundamental for the defense of the region and thus continued to be of great importance for military purposes'.[9] Eudo held the walled cities, towns and strongholds of his territory with garrisons of local men sometimes reinforced with other troops. These troops often included Gascons (Basques), Franks from Charles Martel's military colonies and the descendants of Roman colonists. The latter often supplied needed technical skills. After the Muslim invaders destroyed the Visigothic kingdom of Iberia and established Al-Andalus (Muslim Spain), they occupied Catalonia between 713 and 714. The Muslim governor Al-Samh ibn Malik al-Khawlani crossed the Pyrenees in 720 to take over

Visigothic Septimania, which he used as a base to march into Aquitaine. That year, he laid siege to Toulouse forcing Eudo to seek aid from his Frankish rival, Charles Martel. Charles opted to wait and see what happened. The Saracen army, equipped with siege machines, was bringing Toulouse to the point of surrender when Eudo, who had left months earlier to get help, returned with reinforcements and attacked it on 9 June 721. The Arabs had let down their guard believing that Eudo had given up when he had fled. His attack took them by surprise and broke the siege. The Islamic forces retreated, but returned for a new campaign in 725. This time, they took Carcassonne and held it for thirty-four years. They also took Nimes, which offered no resistance. Advancing north, they laid siege to Autun and sacked the city to crown their victory. The Saracen leader died in battle in January 726 and his army withdrew to Spain. In 730, Eudo formed an alliance with a Berber named Uthman ibn Naissa – nicknamed Munuza by the Franks – who was trying to establish his own Muslim kingdom in Catalonia. This caused Charles Martel to break his alliance with Eudo and raid Aquitaine twice, seize Bourges and defeat Eudo in 731.[10] Meanwhile, the Muslim governor of the Umayyad Caliphate, Emir Abd al Rahman Al Ghafiqi, put Munuza's capital under siege and cut its water supply. Munuza escaped, but committed suicide when he was pursued. After he defeated Munuza, Abd al Rahman invaded the Frankish lands in 732.

The small professional core of Charles' Frankish army easily defeated most of his enemies. Eudo's army was unable to hold back the Arab invaders after he was soundly defeated at the Garonne River in 732 and lost Bordeaux to Abd al Rahman. Eudo joined forces with Charles Martel as the Muslim forces advanced up the old Roman road bypassing the fortified city of Poitiers and marching on Tours.[11] The armies met in October 732 and the victory at Poitiers turned the tide when Emir Abd al Rahman fell on the battlefield. The Saracen cavalry was unable to break the solid Frankish phalanx.[12] The Moors retreated with Eudo's harassing forces at their heels.

The Saracens returned in 735, this time by sea. They took Arles and then Avignon but not without a fight.[13] Next, they launched raids as far east as Piedmont and north into Burgundy, which impelled Charles Martel to launch a new campaign in 737. The Muslims used the local fortifications to secure their hold, but Charles struck quickly retaking Avignon in 737. His men silently approached the city walls, hurled grappling hooks over the battlements, climbed up and attached rope ladders to allow the rest of their comrades access over the walls before the Moorish guards could sound the alarm. Charles destroyed the defences after taking the city. Narbonne, taken by the Arabs in 719 or 720, was not as easy to capture since Charles lacked the necessary siege machinery.[14] He built a wall around the city to isolate it.[15] In addition to the difficulties associated with the siege, Charles had to face problems with the dukes of Aquitaine when a magnate of Marseilles revolted and the new duke of Aquitaine became hostile, threatening his line of communications. The Arabs in Narbonne were supplied by sea, so starving them out was not an option.[16] Charles decided to ravage the countryside and destroy the defences of Agde, Béziers and Maguelonne (south of Montpellier) to prevent the Muslims from consolidating their hold on Septimania before he broke off the siege. He did not even spare the amphitheatre, which formed part of the walls of Nîmes at the time. Next, he marched on the fortified city of Marseilles and crushed a revolt in Provence with the help of the Lombards.

The Arabs returned in 739, but Charles Martel, allied with the Lombard king, drove them out of Provence.[17] At the death of Charles in 741, his son Pippin the Short eventually became king of the Franks in 751 with the approval of the Pope. Pippin answered the Pope's pleas and smashed one Lombard stronghold after another in 754 and 755, defeated King Aistulf[18] twice in battle and forced a peace. Twice during the Italian campaign, he reached the Lombard fortress capital of Pavia. The first time, he established a fortified camp outside the city and proceeded to eliminate Lombard forts in the region. The second time, he laid siege to the city and built a wall of circumvallation around it forcing Aistulf to surrender. Having saved Rome, Pippin took nothing except the loot his troops captured and left Italy.

Pippin renewed the Frankish campaign against the Arabs in Septimania in 752 with the objective of taking Narbonne. The Umayyad Caliphate that had ruled the Islamic world since 661 collapsed in 750. Abd al-Rahman I escaped and established an Umayyad dynasty in Córdoba in 756. Between 750 and 756, there was no unified Islamic kingdom in Iberia, known as Al Andalus (Muslim Iberia). For a quarter of a century Abd al-Rahman was busy maintaining control and holding back a threat from the Abbasid Caliphate[19] and the Franks. Pippin saw an opportunity and moved against the small Arab garrison of Narbonne.

A Gothic magnate named Ansemundus,[20] who controlled large parts of Septimania, turned over Nimes, Agde and Béziers to Pippin. The lord of Mauguio also pledged allegiance to Pippin, which allowed the Franks to advance directly upon Narbonne in 752. Despite the small garrison, a seven-year siege began. Like his father, Pippin lacked adequate siege equipment to assault the walls. When an uprising took place at Nimes, Duke Waiffre of Aquitaine tried to take advantage of the situation. Finally, in 759, Pippin promised the Christian population of Narbonne a form of autonomy if they turned against the Islamic garrison. Thus Narbonne fell and the Arabs pulled back behind the Pyrenees while Septimania and part of Aquitaine fell under Carolingian rule. Next, it was Waiffre's turn. The duke had to depend on the fortified cities and forts in the mostly rolling and mountainous terrain that separated Aquitaine from the Frankish kingdom. Using a religious excuse, Pippin invaded Aquitaine in 760, first bypassing Bourbon[21] and then returning to take it quickly by storming the walls from all sides. He burned the city, but spared the population. Next, he took Chantelle by a quick assault,[22] which caused a number of other forts and defended towns to surrender to avoid angering the Franks. Next, Pippin took the fortress of Clermont by assault and burned it thus completing his takeover of the Auvergne.[23] In 761, he attacked the fortified city of Berry.

The Franks often used fortified cities as their jumping-off point for their offensive operations. Thus, for the siege of Bourges in 762, Pippin set up his base at Nevers. Pippin encircled Bourges with fortified camps before besieging it. He occupied an old Roman castrum outside a gate of Bourges on the road to Nevers to protect his line of supply. He also set up Roman-style earthworks of turf and timber – walls about 1m (3.2ft) high with a palisade and ditches 3m to 4m (9.8ft to 13.1ft) wide – between his camps to form a line of circumvallation. He had these positions built according to Roman standards. The lines ran within 100m (109 yds) of the city so Pippin's artillery and archers could take an active part from covered positions. There is no record indicating if he created lines of contravallation to protect his forces, but he certainly had the time to do so. His baggage train carried the tools to perform this work and he had a sufficient labour for the task. To cover his siege operations, he ordered a second force to advance from Tours along the left bank of the Loire to the fort of Thouars.[24]

The fourth-century Roman walls of Bourges included forty-six D-shaped projecting towers spaced about 50m (54.6 yds) apart and four gates flanked by towers. The enceinte was about 2.6km (1.6 miles) in length, so this siege was a major operation.[25] Bernard Bachrach estimates that 2,000 men were required to man these defences and that there were actually about 5,000 defenders present, including many professional Gascon troops to reinforce the militia. Based on Bachrach's 4 to 1 ratio needed for success, Pippin would have needed over 20,000 soldiers to assault the walls, not including the men left to hold the lines of circumvallation and other positions. Since Bachrach estimates that Pippin could mobilize a force of up to 60,000, this would not have been a problem. Bachrach thinks that the actual number of men involved in this siege was up to 25,000 troops.[26] Since local resources were too limited for foraging for a force of this size, Pippin must have depended on logistical supply line from Nevers of over 60km (37.3 miles). The Franks mastered logistics and kept wagon trains arriving daily. This is one reason why their government made sure communities in their territories maintained the Roman roads and bridges.[27] According to the chronicler Fredegar,[28] who left the only existing account and details of the siege of Bourges, the Carolingians suffered heavy casualties. Pippin wanted to avoid a protracted siege that would drain his resources and leave him vulnerable to raids from the defenders. He decided, therefore, to breach the walls rather than the gates with battering rams supplemented with catapults and trebuchets. The city fell but did not formally surrender. This siege involved a type of watered-down Roman siege warfare that seemed to be prevalent through most of the era. After the siege, a large part of Pippin's force remained at Bourges to repair major damage to the walls and remove the siege lines to prevent the enemy from using them in an effort to retake the city. The remainder of Pippin's army joined the troops at the siege of Thouars and holding lines of circumvallation. The Gascon troops that held the fort at Thouars surrendered quickly when Pippin arrived. The king had the walls razed.

Between 763 and 766, the fortified cities of Poitiers, Limoges, Saintes, Angouleme and Périgueux fell one after another. Duke Waiffre, unable to stop Pippin's advance, had tried to raze their walls before he abandoned them. It is unlikely, however, that stone walls could be levelled in a short time, so the duke's

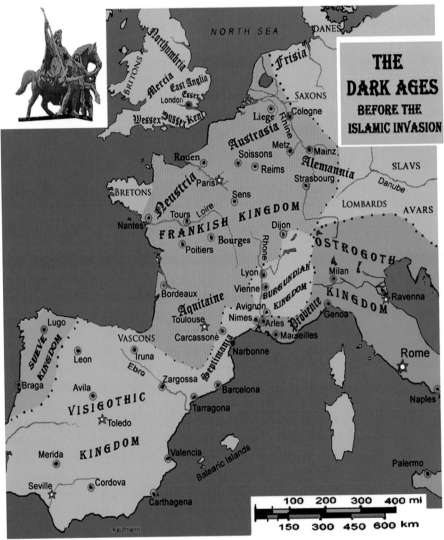

Map of Western Europe in the Dark Ages before the Islamic invasion. Top left: Statue of Charlemagne in Paris.

version of 'Scorched Earth' had little effect on these fortifications. As Pippin took these cities and many forts, he destroyed the existing defences of those he could not garrison and repaired the walls of those he could. To break Pippin's hold on those newly-occupied areas, Waiffre tried to recapture forts that had fallen into the Franks' hands and ordered their defences levelled. Aquitaine suffered heavily from the destruction wrought by the belligerents. No great battles punctuated the Dark Ages, which were mostly defined by the capture, defence or demolition of many fortified sites and the destruction of economic resources.

By 768, most of the leaders of Aquitaine had surrendered to Pippin. Duke Waiffre was killed near Périgord. Pippin died soon after he conquered Aquitaine. However, before his death, he repaired most of the damaged fortifications to maintain his hold on the region. Waiffre's son,[29] Hunoald, led a revolt against the Franks, but Pippin's heirs put it down and supposedly built their own fortress (which remains undescribed) in the Dordogne to aid in an invasion of Basque territory. The war concluded when the Basques turned Hunoald over to the Franks.

House of Cards: Europe on the Verge of Collapse

The eighth century almost saw the end of Christian Europe when a new religion emerged in the Arabian Desert in the early seventh century and spread like wildfire throughout the Middle East and North Africa. Before the end of the century, Islamic armies were threatening Europe. In 711, an army of the Umayyad Caliphate crossed the Straits of Gibraltar and quickly overwhelmed the Visigothic kingdom. Only Charles Martel's unification of the Frankish kingdom allowed him to check the Saracens' advance beyond the Pyrenees in 732. In the East, both old and new enemies kept Byzantium fully occupied in the Balkans and Asia Minor. An Arab army placed Constantinople under siege from 674 to 678[30] and from 717 to 718, but both attempts were unsuccessful. The situation in the Italian Peninsula was not much better as the Lombard king threatened Rome while he faced his own internal problems and the arrival of Pippin.

The Lombards

King Alboin led the Lombards from Pannonia into northern Italy in 568 filling a vacuum left by the Ostrogoths. He advanced through Venetia along the Po and put Pavia (Ticinum) under siege in 569. Frustrated and unable to storm the fortress, Alboin threatened to slaughter the Byzantine garrison, which surrendered only when it reached the point of starvation in 572.[31] Pavia, at the confluence of the Ticino and Po rivers, became the capital for the Lombards, but little detail on its fortifications exists. During the siege, the Lombards ravaged northern Italy, took Milan and most of the Po valley and crossed the Apennines into Tuscany and Umbria. Other groups of Lombards moved into southern Italy founding the duchies of Spoleto and Benevento. The Byzantine forces, which were too weak, could only cling to fortified coastal enclaves like Ravenna, Ancona and Genoa and to the island Sicily, which they could supply with their fleet. They also held Cremona and Piacenza, which they could reach by river. They maintained the fortified position of Perugia high above the main route, the Via Flaminia, between Rome and Ravenna. The Lombards surrounded Rome in 574 isolating it from Constantinople for about a year, but did not lay a formal siege. Things took a bad turn for the Lombards when the wife of King Albion arranged for his assassination at Verona in 572. A new king was selected at Pavia but a slave killed him in 574. The Lombards formed a confederacy of about thirty-six counts who ruled until 584. The Duke of Spoleto was paid off by the Byzantines to loosen his hold on Rome. In 579, however, he marched on Classis, the seaport of Ravenna. He also took the city and sacked it. It took the Byzantines nine years to recapture the city.

The Franks unsuccessfully put the Lombard capital of Pavia under siege in 590. King Authari, also known as Agilolf, who had replaced the ruling dukes in 584, resisted both the Franks and the Byzantines while he also subdued Lombard rebels, a feat he could not have accomplished without relying on his fortress cities. After he was poisoned in 590, he was succeeded by Agilulf who took Perugia in 592, but lost it to the Byzantines the next year through treachery. The Lombards took Perugia back in 594 in a siege that lasted only a few days, but returned it to the Byzantines when peace came in 599. King Agilulf put Rome under siege while he still held Perugia in 593. Although legend attributes his decision to desist from the siege to Pope Gregory the Great's prayers and leadership, it must be pointed out that Agilulf never put up an effective blockade nor made any attempt to assault the walls before he decided to return to Milan. In 601, he put down a revolt in Padua (Patavium) breaking the resistance of the defenders by throwing fire into the city, according to Paul the Deacon. It seems that he used catapults to launch incendiary devices over the city walls. Once he gained access to Padua, he levelled it.

When Agiluf's daughter was captured by the Byzantines, he marched out of Milan in July 603 to attack Cremona. He took the city in late August and ordered his men to raze it to the ground. Next, he took Mantua using his battering rams to break through the walls, according to Paul the Deacon. He allowed the Byzantine garrison to return to Ravenna. As his success against fortifications spread, the garrison of Vulturina[32] fled without putting up a resistance. Thus, Agilulf took the Po valley up to Venetia to obtain the return of his daughter.

After 652, the Lombard kingdom fell into a period of anarchy. Finally, Liutprand (712–44) restored the power of the Lombards as he conquered more Byzantine and Roman territory, causing the Pope to seek aid from Charles Martel. Pope Gregory II and his successor, Gregory III, strengthened the walls of Rome. The defences of many other cities, including those under papal control, had suffered heavily from constant warfare. Gregory III had to rebuild the walls of Civitavecchia. In 742, Charles Martel returned the lost territory to Rome. King Aistulf (749–56) restored the power of the Lombards and tried to conquer the entire peninsula taking Ravenna from the Byzantines in 752.[33] Pippin defeated him in 754 during his first siege of Pavia. In 755, Aistulf put Rome under siege for almost two months and, according to Paul the Deacon, he bombarded the city day and night with his siege machines, including catapults. Pippin returned in 755, besieged Aistulf again in Pavia creating a line of circumvallation and forcing the king to surrender. He then returned to the Pope's lost lands. Desiderius succeeded Aistulf, who died in a hunting accident, in late 756. He had a dispute with the new Pope, Adrian I, over Ferrara and other towns in 772. This time, Charlemagne answered the Pope's call for help. He crossed the Alps in 773 and put Pavia under siege in September. Hunger and disease forced Pavia to surrender in May 774. During the siege, Charlemagne rampaged through northern Italy. The city of Verona, whose defences were as strong as Pavia's were, surrendered, like many others, rather than fight. Desiderius' son fled from Verona to Byzantium. Charlemagne ended Lombard power, proclaimed himself king of the Lombards and took most of their Italian lands, allowing Byzantium to retain Venetia.

Charlemagne extended the power of the Frankish kingdom with a well-armed military force. The roots of feudalism had already formed as landholders were expected to owe service to the king, which eventually led to the rise of heavy cavalry.[34] The growing popularity of the stirrup in the West during the reign of Charlemagne increased the importance of heavy cavalry. Thanks to this Chinese invention, the mounted soldier no longer needed to fight like a dragoon by dismounting to fight. Even though these Frankish armies were smaller than Roman armies, they were highly mobile and proved to be an effective strike force. In these early days, they proved especially successful against groups like the Saxons, but not so much so against the Arabs.[35] Outwardly, it appears that Charlemagne had little use for fortifications or siege warfare unless he had no other alternative as in the case of the Lombard strongholds. Between 772 and 803, he engaged in eighteen campaigns to subdue and convert the pagan Saxons who had no formidable defences. He established fortified camps in their territory to help put down revolts. He overcame the Avars and their strong ring forts in modern-day Hungary in campaigns ranging from the 780s to about 804. During this period, the new Pope, Leo III, fled Rome in 797 when the Roman aristocracy turned against him. After Charlemagne restored him to power in Rome, the Pope crowned him Holy Roman Emperor on Christmas Day 800. Charlemagne sent an expedition into Catalonia under his son Louis, who besieged Barcelona from 801 to 802, built lines of circumvallation and contravallation around it and starved the Muslim garrison into submission. In 804, Louis laid siege to Tarragona but he was driven off by an Arab force. He returned in 809 and besieged Tortosa, a port near the mouth of the Ebro, but failed to take it. After another unsuccessful effort in 810, he brought siege equipment and finally succeeded in 811 after forty days.[36] This siege completed Carolingian operations in Catalonia and marked the birth of the Spanish March.[37]

In 799, while he was still engaged in subduing the Saxons, Charlemagne was alerted to the Viking threat when they struck the island of Noirmoutier south-west of the mouth of the Loire. He responded by creating a Frankish navy and a series of fortified ports along the English Channel in the years that followed. There are no details about the nature of these fortifications, but they were most likely turf-and-timber forts except in the case of some of the older ports like Boulogne, which might have had Roman walls. Charlemagne stationed ships at the mouths of all the major rivers from the Garonne in the south-west to the Rhine in the east and created a coastal watch and defence system. Until his death, he had little trouble with the Norsemen.

Louis the Pious, who inherited the throne in 814 when his father passed away, had to defend the frontiers of the realm and put down revolts throughout his reign. He maintained his father's coastal defence system. In the 830s, when he had difficulties with his sons, the Norsemen tried to take advantage of the situation. In 834, the Danes launched the first of many raids on Dorestad, a key trading centre on the Lek River where silver coins were minted. When Louis died in 840 at the age of 62, he left his empire to his three sons who began fighting each other. In 841, Lothair tried to solve the problem along the Frisian coast by giving a Norse chief the island of Walcheren. This was the first of many attempts to turn Vikings into allies. The Treaty of Verdun of 843 brought peace among the brothers when the empire was divided among them. These divisions formed the core of modern day France and German, but the lands in between were disputed for centuries. This middle section ran from northern Italy through Provence, Burgundy and Alsace-Lorraine to the Low Countries. Charles the Bald (843–77), held West Francia. His successors were replaced in 881 by the successors of Charles the Fat (881–8) who was the son of Louis the German (843–77) who held East Francia.[38] The Viking siege of Paris in 885 led to the downfall of Charles the Fat.

The Vikings shifted their raids on back to British Isles until after the death of Charlemagne. Most of these raiders came from modern-day Denmark and Norway.[39] Norwegians mainly assaulted Ireland and the northern half of Great

Britain and created bases in these areas whereas the Danes concentrated mainly on England, France and the Low Countries. The Vikings struck along the Bay of Biscay and into the Mediterranean. They even took Irish and English prisoners to sell as slaves to the Arabs. They preferred to attack undefended monasteries and towns since they travelled without any of the equipment needed for a successful siege. Rather than besiege a town, they preferred to exact a bribe to break off the attack. After the death of Louis the Pious, the Frankish coastal defence system became undermanned and fell into decay. The Vikings moved their raiding west towards the Seine and the Loire. Charles the Bald proved ineffective in stopping them. In 842, a rival count rebelled against him and allied himself with the Vikings. He provided them with guides to navigate the shoals of the mouth of the Loire so they could attack Nantes. They struck the city on a holiday taking the people by surprise and hauling off many captives for ransom. They established a base on the island of Noirmoutier, a centre for the salt and Loire wine trade. The abbey on the island had to be abandoned.[40]

In 842, a large contingent of Danes sailed up the Seine on a plundering expedition. Across the English Channel, Norsemen raided and spilled much blood at London and Rochester. The Roman walls that surrounded most cities and towns in Francia that had been a factor in the previous century failed to deter the Vikings at Nantes, Rouen and a number of other locations. The reorganization of the Frankish military might have been at the root of the problem. The situation continued to deteriorate on both sides of the English Channel. Fortifications apparently were not a serious factor since the Vikings initially avoided them.

Ermentarius, a monk from the abbey of Noirmoutier reported, 'the endless stream of Vikings never ceases to increase' and their pillaging was everywhere. They were unstoppable, he wrote, since they had taken Bordeaux, Périgueux, Limoges, Angoulême, Toulouse, Paris, Beauvais and Meaux. Angers, Tours, Orléans and Rouen were left in ruins and the fortress of Mélun was levelled.[41] Virtually every town was ravaged or besieged.[42]

The Vikings' activities ranged far and wide. On the Bay of Biscay in 844, a large Viking fleet rowed up the Garonne to Toulouse. Next, this same band headed for Asturias on the northern coast of Iberia whence it was driven off. It followed the coast down to the mouth of the Guadalquivir River, plundered Seville, but failed to take its citadel. There is no description of this fortification either, but apparently it proved to be too formidable for the raiders. The Moorish emir, Abd al Rahman II, struck back, inflicting heavy casualties on the Vikings. He kept them bottled up near the mouth of the river until he bought them off, forcing them to return their hostages before allowing them to sail to the Mediterranean.[43]

No one was immune. While the three sons of Louis the Pious fought among themselves, Horik (827–54), the Viking ruler of Denmark, took advantage of the situation to muster a massive fleet of 600 ships that sailed up the Elbe and sacked Hamburg in 845. Viking raids continued on the Frisian coast in 851. The three brothers tried to enlist Viking bands as surrogates to form a buffer on that coast. Louis the German's military skill kept the Danes out of his territory until his death. The other two brothers, Lothair and Charles the Bald (844–77), were not as fortunate. They even gave a Danish leader the island of Walcheren as a fief, but other Danes set up their own forts on the Frisian coast and continued to raid inland.

In 841, Ragnar (probably Ragnar Lobrok of saga fame) sailed up the Seine and burned down the city of Rouen on 14 May. A week after the sack of Rouen, he plundered and destroyed the monastery of Jumiège. In 845, he took Rouen again and pushed deeper into Francia, advancing up the Seine. The army of Charles the Bald tried to block him by occupying both sides of the river. Ragnar attacked the smaller Frankish contingent and, after defeating it, he proceeded to hang over a hundred of his prisoners on an island within sight of their comrades. The vaunted Frankish cavalry was too few and helpless to stop the Vikings.

No Frankish account of an attack on Rouen/Paris exists. If Ragnar actually had 120 ships as claimed in the sagas, he would have had a force of about 8,000 men, which seems a rather high number.[44] The Franks probably had only a few thousand men, enough to make an attack on a fortified city difficult. On Easter Sunday in March 845, the Vikings took Paris by surprise. No one seems to know where the defenders were, how large and in what condition the walls were or why the walls were not defended, even on a holiday when the city was under siege. Fortunately for Paris, Ragnar's camp was struck by disease, but Charles the Bald did not have the will to fight and paid him off in silver to leave. Ragnar lost about 600 men according to an eleventh century source.[45]

The Vikings returned in 851–2, advancing up the Seine and threatening Paris again. According to the *Annals of St-Bertin*, they sacked the city in 856 and 857 as well.[46] More raids followed into the 860s. The Danes continued their raiding and set up bases on the islands of Jeufosse and Oissel in the Seine between Rouen and Paris. In the late 850s, Charles the Bald laid siege to Oissel Island, just above Rouen, where the Danes had entrenched themselves most likely behind typical earth and stockade defences. When this siege failed, Charles hired a Viking chief named Weland in 861 to do the job. This time, the siege bore some fruit and the Danes on the island bribed Weland to allow them to depart.

Charles the Bald finally found an effective way to stop the Norsemen by building fortified bridges at key points. The first one went over the Marne River just east of Paris in 862. This gave him his first victory and forced the Vikings to negotiate. Before long, another fortified bridge was built on the Seine at Pont-de-l'Arch, upstream from Rouen. According to historian Charles Stanton, in July 864, Charles issued the royal Edict of Pîtres, which among other things, called for the fortification of bridges on the kingdom's navigable rivers. It also prohibited the sale of horses to the Norsemen who often used them to raid inland beyond the rivers.

The Vikings built few fortifications in Scandinavia, but they certainly knew how to use those they captured. The remains of fortifications found in Denmark are generally circular with earthen and palisaded ramparts and enclose quarters for 1,000 or more men. These forts may have served as a refuge since there is little evidence that Norsemen preferred fighting from fortifications. During the Dark Ages, Viking settlements tended to be small and large towns were rare in Scandinavia. When they went on extended raids, the Vikings often set up winter camps surrounded with some type of wooden stockade or actual turf-and-timber ramparts where they could protect their longships.

In Denmark, across the base of the Jutland peninsula, the Danes built the 19km (12-mile) long Danewirke. It began on the Baltic side at the large trading centre of Hedeby[47] and ended near the North Sea at a smaller town. Hedeby was exceptional since it had its own defences. Its single gate, located in the dyke where the road passed through, was on the west side of the settlement. Additional defensive ramparts protected Hedeby and the area surrounding it. When they were completed, the ramparts varied in size from about 3.6m to 6m (12ft to 20ft) high and 5.5m to 28m (18ft to 95ft) wide according to Gwyn Jones, author of *A History of the Vikings*. The main section – carbon-dated at 650 AD or earlier – included three ramparts. The main rampart was one 2m (6.8ft) high and 12m (40ft) wide, consisted of a wooden palisade backed by an earthen mound and had a ditch in front of it. A second rampart named Kograben – built between about 770 and 970 – lay to the south of the main work. It consisted of a wooden palisade about 3m (10ft) high backed by a 2m (6.8ft) high and about 7m (24ft) wide earthen bank. In front of the palisade was a 'V' shaped ditch 4m wide and 3m deep. According to Jones, the middle section, which was strengthened several times, included a stone parapet 2.7m by 2.7m (9ft by 9ft). King Valdemar the Great added a buttressed brick wall 1.8m (6ft) thick and 6m (20ft) high in the mid-twelfth century.[48] It is not exactly clear what the Danish King Godfred built, but the main work and the Kograben still existed during his reign. A late addition to the middle section between Hedeby and Kurborg included works that are more impressive. The low, marshy Trene River valley required less for defence. The rampart ended at Hollingsed on the Trene River. There were no other major obstacles along the river to the North Sea. The ninth-century wall was not an impressive obstacle and was probably patrolled but not garrisoned. At that time, it served mainly to regulate trade and movement. In 815, Louis the Pious' Frankish army passed through it with no difficulty.

The Anglo-Saxon kingdoms became easy prey for the Vikings. By the end of the eighth century, Mercia controlled most of the seven Anglo-Saxon kingdoms, including Kent. The Mercian king, Offa, became the first to claim the title King of England. During his reign, he created Offa's Dyke, which was similar to the Danewirke and extended along the Welsh border for about 285km (177 miles). It consisted of a ditch on the west side about 2m (6ft) deep and an earthen dyke with a wooden palisade of about the same height. Like the Danewirke, it was too long to be effectively defended and its few gateways regulated trade. The dyke itself prevented raiders from stealing livestock.[49]

One by one, the Anglo-Saxon kingdoms toppled before the Viking onslaught as the Norsemen established themselves firmly on English soil until only the Kingdom of Wessex was left standing. Alfred the Great, king of Wessex from 871 to 899 brought the Norsemen to a standstill. However, they were not pushed back until the tenth century. Alfred built fortified sites known as burhs to create a web of defences that the Vikings could not overcome. The burhs sheltered the local population. Some of them were located on old Iron Age ring forts, such as South Cadbury and former Roman walled towns where the Saxons incorporated remaining walls. The Saxons repaired and restored the Roman walls at towns like London, Exeter, York, Portchester and Dover. In some cases, they added wooden walls. New towns like Oxford and Wallingford were surrounded with walls. In places where Roman walls did not exist, they added a ditch, embankments faced with timber and a palisade about 3m (10ft) high, which constituted the typical burh fortification. Wherever partial Roman fortifications survived, they were included into a turf-and-timber burh. Most of the burhs covered river crossings and a few roads and were spaced no further than about 30km (20 miles) apart, a day's march from each other. Half of the locals eligible for military duty served in his army and the remainder worked the land. Some of the troops guarded the burhs,[50] most of which were in Mercia and Wessex. However, new burhs were built in areas retaken from the Danes such as London, Canterbury, Cambridge, Northampton, Nottingham, Lincoln and Manchester. In 878, Alfred defeated Guthrum's Great Army[51] and forced him to cry peace. Viking rule persisted only in the Danelaw, the land between the Thames and the southern part of Northumbria. In the tenth century, Saxon noblemen built private fortified residences in some locations. Like most burhs, they were made of turf and timber and sometimes they included a stone church tower. The fighting did not end even after Edward took Danelaw in the tenth century. The Vikings destroyed Exeter in 1003 and Wallingford in 1006. They attacked London in 1010 and captured Canterbury in 1011. At the death of the English king in 1016, King Cnut, a Viking, took over the throne of England.

Confusion and Lack of Evidence

There is a great deal of confusion regarding the types of fortifications built and their use between the fall of the Western Roman Empire and the tenth century. Historians and archaeologists can only be certain that many of the Roman city walls still stood at that time. Some had deteriorated and others had provided building materials for cathedrals and churches. Often only archaeological evidence and extant ruins provide us with incontrovertible information regarding this period since documentary information is rather scarce and frequently based on oral sources such as sagas and legends. The majority of the manuscripts from this period, such as the *History of the Franks* by Gregory of Tours or the anonymous *Royal Frankish Chronicles*, were written in Latin by members of the clergy and they tend to attribute the success or failure of sieges to divine intervention an pay little attention to the fortifications. To add to the problem, translators often translate Latin words incorrectly. One of these terms is castrum/castra, which was assumed to refer to castles leaving the reader with a stereotypical image. Historian Kelly DeVries, who has evaluated the works of many of the best scholars in *Medieval Military Technology*, has found that some experts identify early rural defences in certain defensible areas as castles even though they only consisted of earthworks and natural defences. These included formidable sites like Chastel–Marlhac, which according to Gregory of Tours was a natural fortress not in need of man-made walls. At best, calling any of these sites created for the protection of communities or noblemen castles is a misnomer. Many of these sites were more akin to Iron Age forts than castles whether they were privately owned or not. The castrum was actually a Roman fort in the Roman era and a fort in the Dark Ages.

Another question concerns the role of the Carolingian dynasty in the construction of fortifications. According to De Vries, opinions among prominent historians are divided on whether Charlemagne actually built and used fortifications. There is little to no evidence that he built any fortifications like those of the Romans, preferring the simpler turf-and-timber forts, which are mentioned in the *Royal Frankish Chronicles*. As De Vries points out, Charlemagne mainly focused on conquest rather than defence. However, he did build several coastal forts and created a navy to deter the Viking raiders. He also relied on older Roman walls that the Franks had repaired over the years. Charlemagne's successors certainly needed to improve their defences, but there is no evidence to indicate that they might have built larger fortifications than the Roman castra such as legionary forts and auxiliary forts.

Despite the lack of data, one can glean some information about fortifications from occasional comments interjected in the manuscripts. Thus, Gregory of Tours mentions the amazing condition of Dijon's Roman fortifications in the sixth century. In the *Royal Frankish Chronicles*[52] only a few sentences mention Charlemagne's involvement with fortifications, but the English translator incorrectly translates castra as castle instead of fort. Supposedly, Charlemagne built a castle (fort) at Fronsac[53] in 769 while campaigning in Aquitaine. In previous years, the Franks are said to have restored other damaged forts. When the Saxons rebelled in 776, they 'forced the Franks to give up the castle of Eresburg'. This 'castle' was another Frankish fortified camp and obviously insubstantial since the chronicle claims that the Saxons demolished the buildings and walls as they advanced on the 'castle' of Syburg where the Franks stoutly resisted. Here, the chronicler states that after the Saxons failed to talk the Franks into surrender as at Eresburg, they erected 'war machines to storm the castle' and 'the catapults which they had prepared did more damage to them than to those inside'. The Saxons, realizing how ineffective their weapons were, decided to prepare faggots to take the fort in a single charge. The chronicler does not explain how the faggots (bundles of sticks and brush) were to be used, but it is likely that the Saxons would have thrown them into the ditch in order to reach the ramparts. However, wrote the scribe, the defenders were saved thanks to a heaven-sent event in the church inside the walls that caused the Saxons to flee in terror. The Franks pursued them all the way to the Lippe River and slaughtered them before returning to the fort. King Charles came from Worms and smashed through the Saxon fortifications – which could not have been too formidable – and accepted their surrender at the Lippe River where he built another fortified camp and later had the fort at Eresburg rebuilt.

Another item of interest mentioned in the *Chronicles* took place in the year 789 when Charles marched from Cologne through Saxon lands to the Elbe where he built two bridges. At one bridge, 'he built fortifications of wood and earth at both ends' and from there advanced to subjugate the Slavs. His grandson used the same method of fortifying bridges to prevent the Vikings from advancing along rivers.

These and a few other sources offer only snippets of information on the fortifications of the Dark Ages, which causes much speculation.[54]

The Great Siege of Paris

For much of the century after the death of Louis the Pious, West Francia remained the main target of the Vikings. Information on the great siege of Paris is limited to an account by a monk named Abbo[55] who described the siege in an epic poem written in Church Latin. According to Abbo, in 885, a Danish king named Sigfred came to besiege Paris with 40,000 Norsemen in 700 longships,[56] numbers he probably inflated. It is more likely that there were at most a few thousand Danes. The importance of Paris was that it blocked access to the Marne and Upper Seine, which offered the Norsemen a river road to raid and terrorize the hinterland. In 862, after the raids of 845 and the 850s, Charles the Bald decided to fortify the bridge of Pont de l'Arche over the Seine just above Rouen. On each side of the bridge there was a fortified camp of turf and timber built in the Roman tradition. It appears that the Franks did not build towers on their forts. The stone work, according to historian Peter Sawyer, was not added until 869

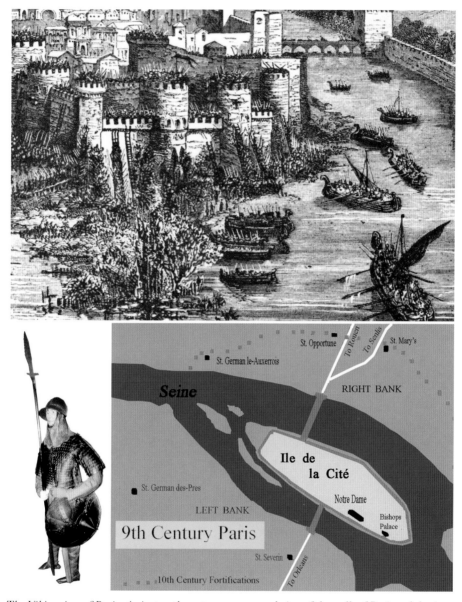

Map labels: St. Opportune · To Rouen · To Senlis · St. Mary's · St. German le-Auxerrois · **Seine** · RIGHT BANK · **Ile de la Cité** · St. German des-Pres · Notre Dame · LEFT BANK · Bishops Palace · **9th Century Paris** · St. Severin · To Orleans · 10th Century Fortifications

The Viking siege of Paris. A nineteenth-century exaggerated view of the walls of Paris and the siege. Lower left: Frankish warrior.

since Viking raiders occupied the incomplete site in 866 and moved up river past Paris as far as Meaux on the Marne and Mélun on the Seine.[57] Charles the Bald tried to isolate the Vikings in their camps to prevent them from raiding, but with mixed success. In 873, after a few years of occupation, he built another fortified bridge at Les Ponts de Cé. After a long siege, he finally drove the Vikings from Angers on the Loire, which had fallen to the Viking leader Hastein[58] in 870. The

Franks completed the work at Pont de l'Arche in 872 and successfully blocked a Norse raiding force in 876.[59]

According to the *Annals of St. Vaast*, which cover the years 875 to 900, the Norsemen ravaged the land of the Franks in 882 and 883, even after King Carloman defeated them in battle in 882. In 883, the Vikings wintered at Amiens and 'devastated all the land to the Seine and on both sides of the Oise' until 884. Carloman died on a boar hunt in December and Emperor Charles the Fat took over his kingdom. The Franks built the fortified bridge at Pontoise on the Oise while Bishop Gauzlein fortified Paris.[60] Unfortunately, the *Annals* do not mention what the bishop did exactly, but he probably fortified the two bridges. The Danes rowed up the Seine in their longships in 885, but the position at Pont de l'Arche delayed them for four months. Both Charles the Fat and his counts had problems mobilizing their vassals, so they avoided battle. The Norsemen finally took and destroyed the fortified position and advanced on Paris. The Franks under the leadership the Count Odo (Eudes) and Bishop Gauzlein were ready. They had fortified the bridges of Grand Pont and Petit Pont leading into the Île de la Cité with a tower on each bank of the Seine.[61] It is not known how many Franks defended Paris, but Abbo mentions a couple of hundred soldiers defending the towers for the two bridges. Also unknown was the number of Franks holding the city or in what condition the walls were.[62] In *Kings and Vikings*, historian Peter Sawyer claims that the Gallic cities had Roman-built walls to meet any possible barbarian threat, but that 'By the ninth century these walls were old and decayed and were being used as quarries for building-stone'.[63] The Archbishop of Sens, he points out, allowed stones from the Roman walls of Sens to be taken for church construction despite the threat of the Norsemen in 859. It is difficult to gauge how many other walls had been quarried during the Charlemagne Renaissance when many stone churches were built and fortifications were largely ignored.

According to a recent study, 5,000 people lived in the Île de la Cité at the time.[64] It is not possible to know the actual number, but the island of about 10 ha (25 acres) could only hold a limited number of people. It is likely that many of the people who lived outside the city walls on the Right and Left Banks had to flee before the onslaught. If the island population consisted of about 5,000 civilians, at least 1,000 of them were able-bodied men who could defend the city walls.[65]

According to Abbo, the tower on the right bank of Grand Pont was 'far from finished, but its foundations were solid and stood firmly grounded', which has been interpreted to mean that the foundation and/or the lower section was built of stone.[66] Abbo also alludes to the fact that the tower may have been part of a more substantial castrum. He does not mention the height of the tower or the number of its levels.[67] Unfortunately such detail is lacking; the castrum may have been mostly turf and timber or possible stone like the position at Pont de l'Arche.[68]

After the Gallo-Roman period, the city spilled over onto both banks of the Seine, but these sections had no known defences and there is no evidence that the Franks added walls to these suburbs. The defences for the Petit Pont on the left bank were smaller and there was no indication of any type of stonework. The condition of the Roman walls of Paris is unknown, especially since there had been previous attacks. It is doubtful that the walls were impressive or that they resembled those shown in the nineteenth-century engravings of the siege of 845. According to Abbo, the walls reached the water's edge, so their weak point would have been the bridges and the gate towers covering them.

The Danes arrived outside Paris on 24 November 885, under the leadership of Sigfred whose objective was not Paris, but rather a free passage for raids further into the interior. The Count of Paris, Odo, refused to let him through. According to Abbo, there were only 200 Franks at the 'tower' of Grand Pont, but there were certainly more troops on the Île de la Cité. Although he claimed that there were 40,000 Norsemen in 700 ships, it is more likely that there were actually only 8,000 to 15,000 in 300 ships.[69] Since the Vikings preferred to attack immediately rather than become involved in long sieges, the assault began on 26 November. Abbo's description has been subject to interpretation. The Danes stormed the defences at the Grand Pont, but failed to take the tower at the entrance to the bridge by the end of the day. That night, Abbo recounted, 'A wooden tier was built all way around the tower, raised atop the old bastion and half as high as before'. This may mean the Franks added another level to the tower giving it three levels as they prepared for the next day's battle. Some of the Norsemen fought their way to the tower and tried to undermine it with iron tools while others tried to burn it down. The Vikings used their boats in the initial attack, wrote Abbo. After the first day, the Danes erected a camp on the Right Bank using stones. When a quick victory eluded them, they settled in and began building siege machines while some of plundered the environs. Early in the New Year, the Danes renewed their assault.[70] The repeated attacks on the Grand Pont failed. The Danes hauled ships overland, set them on fire and let them drift down river to destroy the bridge, but to no avail. The burghers surged out of the city to join the men in the tower. The defenders poured hot liquids onto the Norsemen who tried to fill the ditches and the shallows near the bridges with debris and corpses to get behind the Grand Pont bridge tower. On the other bank, nature did what the Vikings failed to do. Rising waters and debris smashed the Petit Pont on 6 February 886 leaving the defenders on Left Bank surrounded by the Danes. There were only twelve men, claimed Abbo, but that seems too few to have held such a key position. When the bridge went down, reinforcements could not reach the trapped defenders who were soon eliminated by the Norsemen. The Danes built rams and belfries that had 'sixteen monstrous wheels … made of sturdy oak and each wheel had a battering ram, shielded by a roof', but they were unable to get any of them close to the main tower of the Grand Pont. They also tried to approach the walls in testudo formation[71] and under the protection of cats – a shed on wheels covered with hides to make it fireproof – to chip away at them with iron picks. The Danes also used catapults or mangonels to hurl missiles – which included pots of molten lead – into the city and against the towers. The Franks riposted with ballista mounted at a number of locations on the city walls.[72] Spears and arrows were the main type of missiles employed by both sides. 'Dreadful arrows flew thick as a swarm of bees [with] nothing else visible between the sky and tower', wrote Abbo.

The Norsemen 'encircled its [Paris'] walls, so that it had to face constant attacks from all directions', wrote Abbo and 'on the walls, the towers and all the bridges battle was joined'. The sounds of horns and battle filled the air striking the inhabitants with terror and 'the air was woven thick with missiles'. In the end, the Danes were repelled from the walls. Charles the Fat at the head of a relief army and his advanced guard under the Duke of Saxony briefly engaged the enemy. The duke was killed trying to negotiate one of the Vikings defensive ditches. Charles, who reached Paris in October, decided not to fight and negotiated with the Danes giving them a large bribe in silver to leave. They agreed on condition they could move up-river to plunder Burgundy, which Charles agreed to since he was having problems controlling the region. At the end of the siege, the Vikings lost about 3,000 men according to Abbo. The number of Frankish casualties was unspecified, but Count Odo emerged as a hero and Charles the Fat as incompetent. A result of the siege and its conclusion was Charles' reign came to an end and Odo became king of West Francia.

The Danes returned to their pillaging. They besieged Sens in late 886 and Meaux in 888 and several other cities as well. Finally, Odo defeated them at Montfaucon in 888 and when they besieged Paris in 890, he was able to repel them by giving them another bribe, according to Oman. The Great Army, reduced in size, moved on to Brittany where it had no success. Sigfred moved his troops to the Dyle River and built a fortified camp at Louvain. King Arnulf of East Francia attacked this camp in 891 and killed Sigfred. The remnants of the Great Army moved on to England. As the threat to the land of the Franks dwindled, the new rulers could concentrate on fighting among themselves.[73]

All Roads Lead to Reims

The various kingdoms of the Dark Ages tried to keep the old Roman roads, bridges and secondary transportation lines in good condition by integrating maintenance work into the tax system or making it part of the military obligation for vassals. It can only be speculated how successful these efforts were by the ninth century, but this network of roads still provided for a relatively wide and unobstructed pathway for wagons hauling goods. In addition, they allowed military units to move quickly in defence of the kingdom. In the Frankish empire, the old Roman roads came out of the Italian Peninsula along the Mediterranean coast to Arles and also through the Alps from Italy to the Rhône Valley before they turned northward along the west bank of the river to Vienne, Lyon and Paris. From Lyon, one road ran west to Saintes and another to the Loire toward Nantes also intersected with a road from Paris that went to Poitiers, Saintes, Bordeaux, Narbonne and along the Mediterranean to Nimes and Arles.

The road that ran north from Lyon to Paris continued to the mouth of the Seine, but bifurcated at Sens toward Reims before reaching Paris. From Reims, other roads radiated out toward Metz and Strasbourg, to Trier and Mainz on the Rhine. The road that led to the Rhine divided. One branch followed the Rhine to Strasbourg and the other ran along the Rhine to Cologne, Nijmegen and Utrecht. Another road linked Tongres to Boulogne. Halfway to those two towns, the road branched off and returned to Reims. Two other major roads out of Reims ran to Sens and Paris. At this time, only two roads from Sens and Reims passed through Paris. The road from Paris to the mouth of the Seine was on the east bank, the only route the Frankish armies could take to respond to Viking operations in the Lower Seine region since the Vikings relied heavily on the rivers for raiding the interior. The Marne, which joins the Seine near Paris, allowed the Norsemen access deep into the interior to the south of Reims. Down river from Paris, the Oise provided a route into the region north of Reims. The road network from Reims allowed the Franks to counter the Vikings' moves. The roads, combined with the fortified bridges of Charles the Bald, offered the best means of controlling the Norse raiders.

Chapter Five

Transition from The Dark Ages to the High Middle Ages

Emergence of European States and the Castle

A s Western Europe transitioned out of the Dark Ages, the foundations of its future nations were laid. The feudal system that had emerged during the Dark Ages still dominated the social order. However, the first Capetian kings exerted little control over their vassals because the classical form of feudalism among the Franks fostered rebellious counts who could not be effectively contained. Often, these vassals could field larger armies than their king. Furthermore, their feudal obligations allowed them to limit the number of knights and the length of time they had to serve their lord. As a result, the king had to resort to hiring mercenaries to augment the numbers of the royal army.

The threat from the Vikings receded during the tenth century and disappeared late in the eleventh. The French nation emerged after the death in a hunting accident of the last Carolingian king, Louis V, only a few months after he had ascended to the throne in 987. Hugh Capet,[1] who inherited the throne, ruled for nine years and established the first French dynasty. The most important modification to the French kingdom had taken place earlier when the Frankish ruler, Charles III 'the Simple', ceded control of Normandy (named for the Norsemen) to the Viking Rollo[2] in 911. Rollo had operated on the lower Seine since 886 and had captured Rouen. He converted to Christianity and became a vassal of the king before he expanded his holdings.

In 1016, the Danish Viking Canute was elected as King of England. He was challenged by a Saxon rival, Edmund Ironside, whom he defeated in battle. Edmund died one month later, leaving Canute in control of all of England. The kingdom prospered during Canute's reign. Canute was succeeded by his illegitimate son, Harold Harefoot, who died in 1040. His half-brother, Hardicanute, who had replaced their father Canute as King of Denmark in 1035, took the throne until he died in 1042. His passing brought the return of an Anglo-Saxon king, Edward the Confessor, the son of King Ethelred. The situation in England remained stable until Edward's death in 1066 when the line of succession was put in doubt as many of Canute's relatives became involved. Prior to Edward's demise, in 1064, Harold Godwinson, a powerful Anglo-Saxon nobleman, had gone on a hunting expedition by ship along the English coast. A storm had forced his vessel across the Channel where a French nobleman had taken him prisoner. William, Duke of

Normandy[3] had rescued him and entertained him before he returned to England. Harold supposedly had acknowledged William as the future successor to Edward the Confessor. When Edward the Confessor died in January 1066, Godwinson was elected king by the Witan (a council of noblemen), thus becoming Harold II. The election was fraught with family complications because in 1065 Harold Godwinson had removed his brother Tostig Godwinson from the Earldom of Northumbria. Tostig convinced King Harald Hardrada of Norway to back his challenge of his brother's claim to the throne. Thus, Tostig and Harald Hardrada embarked on an invasion of England in the summer of 1066. In the meantime, William prepared to do the same from across the English Channel. Harold II met and defeated the Viking force in September 1066 at Stamford Bridge and marched south to meet William and his Normans.[4] In October, William won the decisive battle of Hastings and took the throne. Although the Duke of Normandy was a vassal of the king of France, he became a king in his own right. During the twelfth century, the English Plantagenets[5] controlled half of France. The French kings established family ties through marriage with most European kingdoms in the West.

Most of the lands bordering on the Rhine, formerly part of the old Roman Empire, came under the control of the Holy Roman Empire, which took form officially under Otto I, the Great.[6] One of his chief rivals on the Italian Peninsula was Berengar II who had wanted to consolidate his power over the region by marrying his son to Adelaide, widow of his co-king, Lothair II. When Adelaide refused the union, Berengar imprisoned her in a formidable tenth-century castle on Lake Garda.[7] According to legend, after four months a priest dug a hole in the walls of the castle and helped Adelaide escape by boat. Adelaide sought refuge in Canossa Castle, built on a rocky hill in the 940s. Berengar pursued her there and laid siege to Canossa for three years. Adelaide offered Otto the Great her hand in marriage if he rescued her from Berengar. Otto accepted her proposal and came to her rescue. After their marriage, which was celebrated in 950, Otto challenged Berengar for control of Lombardy. Berengar built a stronghold at San Marino and invaded the Papal States in 960. Otto came to the Pope's rescue by taking Pavia first and relieving Rome next. He was crowned Holy Roman Emperor in 962 by Pope John XII. However, shortly afterward, Otto turned against Pope John XII and his successor, Benedict V, and starved Rome into submission in 965. At this point, Otto controlled most of Northern Italy except Venice. The Saracens had overrun Sicily at the end of the ninth century while the Byzantines tried to maintain control of southern Italy.

In the eleventh century, Norman adventurers started showing up in southern Italy. They included Robert Guiscard who came in 1048 to help the Lombard Prince of Capua and soon established his own power base. In 1053, he took part in the Battle of Civitate where Pope Leo IX's army of Lombards, Italians and Germans met the outnumbered Normans. Robert, who commanded the Norman

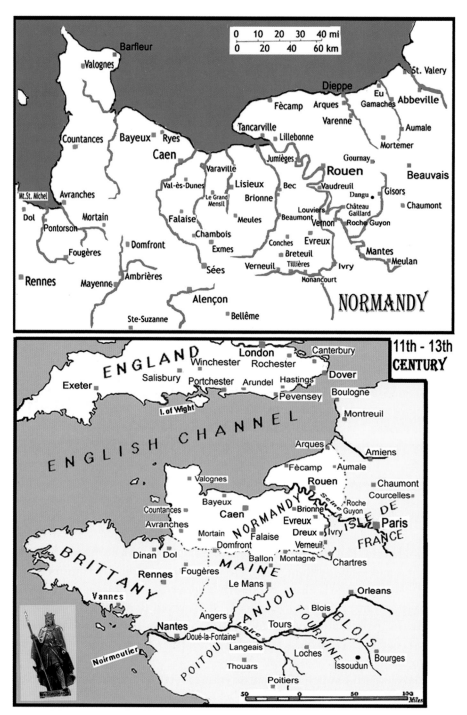

Normandy and north-west France in the High Middle Ages. Statue of Duke Robert I, The Magnificent, father of William the Conqueror.

cavalry, delivered the victory. While, Byzantium's hold in the south dwindled only to Bari, the Normans became dominant in south Italy and established the dukedom of Apulia a few years later.[8] Robert and other Normans tangled with Byzantine, Lombard and Papal forces in their attempt to control the region. By the end of the century, they held most of southern Italy and drove the Saracens from much of Sicily. As the French, English and Spanish nations began to emerge from the old Western Roman Empire during the High Middle Ages, the Italian lands were far from being a strong, unified nation.

In Iberia, the Christian kingdom between the coast and the Cantabrian Mountains known as Asturias survived the Islamic conquest and by the early tenth century had conquered Leon with which it merged. Expansion continued into Castile, the Land of Castles, until the kingdoms of León and Castile united in 1230. During the Dark Ages, many castra secured the kingdom as it advanced. In May 1085, King Alfonso VI took Toledo from the Muslims. The city became the political centre of the kingdom until the end of the Middle Ages. Early in the eleventh century, the kingdom of Aragon emerged and joined with the kingdom of Navarre in driving back the Moors. A Portuguese kingdom emerged in the twelfth century. These Christian kingdoms of Iberia were midway through the Reconquista in the eleventh century and before the close of the Middle Ages Castile and Aragon (united in the fifteenth century) and Portugal controlled the peninsula.

Birth of the Castle

In general, a monarch's soldiers usually built and occupied forts and fortresses, but in the feudal state powerful, and even not so powerful, noblemen built their own private fortifications to protect themselves from local enemies since their sovereign often lacked the resources to defend all parts of his realm. This problem became particularly acute during the tenth-century Viking raids in West Francia (France). These private fortifications, which generally served as a residence for the nobleman and his family, are usually referred to as 'castles' by historians. Powerful noblemen or kings often owned more than one and placed them under the command of a castellan or constable. Often, the term castle is also erroneously applied to similar structures that were not privately owned and should be called forts or fortresses.[9] There is also some confusion regarding the term 'manor' or 'manor house', which was the administrative and judicial centre of a fief.[10] Manors might also be fortified and could be part of an actual castle. Some minor noblemen only controlled a manor house while major noblemen could have several houses and castles. In 864, Charles the Bald's Edict of Pîtres declared, 'Whoever constructs in these times castella, defensive works and palisade without our order … are to have them pulled down …'.[11] Charles was not the first king to warn against building private fortifications or adding crenellations to one's home. In England, between the mid-twelfth century and the seventeenth century, a licence to crenellate was required to fortify a manor, a castle, church buildings or even towns. Philip Davis has catalogued types of licences issued between 1199 and 1567 in England and Wales. It turns out 449 were for private residences, 28 for urban defences and 44 for ecclesiastical sites. Of these, 101 were described as masonry castles, 24 as fortified manor houses, 66 as palaces, 24 as tower houses and 18 as town defences. Of the licences that were issued, eleven were to women, ninety-six to clergymen, twenty-four to townsmen (including six to mayors) and sixty-four to knights. Thirty-one documents used the term castrum for castle. Some licences were issued to convert manors into castles. According to Davis, many noblemen built their fortifications without licence.[12]

Some Roman-era walls of military camps, forts and cities still stood at the end of the Dark Ages; many, however, had been repaired and modified. The most impressive Roman works, however, were not to be found in northern Europe. The Crusaders at the end of the eleventh century and later came across them in Italy, Byzantium and the Middle East. When they returned during the twelfth century – especially the latter half of the century and later – they brought with them knowledge of D-shaped towers, round or drum towers, stone machicolations, beaks and talus slopes on walls, properly placed mural towers and symmetrical enceintes. Some of these features were also probably developed independently in Europe. Military technology involving equipment and types of artillery had not changed significantly in siege warfare. In the mid-twelfth century, the counterweight trebuchet may have been one of the most significant developments. Larger trebuchets that launched heavy rocks were able to bring down towers or sections of wall with a direct hit. The smaller perrier was a traction predecessor of the trebuchet. It was less accurate since 'traction' required men to pull down on several ropes to propel the arm that worked like a sling. The trebuchet was larger than a typical torsion catapult for hurling stones (often called mangonels – from a Greek term for war machine – in the Middle Ages). Mangonels could seldom damage stout stone walls and were more effective against wooden walls and hoardings. When several machines were organized into units, they could engage in bombardments that lasted for hours, possibly inflicting some casualties, but also hurting the morale of the defenders. Due to their limited range, however, they had to be placed close to the fortifications, which often invited the besieged to attack them. The ballista, more of a giant crossbow, had limited value against fortifications since it fired only bolts.

There was little incentive to build new fortifications when there already were older ones that only needed repairs or modifications. New fortifications, which consisted mainly of wood and earth, appeared in the Dark Ages in north-west Europe mainly to protect undefended villages from Viking raids. Fortified manor

Siege engines and missile weapons. Top left: Traction trebuchet. Top right: Ballista at Castelnaud. Centre left: Type of catapult at Castel Sant'Angelo. Centre right: Large crossbow. Bottom left: Crossbow. Bottom right. Counterbalance trebuchet at Castelnaud.

houses and the first medieval castles were also built in the same style. The first significant development to spread throughout Europe was the motte and bailey developed in north-west France. It became dominant in eleventh-century France and England and even spread into southern Italy.

Feudal France

In the tenth century, the Capetian family wrested the elective kingship of West Francia from the Carolingians and established its own ruling dynasty under Hugh Capet. Feudalism in its most classical form took hold in the emerging French kingdom. The king's Royal Domain (demesne) consisted of the Isle de France where many of his vassals were uncontrollable, avoided their feudal obligations and made travel unsafe, even for the king. The Duke of Normandy exerted strong control over Normandy and other conquered counties (comtés). Feudalism was weak in the Duchy of Brittany and the Bretons were often a problem for the dukes of Normandy as well as the kings of France. Other counts including those of Flanders and Blois, like the Dukes of Normandy, gave the crown minimal feudal service. In the south-west, the Duke of Aquitaine and the Count of Toulouse did not even recognize or pay homage to the king until the twelfth century. Most of the king's vassals only sent the minimum required number of men for castle guard. As an example, according to John Beeler, author of *Warfare in Feudal Europe*, the Duke of Normandy, who could raise 1,500 knights from his vassals, only sent ten knights to the king for their annual obligation; other powerful magnates did the same. If all of the king's vassals met their obligations, he could only raise an army of about 500 to 700 knights.[13] When William invaded England in 1066, only about half of the 5,000 knights he took were Norman since their feudal obligation did not require service outside the kingdom. Thus, he had to rely on many mercenaries and adventurers from various parts of France. To avoid the same problems in England, he changed the normal feudal obligations and forbade war between barons, which was rife in France and went on uncontrolled until Louis IX (St. Louis) in the thirteenth century.

The king had to raise peasant levies of dubious quality from his villages to augment his army.[14] Philippe I (ruled 1060–1108) brought the crown to its lowest point as his Royal Domain shrank to its smallest size. His vassal, William the Conqueror, had taken control of England and Philippe could do little to interfere with his activities. His successor, Louis VI the Fat, restored the power of the crown, crushed all opposition in the Royal Domain and expanded his kingdom. His son, Louis VII, took the throne in 1137 and brought new troubles when he married Eleanor of Aquitaine. Eleanor got an annulment of their marriage and married King Henry II of England (Duke of Normandy and Anjou) in 1152. The union placed her lands under English control. Their son, Richard the Lionheart, expanded his own holdings in France and came in conflict with Philippe II Augustus (reigned 1180–1223). Philippe found himself in a strong position after the death of Richard and took advantage of the situation to drive Richard's brother John from his French holdings. He even sent an army to challenge John in England.

Until the end of the twelfth century, the greatest impediment for the French king in controlling his own nobles was the rise of the motte-and-bailey castle, which had sprouted up all over northern France to help hold back the Viking invasions. For the small feudal armies of the king, the dukes and the counts it was easier to go on defence and allow their opponent to attack the castle or put it under siege, which were difficult propositions during this period. If a castle fell, the victors filled the moat and pulled down the palisades, but once the invader was gone, the locals easily rebuilt them. In the eleventh century, stone castles gained increasing popularity.

The Motte-and-Bailey Castle

Ringworks, consisting of circular-shaped earthworks with ditches and palisades, preceded the motte-and-bailey castle. They often occupied a position on a hill and might have been as complex as the earthwork of Maiden Castle in England.[15] Ringworks remained in use during the Dark Ages and some were converted into a motte-and-bailey with the addition of a motte and tower. In *Castles: Their Construction and History*, Sidney Toy defines the typical motte and bailey as consisting of a mound 3m (10ft) to 33m (108ft) high with a level top surrounded by a palisade used for the final defensive position. This mound could be a natural hillock, a man-made hill, or a combination of both. Below the motte, there often were one or more baileys or wards surrounded by walls and ditches. The walls usually consisted of a wooden palisade on an earthen embankment, but could also be of stone. Ring works and the motte and bailey probably account for most of the castles built in Europe. During the eleventh century, this type of 'castle' spread from north-west Europe to Denmark, the Holy Roman Empire and southern Italy. A donjon usually occupied the top of the motte.[16] Late in the tenth century, the first stone keeps or donjons appeared north of the Loire. Only noblemen with sufficient resources could afford to build in stone; lesser nobles had to settle for timber and earth castles. The tower on the motte was replaced with a shell keep consisting of a wall that surrounded the top of the motte and included facilities in the walls. Noblemen with adequate resources built rectangular or square keeps with two or more levels that could serve as a home and a refuge. Gradually other layouts were adopted, including L-shaped and polygonal keeps that often had a forebuilding that covered the entrance. Round keeps appeared in the twelfth century and became particular favourites of Philippe Augustus. After the late eleventh century, the keeps of kings and powerful noblemen became larger and the defences of the bailey increased in size and complexity. Two or three baileys to a castle with fortified gates and towers became more common. However, the keep remained the key position of the defences. When a nobleman could afford to build a stone keep, he usually opted for stone walls rather than wooden palisades for the bailey.

Motte-and-bailey castles: Top: Langeais. (Photo courtesy of Rupert Harding). *Bottom: Gisors*

The Count of Blois built the first stone donjon at Doué-la-Fontaine when he converted and fortified a single-floor structure into a two-storey castle in about 950.[17] Fulk Nerra, the Count of Anjou, who had a motte-and-bailey castle at Langeais that withstood a siege in 992, rebuilt the keep in stone in the mid-990s. Langeais resisted two more sieges by the Count of Blois. The counts of Blois and

Anjou often fought and in the last siege of Langeais in the 990s King Henri I had to rescue Fulk Nerra from Count Odo of Blois. Neither side was able to field large armies in these localized contests. If the aggressor failed to meet and defeat the defender in open battle, the latter could quickly take refuge in a castle. Once the drawbridge went up on a timber-and-turf motte and bailey the option to storm the castle could result in the attackers suffering heavy losses. The alternative was a long and usually unsuccessful siege since most noblemen could not completely isolate and besiege a castle for an extended period with their small armies. Since building and employing siege engines generally required a large body of men, this was not an option. The best they could do was to ravage the countryside and hope the defender would come to terms. In north-west France during the tenth and eleventh centuries, most noblemen could only afford small armies and when they were not dealing with raiders, they marched against each other in petty rivalries like those of the Count of Anjou and the Count of Blois. Larger armies could have quickly dispatched these non-masonry castles.

Fulk Nerra, a prolific builder, is said to have erected nearly a hundred castles, but the actual number may have been closer to a dozen. He used his castles as part of a military strategy against his neighbours.[18] In the latter part of the eleventh century, William the Conqueror and his successors secured their hold of England by building many castles with impressive keeps in London (the White Tower of the Tower of London), Dover, Rochester and other sites. They also built castles in their French holdings. The keep remained the dominant feature of most castles through the thirteenth century in the West.

Some elements of ancient fortifications never lost their importance in the Middle Ages. Thus, the ditch remained a standard feature in medieval castles although it underwent some odifications during the medieval period. Thus, whereas the Roman period ditch could be narrow and shallow, the medieval moat was almost invariably wider and deeper than the average height of a man. In addition, the Roman type ditch tended to be V-shaped, whereas the medieval moat was usually U-shaped. Although moats are filled with water in common imagination, in the fact, in the typical European castle, wet moats were less common than dry ones because they required ideal hydrologic conditions. A high water table (water level close to the surface) made it easier to create a wet moat, which was common in low-lying regions such as Belgium and the Netherlands. If there was a nearby river or water source, a man-made channel easily diverted water into a moat. In most cases, the enemy could fill in part of the moat before an assault. Where the water table was high, it was more difficult, if not impossible, to tunnel beneath a wet moat. In mountainous and hilly areas, wet moats were less feasible, but dry moats were often deeper if the engineers could excavate into the rock, making it more difficult, if not impossible, for the attacker to fill in or tunnel under. In such rugged areas, wet moats were rare. In places where natural features such as cliffs or rivers afforded protection to sections of the

Tour sign on the site with detail of entrance to Inner Bailey

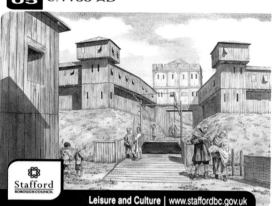

Stafford Castle. Top: Recreation of the recessed entrance to the inner bailey. Bottom: Recreation of the village and castle. (By permission of Stafford Borough Council)

enceinte (enclosing wall), partial moats were sufficient. The moat and the outer wall served as the first line of defence against enemy assault. If a castle had a motte, it usually had its own encircling moat at its base. The defenders on the bailey walls and towers, if any, covered the moat, which attackers had to negotiate first before reaching them. One of the weakest spots of the moat was the access point into the castle, usually some kind of bridge. A removable bridge such as a drawbridge worked best. If the moat was not too wide, the drawbridge spanned its entire width; if it was too wide, it spanned only part of it. When it was raised, the drawbridge usually closed the gateway. The inner wall of the moat (scarp) and the outer wall (counterscarp) were most effective when they were made of masonry or some type of revetment to prevent collapse. A better option was a moat cut into a natural rock formation that did not require any type of revetment.

Wooden palisades surrounded the bailey and often were at both the base and top of the motte. Although their heights varied, the walls were normally greater than the height of a man. The palisade on top of the motte had the advantage of the height of the motte, which was usually steep enough to make access to the top difficult and included a stairway or a bridge-like walkway (a flying bridge) that gave the defenders a gentler slope to make their routine ascent less difficult.

Masonry walls often were higher than typical wooden palisades. Stone walls required a masonry ditch scarp unless the subsurface consisted of some form of solid material.[19] The use of stone, bricks and mortar required skilled masons that many of lesser noblemen could not afford. Thus, timber and turf motte-and-bailey castles proliferated even as masonry types appeared because of excessive costs and manpower requirements.

The bailey[20] generally served as a refuge for the villagers. It often included quarters for the garrison, a blacksmith's forge, an armoury, a chapel, a well, pens for livestock, stables, storage sheds and bakeries, etc. Some castles had several baileys such as an inner, outer and even a middle bailey. Sometimes these baileys are identified as upper and lower bailey, eastern and western or some other combination based on their location relative to each other. Sometimes a walled town grew next to the castle. Depending on the resources available, gate towers and mural towers were added to the enclosing walls. These features were generally simple structures when the enceinte consisted of wooden palisades instead of masonry, but they could be impressive on large timber castles.

The addition of a tower to the top of the motte turned the motte and bailey into a castle.[21] This tower, known as the donjon[22] or bergfried in German, served as the last-stand position and a residence for the owner. Its dimensions depended on the wealth of the nobleman and the size of the area on top of the motte. Since most motte-and-bailey castles were owned by lesser noblemen, they were often two-level timber structures. Until the twelfth century, wood and masonry keeps were square and often of two to three levels with living quarters and storage on the first two floors.[23] The basement usually served for storage and was often the ground floor. In the eleventh century and later, noblemen with sufficient wealth and resources built stone keeps, which reflected their wealth and power. Stone walls and buildings were likewise a status symbol. Fulk Nerra built one of the tallest stone keeps in Europe at Loches, Indre-et-Loire. Although it was previously thought that it was built in the twelfth century, dendrochronology applied to some of its timbers has shown that the keep of Loches was actually built

Loches Castle. Photo by Lieven Smits. (Wikipedia Commons)

during the first quarter of the eleventh century.[24] The keep is 37.2m (122ft) high and divided into four storeys, with the great hall on the lower level. Its very thick walls were held up with semicircular buttresses that ran from the ground floor to the battlements. An adjacent three-level forebuilding housed the entrance stairs that accessed the keep on the second storey and a chapel the third storey. The interior of great hall measures are 8.25m x 19.8m (27ft x 65ft). The keep walls are about 2.5m (8ft) thick, but are 2.8m (9ft) at the thickest sections. Narrow windows on each side of these thick walls poorly light the interior. The ground floor was a windowless basement and the first floor (second storey) included the entrance. This type of arrangement was typical of other keeps. However, size, thickness of walls and height varied from keep to keep. The building of a stone keep on top of a motte presented special problems when the mound was man-made. The builder had to consider subsidence since the weight of the stone was much greater than timber. Depending on the composition of the motte, heavy rains and the pressure of large stone fortifications could cause it to compress or shift and even collapse in sections.

The man-made motte was a complex structure. Generally, it was shaped like a truncated cone and its size and composition varied from site to site. A study done by Malcolm Hislop, found most mottes range from 40m to 60m (131ft to 197ft) in diameter at the base and 15m to 27m (49ft to 89ft) at the top. Their heights range from 8m (26ft) to 12m (39ft). Most mottes have slopes of about 40 degrees but in some cases only 25 degrees. There were, however, larger mottes. The one at Tutbury Castle (south-west of Nottingham) was slightly over 80m (263ft) wide at the base and 25m (82ft) at the top and 12m (39ft) high with an incline of 40 degrees into the bailey and 50 degrees where it forms the exterior of the defences. The slope was generally steep enough to make it difficult for an assailant to reach the walls at the top. Steps were often cut into the slope, but if the angle was too steep, a wooden causeway was built instead.[25]

No records remain to indicate how soon after the completion of the motte that work began on the keep, but the motte alone took from a few months to a year to create depending on the labour force available. Since the weight of a wooden keep did not pose serious problems for the motte, work could have begun quickly. The materials used to build the motte usually included a large percentage of dirt and rock excavated from the ditch. After a considerable amount of time subsidence took place making it possible to successfully build a stone keep. Archaeological research shows that by the twelfth century builders layered the building material for the motte to increase stability. Depending on the composition of the surrounding terrain, the ditch or even the motte might require a revetment.

Not all motte-and-bailey castles with wooden walls and keeps were trifling affairs. Robert de Tosny, a knight of William the Conqueror, built a massive wooden castle in 1072 near the town of Stafford.[26] Stafford Castle covered 4 ha (10 acres) including an inner and outer bailey with wooden walls built on a ridge with a man-made motte for the keep. The walls of the inner bailey were much larger than the walls of the outer bailey. There was an enclosed settlement outside the outer bailey and the palisades of both rested on the spoil from the ditches. The outer bailey covered 1.69 ha (4.18 acres) and included four gates with its western gate leading to the inner bailey. Skilled workers, manual labourers and soldiers resided in the outer bailey. This area served as a site for food stores, stables and animal pens. Recreations of the site show the walls of the inner bailey with overhanging galleries on the battlements and an entrance gate set a distance back with the walls turning inward forming a U-shaped indentation in the enceinte. This setup exposed both flanks of an attacking force to the walls that turned inward toward the gate.[27] The main gate of the outer bailey was similar, but it was not set as far back. Both may have been gate towers. The inner bailey covered 1.15 ha (2.83 acres) and included domestic structures that served the castle: a chapel, a great hall, storage, quarters and stables. Behind the massive wooden walls of the inner bailey was a 15m (49.2ft) high motte crowned with wooden walls and a large wooden multi-level keep. Recreations of the site show walls of up to 4m in height. The walls on the motte ditch opened to the rear allowing the defenders on top of the motte to dominate them should they fall to the enemy. Little remains of the original Stafford Castle, one of the largest timber castles discovered. Two centuries later the owners converted it into a stone castle.

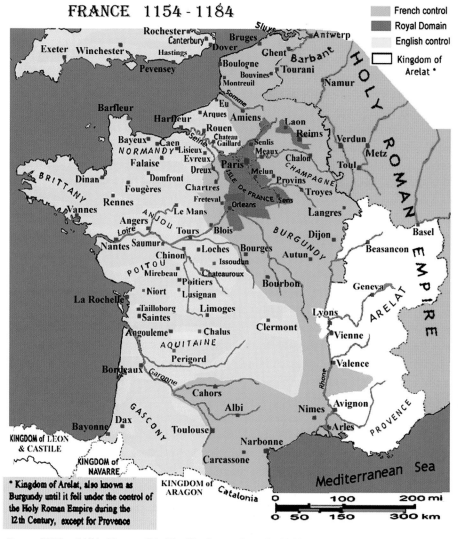

France 1154 to 1184. Map modified by Kaufmann from the 1911 atlas by Shepard.

The Midi and Catalonia

The Midi is a French term derived from the Latin for 'midday' and 'south'. Today it refers to the part of France between the Mediterranean and the Atlantic, from Spain in the south to the Loire in the north and Valence in the east. It includes Aquitaine, Languedoc, Provence, parts of Poitou and the Alps. This region had been more heavily Romanised than northern France had, a fact that was reflected in its culture and languages. Formidable Roman fortifications survived in many places such as Carcassonne, Arles and Nîmes. They were much larger and more extensive than the walls of Paris. In this region, where Islamic invaders challenged Frankish control during the Dark Ages, traditional feudalism did not appear as it had in north-western France. Not all fortifications identified as castles here were privately owned residences.

Catalonia formed along the Spanish Marches, but, like the Midi, it did not follow a traditional form of feudalism. In 'Feudalism in Twelfth-Century Catalonia', Thomas Bisson pointed out that the Catalonian fief was an administrative tenure of land until the 1020s when the count's authority weakened 'with the growth of a military class and the multiplication of castles to bring on a generation of disorder'.[30] Count Ramón Berenguer I (1035–76) restored order by giving his clients sufficient castles so that none could gain enough strength to turn on him the way the Normans acted against their own counts. He could take ownership of any castles by agreement with their owners who swore allegiance to him. The lords of the castles received taxes from the surrounding fiefs to pay for the knights and garrisons. They were his allies rather than his vassals as in traditional feudalism.

In these regions, a strong centralized feudal state such as in Normandy did not exist until Berenguer began to change the situation because many knights and lesser nobles owned the land they held without a feudal obligation. With so much allodial property (property owned without a feudal obligation) in southern France, like in Germany and Italy, most high-ranking noblemen had fewer vassals that owed them feudal military service. During the time of the Franks in the Dark Ages, Frankish soldiers usually had to garrison forts of the Midi. Many of those who obtained these land grants in the Midi and Catalonia had no obligation beyond serving in their count's army when the need arose instead of providing a certain number of days of service. Due to this apparent lack of organization and leadership, according to Beeler, no army in the region won a major victory during most of the ninth century. During the tenth and eleventh centuries, a new class of professional soldier garrisoned the numerous castles that sprouted from the Alps to the Pyrenees. Since these soldiers – both noble and free serfs – held no land, they had to depend on the people living on the lands near the castle for support. These mercenaries also sold their services to feudal lords in northern France.[31]

Higham and Barker, authors of *Timber Castles*, point out that some motte castles display no evidence of a bailey. They conclude that since the keep alone was not sufficient to accommodate the needs of a residence, many of these structures may have actually had surrounding palisades. However, since no earth works have been identified so far, archaeologists cannot delineate the bailey. On the other hand, they also concede such isolated bastions may have served as watchtowers or had a hitherto unidentified function.[28] The main problem for the military historian is that he can never be certain of the size and scope of the defences built from the tenth through twelfth centuries even when they are mentioned in chronicles of the time. In the absence of contemporary detailed descriptions, it is difficult to know what they looked like, particularly since they often underwent many modifications during the High Middle Ages, which can often be dated based on style.[29]

From Motte and Bailey to the Classic Castle

Between the twelfth and thirteenth centuries, castles began to take on a more classic form. In many cases, such as the castles of Arundel and Langeais, new works appeared relegating the old motte-and-bailey keep to an insignificant part of the castle defences. In other locations, castles replaced the old motte and bailey or appeared where no motte and bailey had previously existed. Often dukes and kings had located the motte-and-bailey castles to control important trade roads, rivers or towns. As time passed, it became imperative to improve these positions in order to secure their control of the surrounding regions. Since many modifications took place during the twelfth century and later, it is not possible to know exactly what castles looked like at any single point in the High Middle Ages. Although historians can date some new features to the time of their first appearance, that does not mean they appeared on all castles at the same time or even in the same century. Depending on the location of a castle and its involvement in conflict, it may have undergone numerous changes in a period of a hundred years or more. Sometimes, works of art provide more clues than plans, but this kind of information is scant.

By the thirteenth century, significant changes had taken place in castle building. Formidable defences were added to prevent the enemy from reaching the keep, which was changing shape and acquiring new features. For instance, Château Gaillard had round towers, and its keep included a beak or prow and machicolations. It is said that the design of this castle on the Seine reflects Middle Eastern influence on King Richard I, the Lionheart, of England acquired during the Third Crusade. According to Malcolm Hislop, the beaked donjon and lines of concentric defences first appeared at La Roche-Guyon, further up the Seine from Château Gaillard. Both castles date from the 1190s and show decisive changes in design. Round mural towers and keeps gave better protection against

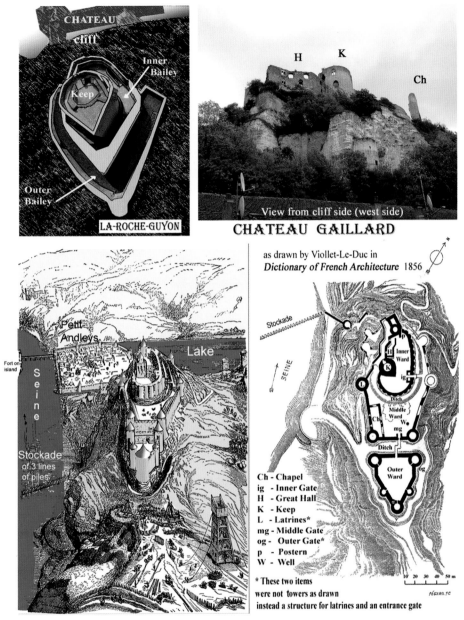

La Roche Guyon and photo of Château Gaillard. Plans of Château Gaillard by Viollet-le-Duc, 1856.

mining and enemy sappers trying to break the towers at their vulnerable corners. The mural towers at Château Gaillard were round and the inner bailey wall had an unusual corrugated shape. The spur, the plinth, the batter, the beak and the talus slope strengthened the base of the towers and protected them from mining and battering.[32] Concentric defences were already in use in older motte-and-bailey castles with two or more baileys, but they became more elaborate as a ring of works was built within another ring. The keep of La Roche Guyon towered over the walls of the inner bailey, whose walls in turn dominated the defences of the outer bailey. At Château Gaillard, the design is similar for the keep and the inner and middle baileys, but not for the outer bailey. In both cases, the walls of the inner bailey included a section overlooking a cliff. Later classic concentric castles such as Coca and La Mota in Spain consist of a ring within a ring.

The keeps of the first motte-and-bailey castles served as residences and had to include basic features such as a garderobe, a cistern, fireplaces and quarters for the lord and his family. The most basic keeps consisted of a storage area, often called the basement, located on the first level (ground level) rather than below ground. The entrance was usually on the first floor (second level), which also included the hall. The private apartments were on the second floor (third level). Not all of the basic features were found inside the keep. In some cases, they were situated in attached structures or even in the inner bailey. Usually the ground floor (storage area) had a vaulted masonry ceiling that served as the floor of the level above. The other storeys usually had wooden floors and ceilings, although there are exceptions such as Provins where all levels have vaulted ceilings. Wooden beams and/or corbels that supported the wooden ceilings and floors were inserted into special sockets in the walls. In some cases, the walls of the upper level were offset, leaving a ledge on the next level so corbels were not needed. If the keep was very large and too wide for a single wooden beam to span the space between walls, a cross wall supported the beams. A large keep often had a wooden stairway, but in most keeps, there were one or more stone spiral staircases in the walls or corner turrets. Stairwells usually turned clockwise going up supposedly to allow the defender to wield his sword unimpaired by the newel (central supporting pillar). However, there are some examples of counter-clockwise stairs like one of four staircases at the new castle of Langeais.[33] Keeps were not designed to have windows; usually narrow slits provided light and ventilation in stairwells, in the ground-floor storage areas and at other levels. Sometimes upper levels had small windows. The keep usually included a chapel on an upper level, often with a pair of arched windows facing a non-threatened section of the structure. Since glass was an expensive luxury, it was not widely in use until the Late Middle Ages, except in the chapel. The basement level often served as a storage area, but in some cases, the entire area or part of it was a cesspool depending on the type of garderobes used. The most common type of garderobe projected outside the wall and the excrement dropped into the surrounding ditch or wet moat. In some case, a pipe system dropped the waste into a cesspool in the basement, which had to be cleaned out periodically.

The entrance was normally on first floor, the level above the ground floor, to render access more difficult. Large keeps could have a forebuilding as part of the entrance. Sometimes this structure housed stairs to the entrance, but usually a wooden or stone stairway was located outside of it. The private rooms above the first floor were called solars.[34] One or more fireplaces served the hall or great hall and quarters, but chimneys did not come into use until about the eleventh century. Prior to that, the smoke exited through vents in the wall. The

CHAMBOIS

Corbels to support roofing

Sockets for floor timbers

Indentation for floor boards

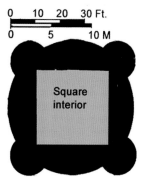

0   10   20   30 Ft.

0   5   10 M

Square interior

Circular donjon with corner towers

HOUDAN

The keeps of Chambois and Houdan.

main fighting positions were on the roof with the battlements. Except for the entranceway, there were no accessible points of entry in the walls. The windows, if there were any, were generally too narrow and almost impossible to reach from ground level. The roofs varied in style and often consisted of wood with lead tiles.

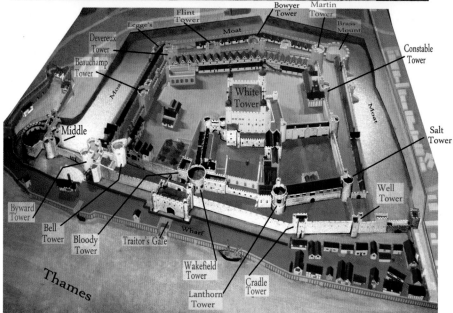

TOWER OF LONDON |

Tower of London. Photo from the Thames and model from Wikipedia.

The French preferred conical roofs, but other types were also used, including a conical roof that began below the battlements so as not to protrude above them.

The shape of keeps evolved from the earliest square and rectangular types to the multi-sided polygonal and cylindrical styles of the twelfth century like the eight-sided donjon of Gisors and the round keep of Château Gaillard. Sometimes, circular keeps had a rectangular base. Some keeps, like the rectangular one of Chambois and the circular one of Houdan, had corner turrets. Many keeps had some form of buttress, usually in the style associated with Romanesque architecture. Heavy buttresses thick at the base and tapering off as they rose supported many fortification walls. A more decorative as well as functional type was the pilaster buttress, which maintained the same thickness throughout its height and generally ran from the bottom of the wall of a keep to the top of it. It looked like a thin column and was often associated with church architecture. This type of buttress is found on the White Tower in London. The buttresses of the keep at Château Gaillard were more unusual as they widened as they neared the top and formed slot machicolations.

The Tower of London's White Tower is one of the best surviving examples of a great keep since it is complete and well documented. Gundulf, the Bishop of Rochester, designed and built it for William the Conqueror to replace the wooden motte and bailey castle in the south-east corner of London. It was located at the point where the Roman city wall, last repaired in 885 by Alfred the Great, ended. Gundulf copied some features from other Norman donjons. As a young Norman monk, he had studied at Rouen where, many historians believe, there was a castle destroyed after 1200, which served as his model for the design of the White Tower.[35] Work began in the late 1070s and neared completion at the beginning of the next century. The ground floor is a storage area and includes a well. An area below the crypt had a stone vaulted ceiling and later served as a prison.[36] The entrance is above on the first floor through a forebuilding. Originally, the tower had a first and second floor above the ground floor. The second floor had a gallery level above which in the fifteenth century had a wooden floor placed between the walls creating a third storey at the gallery level. A 2.1m (7ft) thick cross wall, also known as a spine wall, divided each level into two unequal sized sections; an eastern section with the chapel and a wider western section. Smoke from the fireplaces exited though vents in the walls. There were garderobes on each floor above the basement. The large chapel in the south-east corner has an impressive projecting apse. The decorative interior and exterior pilaster buttresses are indicators of opulence, which may indicate that the tower served as a palace and a residence. The upper floor (third floor) included a passageway through the walls (the gallery) with openings to the two large room sections between the cross wall. The passage ended on both ends at entrances to the gallery looking down on the chapel. After the medieval period, this upper floor housed a council room in the western chamber and a residence in the eastern chamber. The second floor contains the St. John chapel (extending up the third floor above) and the western chamber served as a banqueting hall. The monarch held court in the smaller eastern section. Three spiral staircases in each corner of the second floor led to third floor and the roof. The first floor with its two large chambers and the chapel had a single spiral staircase leading up to the second floor and down to the ground floor. On this level, underneath the chapel, is a crypt. Here the two large rooms accommodated the garrison. The original entrance was on the south side of this floor. Below this, the basement is only below ground level on the north side. Each corner of the tower had a turret. The one on the chapel side was set back.

The White Tower was built of local stone and its exterior sections were faced with limestone brought from Caen. It is thickest at the bottom with 4.6m (15ft) thick walls narrowing to 3.3m (11ft) at the top, measured 32.6m x 35.9m (107ft x 118ft). The structure rose from its ground floor (partially below ground level on its north side) to 27.4m (90ft). In 1241, Henry III had the tower whitewashed, turning it into the 'White' Tower. He also had stained glass put in the chapel windows. The bailey wall was originally earthen with a wooden palisade, but it was converted into a stone wall, only a small section of which remains today. The large windows are later replacements of the narrower ones. In the sixteenth century, Henry VIII modified the roof battlements to accommodate artillery. The massive concentric lines of towers and walls that evolved over the centuries nearly eclipse the White Tower, which still manages to rise above the whole complex.

During the early part of the twelfth century, cylindrical keeps began to occur, following the earlier appearance of round mural towers. According to Malcom Hislop, cylindrical keeps, which were not as complex as the rectangular ones, were not as popular in England as they were on the Continent. In one location where flint was the prevalent building stone, this type of tower was used because flint was not good for making angles. In England and Germany, churches had round towers long before keeps acquired this shape. The keep remained the centrepiece of castle construction long after the traditional motte and bailey went out of style and it was often called the Great Tower.[37] Houdan, built in France in about 1120, was one of the first cylindrical keeps. It had a square interior and four semicircular corner towers. Philippe Augustus is credited with introducing the round design in France and this type of keep was given the name of 'Tour Phillipienne'. It is characterized by its Gothic style and it was meant to rival the Angevin rectangular towers of France and England. Philippe Augustus built at least twenty circular keeps by 1220. Not to be outdone, the English moved away from the Romanesque to the Gothic style and developed polygonal keeps or keeps that combined rectangular and circular shapes. Earlier in the mid-twelfth century, the French had created the quatrefoil ('four leaves', i.e. four lobes) Guinette Tower for the king at Étampes and the unique César Tower for the Count of Champagne at Provins. At the end of the twelfth century, keep designs multiplied from Iberia to Britain, as the tenth and eleventh century motte-and-bailey donjons were updated with increasingly complex defensive systems.

The keep's battlements generally dominated other castle positions and could serve as a command centre for directing operations. Sometimes, ballista or mangonels were placed on the roof, but usually only archers were stationed there because it was out of reach of scaling ladders. The best and fastest procedure to take a keep was to breach the entrance, which was hard to reach once the defenders had removed the wooden stairway or lifted the drawbridge that linked stone stairs to the great door looming above the ground floor. Once the enemy managed to break into the keep, there was little the defenders could do beyond engaging in hand-to-hand combat with swords, spears and other such weapons. Contrary to a common misconception, archers could not fire from the narrow slits or windows of most keeps. Regular windows were normally located in less accessible parts of the keep, but over the centuries, as the donjon lost its military function, windows were added and enlarged. The entrance door and accessible windows were defended by an overhanging stone position called a bretèche or by a hoarding. The bretèche, which usually looked like a balcony, was large enough to hold one or two men. It had a hole in the floor through which it was possible to drop projectiles on hapless assailants below. Some bretèches also had one or more openings in the sides for viewing. From the outside, a small bretèche looked much like a garderobe, which would not be placed to empty over an opening. In some keeps, wooden hoardings or stone machicolations were added to the battlements on the roof.[38] The machicoulis was similar to the bretèche, but it formed a long continuous balcony-like position that included merlons and crenels. The wooden hoardings were similar, but included a continuous roofed gallery with the stone wall's merlons and crenels behind it.

Often a wall with its own battlements, called a chemise, surrounded the keep. This actually served as the last major defensive position. A stone chemise was more formidable than a wooden palisade and, in some cases, reached impressive sizes like the one at Cesar's Tower at Provins.

The stone walls of the baileys could also include machicoulis or wooden hoardings and round, rectangular, square, semicircular or D-shaped towers usually open at the rear. Towers had fighting positions on the battlements and sometimes on different levels. Some towers resembled keeps, but they were not residences. The most important and most heavily-defended feature of a castle was the gate, which included a gatehouse often flanked by a tower on each side. Later in the Middle Ages, it was quite common for the gatehouse to become more important than the keep and even replace it as a residence. Such was the case at Harlech Castle.

Construction Materials and the Builders

The stone used for constructing various parts of the castle came from local quarries and/or other locations. Some local stones were of excellent quality, depending on the region. Local stone of poor quality was called rubble, but it was used in wall construction nonetheless. This material, cut to various sizes, was usually roughly squared and laid out with mortar. Smaller pieces held together with mortar filled the gaps. Better-quality stone was cut into standard-sized blocks called ashlars,[39] which were used as the facing stone instead of courses of cut rubble or bricks. Ashlars used to cover corners made of cut rubble were called quoins. When walls were not faced with ashlars, the high-quality stone was used to frame windows, arrow loops and corners where it served as reinforcement. As in Roman times, an effective and economic method of building a thick wall was to lay out the inner and outer faces of a wall and fill the space in between with rubble and mortar to create a type of concrete. Granite, marble or some other decorative rocks were used to create ornamental and opulent effects in interior walls. During the twelfth century, masons started using rusticated (bossed) masonry to give outer castle walls an aesthetic finish. This method involved cutting into the edges of the block leaving a rough raised surface that sometimes included a design.[40] A much older style of masonry was herringbone style, which consisted of bricks or cut stone laid out at an angle in courses. The adjacent courses were laid at opposite angles. Occasionally, a horizontal line was placed between the herringbone design.

Usually, the timber used for floors, bracing, roofs and hoardings came from local forests. Some keeps required cross walls because the nearby forests did not have trees large enough to make beams long enough to span the interior. Most towers and donjons had either spiral or standard staircases made of stone. Straight staircases and those leading to the entrance were generally made of wood. Roofs were usually made of wooden or slate shingles depending on availability. A wealthy nobleman could afford lead on the roof.

Interior walls were made of wattle and daub, which had little defensive value and consisted of a woven lattice or matrix of wooden strips (wattle) covered with a sticky material (daub) that included components such as sand, clay, animal dung, etc. to form a wall. Wattle and daub was also standard for houses and many buildings.

The men who designed and built the castles and other great structures such as cathedrals had skills not much different from engineers and architects today. The Gothic period, which followed the Romanesque in the twelfth century, was characterized by semicircular and circular arches, thick walls and the use of pillars and groin vaults. These features resulted from a fusion of Roman, Carolingian and Byzantine architecture of the Dark Ages. The builders did not master the stone arch until the era of the stone keep when they began to use the simple barrel vault for ceilings and floors. Arches and vaulting created galleries within the walls of a keep or the enceinte. Large cylindrical donjons included a series of arched recesses along the walls at each level. The piers on which the arches stood served as buttresses for the wall. Decorative arcading was found in churches and the castles of wealthy noblemen. In some cases, different colours of stone formed bands or layers to enhance the look of the walls. Decoration was usually confined to geometric shapes. William the Conqueror introduced Norman architecture in Britain with his Romanesque-style donjon. Gothic architecture, which remained in use until the Renaissance, was the hallmark of the High Middle Ages. It is best known for its cathedral pinnacles and spires that reach to the heavens, flying buttress and pointed arches for ceilings, windows and doors. Although most of these features were not practical in castles, but one does find the pointed arch and rib vaulting in the chapels. Some of the earliest examples of castles in the Gothic style are the round towers of Philippe Augustus. The fortified Palace of the Popes in Avignon represents a later and more spectacular phase of Gothic architecture.

Like most artists and artisans of the period, most of the medieval master builders remain anonymous. The master masons who worked on the stone left their mark on the sections they built, but master carpenters remain nameless like the master dykers who designed and worked on moats, which required specialists. Few names of the men in charge of construction appear in the records. Bishop Gundulf (circa 1024–1108) of Rochester was responsible for the design and construction of several castles in England including Rochester, Colchester and the White Tower. Edward I brought Master James of St. George (1230–1309) from Savoy to England after seeing his work. Some records identify Master James as an 'ingeniator' or engineer and mason. He was developed the Edwardian style, which was characterized by concentric castles, and he built Caernarfon, Conwy and Beaumaris castles among others. Master Ailnoth handled the work at Orford castle. Maurice the Engineer worked on the keep and enceinte at Dover. Henry Yeverly (1325–99) was the master stonemason and chief architect of Edward III and was responsible for the Bloody Tower at the Tower of London. A more complete list of these engineers can be found in Malcom Hislop's *Castle Builders*.

Chapter Six

Beginning of the Classic Age of Castles –
the Twelfth Century

The Rivals

The enmity between France and England has its roots in William the Conqueror's reign and in the rivalry that developed between his three sons. The eldest, Robert Curthose (Short Stockings), became Duke of Normandy and William II Rufus (The Red) took the throne of England on their father's death in 1087.[1] The Baron's Revolt of 1088 in England, incited by Robert, caused Rufus to retaliate by invading Normandy in 1091. After suffering a defeat, the two brothers cried peace. In 1096, Robert took up the Cross and left his dukedom to join the First Crusade. Rufus died in a hunting accident in 1100 when Robert returned from the Holy Land. Their younger brother Henry I took the throne. In 1101, Robert invaded England and tried to march on London, but Henry renounced his claim to Normandy and Robert returned home. Despite the pledge, Henry I invaded Normandy in 1105, taking Caen and Bayeux. At the siege of Tinchebray Castle, the two brothers engaged in the battle and Robert lost Normandy.[2] The Norman overlords in England maintained their French lands as vassals of the Capetian king and launched campaigns of conquest against the Celts of Scotland, Wales and Ireland in the twelfth century and later. Both French and English monarchs spent much of the medieval era subduing their homegrown rivals and consolidating their power. Castles played an important role in these conflicts. Kings built them to control towns and strategic points (fords, bridges, defiles, etc.) whereas noblemen used them to control their lands and often did not locate them in places of strategic value. Through marriage and war, the boundaries of England and France expanded and retracted. The greatest bone of contention between the two nations extended from Normandy to Aquitaine.

William the Conqueror subdued the Saxons of England by building motte-and-bailey castles to crush their power. Since these castles appeared so swiftly, they must have been made of wood rather than stone. William also built a motte-and-bailey castle in London and later rebuilt it as the White Tower. King Louis VI and the Counts of Flanders and Anjou challenged the hold of William and his sons on Normandy. When peace was declared in 1120, Henry I controlled both Normandy and England. He solidified his hold on England by adopting the Anglo-Saxon justice system and by creating the Exchequer. He proceeded in the similar fashion in Normandy since castles alone were not enough to consolidate his power. The influence of Byzantium and the Levant on military architecture was felt in the West shortly after the First Crusade. The innovations increased the expense of building and garrissoning castles.

Henry's death in 1135 set off a problem of succession. His daughter Matilda[3] vied for the throne and engaged in a civil war with her cousin Stephen, the barons' candidate. Matilda's husband, Geoffrey Plantagenet Count of Anjou, won all of Normandy, which he bequeathed to their son upon his death. Henry Plantagenet, Duke of Normandy and Count of Anjou, became England's Henry II in 1154 and founded a dynasty that fought for control of north-western and south-western France until 1453.

Until Louis VII (reigned 1137–80), the French kings had been mostly ineffective. His father, Louis the Fat, consolidated his power after supressing rebellious nobles and winning the favour of the Papacy. Louis VII, who faced difficulties early in his reign, resorted to his father's policies for crushing the opposition. To establish his virility and piety, he joined the Second Crusade (1147–9) where he proved to be a good knight, but not a good leader. His marriage to Eleanor ended a few years later with an annulment and lost him the wealth of Aquitaine, but Paris emerged as the centre of culture in the West.

After the annulment, Eleanor of Aquitaine married King Henry II of England in 1152, which made Henry Duke of Aquitaine and doubly beholden to Louis VII as a vassal. In 1159, the French king blocked Henry's efforts to take Toulouse. Henry put down a revolt by his sons in the 1170s and then made a pact with the French king. In 1180, Louis VII's son, Philippe II 'Augustus', ascended to the throne at the age of 15 and ruled until 1223. The rivalry between France and England increased during his reign.

Henry II had to contend again with his rebellious sons in the 1180s. Prince Richard joined Philippe and defeated Henry's forces throughout France forcing Henry to withdraw to Château Chinon where he soon died in 1189 a broken man,[4] but not before reconciling with his son. Soon afterward, Richard the Lionheart took the throne and departed for the Third Crusade.[5] As Duke of Aquitaine, he had revolted against his father more than once and allied himself with Philippe II. In 1190, Richard and Philippe joined the Third Crusade and agreed to share the spoils they would take. The two kings had a falling-out after the capture of Acre and Philippe returned home. Richard fought on, made peace with Saladin and embarked for England only to be taken hostage by a rival, Leopold of Austria, and held for ransom in the Holy Roman Empire. Meanwhile, Philippe expanded his control into Flanders since the Count of Flanders had died at the siege of Acre. He allied himself with King Richard's nephew Arthur, who ruled Brittany and launched the conquest of eastern Normandy. When Richard was freed in 1194, he returned to England in March, put down his brother John's revolt and set off within two months to recapture the lands his brother had lost to Philippe

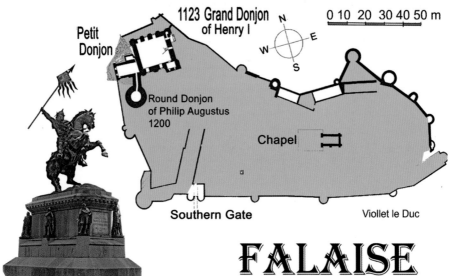

The keep of Falaise and a statue of William the Conqueror.

in eastern Normandy. His war with the French king lasted until his death in 1199 when he was killed by a crossbowman at the siege of Chalus-Chabrol.[6] Richard's death allowed the ambitious Phillipe Augustus to pursue the conquest of Angevin controlled France. King John, who was not a great warrior like Richard and was unpopular in England, was unable to stave off Phillipe's encroachments on his

French domains. Normandy began to slip from his grasp between 1202 and 1204 as Philippe took the castles at Falaise and between Mortain and Pontorson.

Meanwhile, the French besieged Rouen, forcing the garrison to surrender in June 1204. Rouen had grown in size as a walled city on the right bank of the Seine. It had acquired a stone bridge with a barbican on the left bank in 1160. A castle Richard had built on the south side of the city burned down in 1200. After the city fell, Philippe Augustus built a new castle on the north side of the city and expanded the enceinte. During the siege of Rouen, when they occupied most of Normandy, the French laid siege to Château Gaillard from 1203 until March 1204.

Castle Warfare

Most conflicts in Western Europe during the High Middle Ages seldom involved massive armies. Today, most of these battles would be considered mere skirmishes. Most wars involved sieges rather than two armies clashing on the battlefield. Kings and powerful lords relied on feudal service owed by their vassals and on mercenaries to muster their armies. Due to the expense, most royal castles had small garrisons, but they were well stocked with weapons and supplies. Army sizes varied, but they seldom reached the magnitude of the army of the First Crusade, which numbered over 10,000 men when it got to the Holy Land. At the Battle of Brémule in 1119, Henry I defeated Louis VI's 400 men with 500 soldiers. Unfortunately, most chroniclers and medieval historians have no idea how many troops took part in most battles and tend grossly to exaggerate their numbers. In *Medieval Sieges,* Jim Bradbury points out that Henry I of England, one of the great castle-builders of the era, often intimidated his enemies with the mere threat of war. He also concludes that in the High Middle Ages 'warfare consisted of perhaps one percent battles and ninety-nine percent sieges' from England to Italy and Iberia.[7] The number of combatants in any given battle varies widely from source to source making it difficult to determine the actual size of the forces involved. However, it must be noted that the chroniclers tend to give numbers of about 100 to 300 men for the defence of key fortifications. The twelfth-century English kings controlled dozens of castles in England and their French lands. The smallest castles might have maintained a garrison of a dozen or more men and an average-size castle at least 100 men in time of war. Thus, castle garrisons might easily absorb several thousand men in time of war. No warlord could remove every knight and soldier from these sites for a campaign because some had to remain behind to maintain control and to protect the site from the enemy. Thus, it may be safe to assume that the English king could safely field a force of about 3,000 men in addition to mercenaries. According to Bradbury, Geoffrey V of Anjou, father of King Henry II, conquered Normandy in a ten-year period without fighting a major battle before finally taking Rouen in 1144.[8] Henry II put down a rebellion between 1173 and 1174 after some skirmishes and many sieges.

The belligerents had no desire to risk their small armies in a crippling battle since assembling large numbers of men was expensive and losses were difficult to replace. In addition, there was often little to be gained from such battles because the opponents' castles and fortified towns might continue to resist. A campaign consisted mainly of manoeuvring and attacking the enemy's strong points where a resolution to the conflict seldom happened within a few days. The besiegers and besieged seldom took heavy losses in combat unless they engaged in an actual assault. If the cost became too high, either the aggressors lifted the siege and went home or the defenders surrendered. From the time of Henry II to the death of Richard I, only a few notable engagements were fought in England and France. In England in 1173, Henry's commanders defeated a rebel force consisting mainly of 3,000 Flemish mercenaries with several hundred troops at the Battle of Fornham. Richard won a victory in 1194 at Fréteval and at Gisors in 1198 in battles that involved a small number of troops and amounted to skirmishes. In 1176, Emperor Frederick Barbarossa, at war with the Lombard League, engaged about 2,500 men against a force of similar size at Legnano in one of the largest battles of the period. Between 1194 and 1199, Richard I and Philippe II faced off in two dozen sieges and assaults on castles. The number of battles involving castles and fortified towns during the twelfth century dwarfs the number of major battles between armies in the West. The situation did not change much until the end of the Hundred Years War in 1453.

A careful look at the military career of Richard the Lionheart in France highlights the dominance of castle warfare in the twelfth century. In 1173, Henry II's sons revolted. Richard's brother, 'Young King Henry', placed the castle of Gournay under siege, while Louis VII, who was in league with him, laid siege to Verneuil and Philip of Flanders, another ally, attacked the castle of Drincourt. Meanwhile in 1174, a Scottish invasion in the north resulted in the fall of the castles at Liddell, Burgh, Appleby, Harbottle and Warkworth and ended with the siege of Carlisle. While Henry was back in England, Louis VII placed Rouen under siege, which he lifted when Henry returned to the continent. In 1176, after Henry quelled the revolt and Richard returned to the fold, he sent his son against the castle of Limoges, which fell to the 19-year-old warrior prince in two days. Later, Richard took Châteauneuf and Moulinef. Next, he stormed the fortress of Angoulême in only six days and captured several powerful noblemen. At the end of the campaign in January 1077, he turned south to besiege Dax. After this, he moved north to take the castle of Pons, about 20km (12.4 miles) south of Saintes, where unfriendly magnates threatened the English lines of communication. Geoffrey of Rancon, the leader of the revolt, prepared Pons castle with a strong and well-provisioned garrison. Richard decided that the position was too strong to overcome and withdrew, but swiftly took and demolished five small castles.[9] The 22-year-old prince next applied his skills to Rancon's formidable castle of Taillebourg[10] perched on an outcrop above the village on the Charente River.

Steep slopes protected three sides of this castle and three walls and ditches facing marshy ground protected it on the marshy side. The only approach was from the town of the same name. In May, Richard lured the garrison out by devastating the countryside. That allowed him to charge the enemy forces in the field and drive them back into town with his men close on their heels. Before the defenders could close the gates, Richard's men raced into the town to plunder and pillage. The castle garrison capitulated within days. Geoffrey of Rancon surrendered Taillebourg and Pons in May 1079 and Richard razed both castles.[11] Awed, Rancon's ally quickly surrendered the castles of Angoulême and Montignac, which Richard demolished as well.[12] In 1182 again in south-west France, Richard attacked the fortifications of Périgueux. He took four more castles and demolished several fortifications. In March 1183, Young Henry revolted against his father once more. Henry and Richard laid siege to the fortress of St. Martial at Limoges. However, the position was too strong and the demoralized besiegers[13] lifted the siege in May. The next month, Young Henry died and the revolt collapsed. They returned to Limoges where the fortress surrendered at the end of June 1183 and the victors demolished the fortifications. In 1187, Philippe II of France placed Richard and John under siege at Châteauroux until their father Henry came to the rescue.

Richard ascended the throne of England at his father's death, but shortly after that, he set off for the Holy Land to conduct more sieges and engage in a few major battles. He returned to England in 1194, only to find many of his Norman castles in the hands of Philippe and his kingdom in turmoil. His brother John had usurped power in England and clung to two castles: Tickhill, which quickly surrendered to Richard, and Nottingham, which did not. His father Henry II had replaced the motte-and-bailey at Nottingham with a larger castle with a middle bailey that included the royal apartments built next to the original bailey (the inner bailey) on Castle Hill and a dry moat to protect the sides of the hill where the slope was not steep. Beyond the moat on lower ground was the outer bailey with a barbican that covered the castle's eastern side. Richard arrived on 25 March 1194 and he invested the castle that very evening, taking the barbican and occupying the outer bailey. The defenders set fire to the outer works as they fell back. Richard bombarded the castle with two siege engines and Greek Fire until it surrendered a couple of days later[14] and John reconciled with his brother. However, on 10 May, Philippe II placed Verneuil under siege, forcing Richard to return to Normandy. Richard broke the siege on 30 May. Philippe withdrew, only to lay siege to the castle of Fontaines, a few miles from Rouen, and taking it in four days. Richard retaliated by taking three castles including Loches, which he captured in one day in June,[15] and Montmirail (between Reims and Paris). Meanwhile, while John was besieging the castle at Vaudreuil, Philippe captured his siege engines and took many prisoners in a surprise attack. In July, Richard advanced into Aquitaine and defeated Philippe at Fréteval.[16] The two adversaries negotiated a truce that lasted from late July 1194 to November 1195 and gave Philippe control of the Vexin, home of the castles of Vaudreuil and Gisors. The truce ended when Philippe stormed the town of Issoudun, east of Loches and besieged the castle. In that autumn of 1195, Richard attacked Arques, which fell by year's end, and Philippe raided and burned the port of Dieppe in November of that year.[17] Philippe, who still had the castle at Issoudun under siege, watched Richard lead a small relief force into the castle. As the siege went on, a unit of Richard's mercenaries caught Philippe from behind forcing him to abandon his siege lines. In December, the two kings cried truce once more.

Fighting resumed in July 1196 as Philippe struck at Aumale and Richard took Nonancourt where he bribed the castellan into surrendering without resisting. In August, Richard tried to break the siege of Aumale, but he was heavily outnumbered. He tried unsuccessfully to break through the French lines, but managed to inflict heavy losses on the enemy. After Aumale fell on 20 August, Philippe levelled it. Before the end of the summer, Phillipe retook Nonancourt where Richard was wounded. The only consolation for the English was that John took Gamaches.

In 1196, Richard added a new piece to this game of castles by initiating construction of Château Gaillard to create, he hoped, an impregnable bridgehead on the Seine into the Vexin, which would protect Rouen and threaten the Île de France. This was in violation of an agreement Henry II had made not to build new fortifications in the Vexin. When the castle was completed in 1198, he was convinced it was impregnable. As work continued on his fortress, in the summer of 1197, he seized ten of Philippe's castles including the one at Dangu (about 6.4km [3.9 miles] from Gisors), which covered a crossing of the Epte and Courcelles. Phillipe retook Dangu before the end of the summer. Richard began his summer offensive with his ally, Baldwin of Flanders, who attacked in the Artois and put Arras under siege to help divert Philippe's attention. Philippe hurried to relieve Arras after taking Dangu and fell into the trap. No great battle ensued because Baldwin outmanoeuvred the French king, destroyed the bridges and cut his supply lines. Philippe was forced to yield and arranged a truce in September.

In September of 1198, Richard and his ally launched a new offensive. Baldwin laid siege to St. Omer in Flanders to distract Philippe. Richard, in the meantime, burned Neufbourg, lured a French contingent into a trap and captured thirty French knights. Shortly afterward, he invested the castles of Dangu and Courcelles. This time, Philippe decided to ignore the situation in Flanders and head for the Vexin with a relief force of about 300 knights only to find Courcelles had already fallen. Faced by Richard's force, he tried to retreat. The two kings clashed at the Battle of Gisors where Philippe lost 150 knights. He was thrown into the Epte River when the bridge outside the gates of Gisors collapsed, but made it back to the castle with the remainder of his force. Richard, who did not have any siege equipment, had to withdraw. In mid-October, St. Omer fell to Baldwin after a six-week siege. Philippe accepted another truce as he licked his wounds. His luck changed when Richard suffered a mortal wound at the siege of the small castle of Chalus in Aquitaine in March 1199.

Henry II, England's Imperialist

When Henry Plantagenet (1133–89) took the throne of England, he altered the relationship between England and France for centuries. On the death of his father in 1151, the teenaged Henry inherited the titles of Count of Anjou, Count of Maine and Duke of Normandy. He sailed for England in 1153 and ascended to the throne when his cousin Stephen died the following year. The king of France, who had been an ally at times, became an enemy after Henry subdued the barons. During the same decade, Henry made incursions into Scotland, Wales and Ireland. In 1158, he also found the time to take over Nantes as he moved into the Duchy of Brittany. The Vexin, a strategic plateau situated between Rouen[18] and Paris on the right bank of the Seine came to him as a dowry for the marriage of his son to the daughter of Louis VII. In 1159, secure in the British Isles, Henry formed a large army by employing many mercenaries and marched south through Cahors leaving a path of destruction as he tried to seize Toulouse. Even his former enemy, the King of Scotland supported him. Other assistance came from the Count of Barcelona and the magnates controlling Béziers and Carcassonne.

Toulouse, which had been fortified by the Romans since the first century, was on the east bank of the Garonne. On the west side of the old city, a wall enclosed a new area built in the twelfth century. The city had a 3km (1.8-mile) long enceinte about 2.5m (8ft) thick with towers every 35m to 40m (38 yds to 43 yds). The brick-lined walls rose from 5m to 8m (16.4ft to 26.2ft) with three gates and sheltered over 35,000 people. The siege began in June 1159 when Henry tried to batter the city into submission with his siege engines. The siege ended in September as Louis VII, who had failed to take Toulouse in 1141 and who feared that Henry's success would weaken his authority over his vassals, came to the rescue. Before long, Henry engaged in a personal war with the Church that reached its climax with the assassination of Thomas Becket in 1170.[19] War with masters of the Church proved more difficult and disastrous than war with lords of the castles.

The enmity between the two monarchs grew as Henry II tried to expand his kingdom into Louis' dominions. Philippe II, the son of Louis VII, was born in 1165, two years before John Lackland, Henry's last son. The rivalry between the two kings intensified. John and Philippe later spent a great deal of time fighting from castle to castle in France. Meanwhile, Henry II won the title of Duke of Brittany for his son Geoffrey by marrying him to Constance.[20] In the late 1160s, Henry campaigned in Brittany, crushing rebellions and attacking vassals of the French king on the borders of his own French lands. Early in the 1170s, he forced the lords in Ireland into submission. After the death of Becket in 1173, three of his sons and his wife, Eleanor of Aquitaine, rebelled against him.[21] Louis VII encouraged his son-in-law, 'Young' Henry, to rise against his father. His younger brother, John Lackland, had received three castles including the strategic fortress of Chinon, which spurred 'Young' Henry (Henry II's eldest son) to rebel. Even his brothers Richard and Geoffrey, both in their mid-teens, joined the rebellion encouraged by their mother. Henry II locked Eleanor up at Chinon while her sons received Louis VII's support. The revolt failed in the Vexin in 1173 and 'Young' Henry laid siege to Verneuil castle, but his father drove him off. The Scots entered the fray, but failed to take the castle at Wark and they were stopped at Carlisle where they agreed to a truce.[22]

After that, Henry took on the rebellious barons in England until the winter brought a lull that lasted until the spring of 1174. The Normans had built castles in England to consolidate their power over the newly-conquered lands. However, by the time the Plantagenets inherited the crown, these castles had become seats of power for the barons and served as obstacles to the King's control.[23] In addition, Henry had to defend England from Scots and rebels.

Wark (on Tweed) Castle, was originally destroyed by the Scots in 1138 and was rebuilt by Henry II between 1158 and 1161. It consisted of a polygonal shell keep on a motte, stone curtains and a gatehouse. Roger de Stuteville, one of the northern barons, held out there in 1174 against the Scottish king, William the Lion. The siege of Wark had an ominous beginning for Stuteville when one of the catapults failed and the first stone rolled out of its sling taking down one of his own knights.[24] The defenders, only ten knights and forty squires, refused to submit, so William lifted the siege and moved on to Carlisle whose garrison also refused to surrender to an army of supposedly 80,000 (an exaggerated number). William proceeded to take other poorly-defended castles that lacked provisions and headed on to Brough, a castle built on a strategic pass and the site of an old Roman fort. His troops took the outer defences forcing the garrison of only six knights back into the wooden keep. When the keep was set on fire, resistance was short. The Scots levelled the remaining fortifications and marched first on Harbottle, which fell and to Warkworth castle – another motte-and-bailey castle occupying the neck of a loop in the river with the town behind it – which also surrendered.[25] William met stiff resistance at Prudhoe, located on a promontory 46m (150ft) above the south bank of the Tyne River. This castle had a gatehouse and a deep moat on its south side and an inner moat. Its stone walls 8m (26.2ft) high

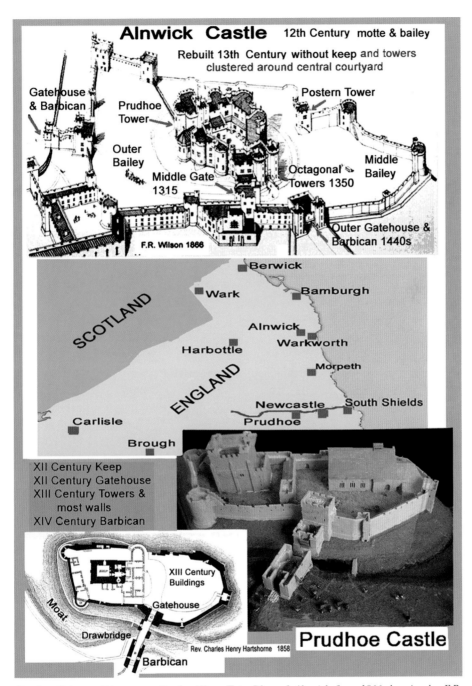

Castles of the twelfth-century Border Wars. Top: Plan of Alnwick from 1866 drawing by F.R. Wilson. Middle: Map showing location of border castles. Bottom: 1858 plan by C.H. Hartshome and model of Prudhoe Castle.

1173 - 1210
FRANCE

FLANDERS
Somme

Eu

NORMANDY

Arques
Dieppe Mortemer   Aumale
Drincourt

Gournay
Beauvais
ROUEN   Neufmarché
Seine
Epte
Pont de Arche Courcelles Gisors
Vaudreuil   G   Gamaches
Dangu
Neubourg   Evreux
VEXIN
Beaufort-le-Roger
Conches   Pacy   Seine
Breteuil   Ivry
Eure
PARIS
Monancourt
Verneuil
Seine

Radepont
Pont de Arch
Vaudreuil
Chateau Gaillard
Louviers
Seine
Gaillon
Neubourg
Vernon
Roche Guyon
Evreux

Chartres

Montmirail
Fréteval

Le Mans

Vendome   BLOIS

Loir   Loire

ANJOU   TOURAINE   Loire

MAINE

Angers   Tours   Cher

Loire

Chinon   Loches   Issoudun

Vienne   BERRY

Major Fortification   Mirebeau
Castles   Poitiers   Indre
Chateau Gaillard   G

0   50 km   Kaufmann

Northern France under Philippe Augustus from 1173 to 1210. Statue of Richard the Lionheart.

and 1.5m (4.9ft) thick had replaced the timber palisade in around 1100 and a two-storey stone keep had taken the place of a wooden one in the 1150s.[26] Foiled once again from taking this castle, the Scottish king retreated north to invest the stone castle at Alnwick held by William I de Vesci. This castle had two rings of buildings instead of a keep. The inner ring had a small courtyard surrounded by a cluster of towers, a design used in a few other castles of the era. The outer bailey included towers along its walls.[27] Here, a relief force surprised and captured William the Lion, breaking the back of the rebellion. The campaign was almost typical of the era with an army trudging along the limited invasion routes facing one castle and fortified town after another, having to either take or neutralize those sites to protect their own line of communications. In many respects, it was easier to face an enemy army on the battlefield.

Henry returned to Normandy with Welsh and Brabant mercenaries in August 1174 where his son and the French king were still besieging Rouen. He forced them to end the siege and Louis VII sued for peace. The rebellion was over and Henry restored power to his sons and rewarded them with castles and revenues, but not with power. Eleanor, who conspired with Louis VII and her son, was virtually imprisoned until Henry's death. Scotland's king became a vassal until Richard I changed his status in exchange for money to finance his crusade. Henry took control of all the castles in England and France and removed the disloyal castellans who had opposed him and even took over the castles of his supporters. He destroyed some of the strongholds and he rebuilt others, replacing timber with stone. Henry II, like William the Conqueror, used castles to strengthen his hold.

Three Fortresses and the Impregnable Castle

At the end of the twelfth century, three castles in north-west Europe stood as the key to English supremacy: Dover, Chinon and Gisors. A fourth, Château Gaillard, appeared at the end of the century. Except for Dover, all were lost to the French in the thirteenth century.

The English Benedictine monk and chronicler, Matthew of Paris, identified Dover as 'The key of England' in the thirteenth century. Henry II, England's great castle-builder, built his great fortress built on a dominant point on the headlands that had been a fortified since the Iron Age. It dominated the harbour below from an almost unassailable site at the top of the chalk headland with white jagged cliffs on its south side and steep slopes on the east and west sides. The massive fortress blocked the most direct invasion route from the Continent and intimidated any invader viewing it from the sea. Henry's castle dwarfed the remains of old Roman lighthouses and a small fort[28] and the Anglo-Saxon fortifications on the site. England's best builder, Maurice the Engineer,[29] who handled the construction, was paid six times more than others with similar skills were. By the time of his death in 1189, Henry had spent over 15 per cent of his yearly revenues on Dover.[30] The construction of the great keep took place between 1181 and 1187. Maurice imported construction materials from all over the Angevine Empire since the local chalk was of little value. He used the very hard and dark-coloured Kentish

View inside Avranches tower

Courtesy of Stephen & Lucy Dawson

1 Barbican
2 Avranches Tower
3 North Gate
4 King's Gate
5 Palace Gate
6 St John's Tower
7 Constable's Tower
8 Fitzwilliam Gate
9 Keep
10 Pharos
11 Church
12 Inner Bailey
13 Outer Bailey

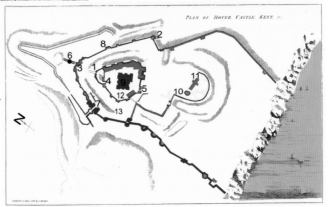

Dover Castle. Top: The castle. Centre left: The Avranches Tower and view inside showing low height of arrow slit that could only accommodate crossbows. (Courtesy of Stephen and Lucy Dawson) *Bottom: Plan.*

ragstone and local flint and brought the cream-coloured limestone from Caen to form decorative grey and light-coloured horizontal bands on the keep. He used white ashlar from Caen for the corners (quoins). He used a design similar to an earlier one he had employed at Newcastle. Although the entrance was above the ground on the level of the first storey in most keeps, at Dover the entrance was on the level of the second storey. A forebuilding that began on the south-east wall and ran along the north-east wall included three doors (or gateways) with a drawbridge between the last two that blocked the stairs. The actual keep entrance was at the end of the stairway. The forebuilding had no roof to allow the defenders to fire down upon assailants from battlements on both sides.[31] The well, which was on the second floor, was about 122m (400ft) deep, which went below sea level. The water was hauled up and poured into a system of pipes embedded in the walls and distributed throughout the keep.[32] The second storey included a great hall, the king's chambers, garderobes and windows so it could serve as a palace. The first storey also contained similar facilities, but not on as grand a scale. The ground floor was mainly for storage. Spiral staircases in two towers at opposite corners (north-east and south-west) led down to the first floor and the basement and up to the roof with its battlements and corner towers.[33] This great rectangular keep, which was 27.4m (90ft) high and the walls from 5m to 6.7m (16.4ft to 21.9ft) thick and 29.9m by 29.3m (98ft to 96ft), was the last square keep built in England. Like the Tower of London, the centre of each wall had a pilaster buttress and corner towers. The roof rose from the second floor and remained below the level of the battlements.[34]

Maurice also worked on the walls that eventually formed the inner bailey, beginning in 1185. The keep was garrisoned before it was completed. The curtain wall included fourteen square flanking towers, about 20m (65.6ft) in height with arrow slits at a lower level. Archers could protect the walls from escalade from these projecting towers, a feature found in many of Henry's castles. A northern and southern gatehouse had a barbican each. The northern one covered the most vulnerable part of the castle and consisted of a double tower gatehouse known as the King's Gate in front of which there was a courtyard formed by the barbican. A zigzag approach that linked the barbican gate to the King's Gate made it nearly impossible for the enemy to push a ram up to the gate. The curtain wall of the outer bailey was started during the reign of Henry II, but it is not known how much of it was completed at the time of his death. The Avranches Tower at an angle on the outer wall on the east side was a unique feature. It consisted of three levels (the top level is now gone) each of which had positions for three crossbowmen. The slits are not of sufficient height for a bowman. The position for each archer had triple arrow slits giving these nine men twenty-seven fields of fire. Additional crossbowmen were posted in the tower to maintain an almost continuous rain of fire by alternating positions.[35] The tower allowed a small number of archers to cover a large angle of outer wall. The outer wall took over thirty years to complete. The first towers were square, but subsequent towers built in the times of Kings John and Henry III were round or D-shaped. Today, only nine of possibly twenty towers remain on the outer bailey. Two massive D-shaped towers at the entrance of the outer bailey wall were destroyed in the

Chinon on the Loire. Photos from riverside and plan by Agnes Dahan. (Wikipedia Commons).

siege of 1216 and replaced later. The period of construction under Henry III in the 1220s included the Constable's Gate – England's most elaborate gateway – which had five towers, including one from the time of King John that had been modified. Work on Dover castle continued past the thirteenth century creating a medieval masterpiece of a concentric fortress. Dover withstood major sieges by Prince Louis of France in 1216 and 1217 during the First Baron's Revolt, a critical period that began when John lost Normandy after the fall of Château Gaillard (see section on this castle below).

Chinon Castle dates back the mid-tenth century when Theobald I, Count of Blois, fortified the site of an old Roman fort on a rocky spur above the Vienne River, several kilometres from its confluence with the Loire. The castle stands above the north bank of the Loire and the town between the ridge and the river. The eleventh-century castle included a keep, which later became the eastern side of the Middle Castle and was in ruins when the Count of Blois built the main works around a keep known as the Coudray Tower. The old walls were only about 5m (16.4ft) high. In the twelfth century, Henry II took possession of the castle and made a number of changes and additions including the Mill Tower (Tour de Moulin)[36] on the western corner and about a dozen circular towers built on square or rectangular bases. The rectangular Treasury Tower on the south side was unusual for a curtain tower because it included abutments, probably due to its location on the steep southern slope. Henry also ordered the construction of a higher mural wall with loopholes for archers, especially on the east side by the remains of the old keep. In the 1160s, Henry built a palace on the eastern side of the Middle Castle and the main approach to the castle. His son, John, fortified the section of the site which became known as Fort St. Georges.

From its location on the Loire, Chinon, the jewel of Henry II's castles, allowed him to rule his French dominions conveniently. When he gave it to John, his unhappy eldest son, Young Henry, turned to Louis VII of France and plotted against him. It was here, after fighting for over a decade with his son Richard and King Philippe that Henry died. After wresting the castle from King John in 1204, Philippe Augustus implemented his own changes. He added towers, the most notable of which are the Boisy and the Dogs' Towers, to the Middle Castle. The entrance to the Middle Castle was on the south-east corner at the Clock Tower, which he enlarged and to which he added a portcullis and a drawbridge. He also enhanced the separation between the Coudray Fort and the Middle Castle by putting a deep moat between them.

The Coudray Tower and the Tour du Moulin (Mill Tower) are 20m (66ft) high whereas the Tour de Boisy is 30m (98ft) high. Natural features protected the castle on three sides and the eastern side of the three forts was covered by man-made ditches and moats. The fortifications are 396m (433 yds) long and 70m (230ft) wide. Work continued on the defences through the fifteenth century, including

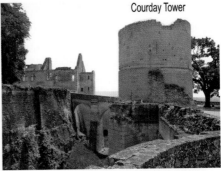

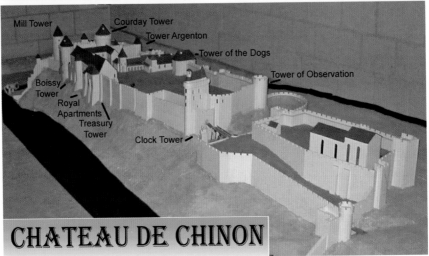

Chinon. Photos of various towers and plan. Model from Wikipedia Commons.

the addition of machicoulis in the second half of the fourteenth century. Much of the stone used in the construction of the chateau came from local quarries.

In 1308, in an effort to curtail the power of the Knights Templar and grab their wealth, King Philip IV imprisoned the Grand Master Jacques de Molay and other officials at Chinon before carrying out their death sentence in Paris.[37]

Gisors. Top: Enceinte and gate with keep behind it. Middle: Devil's Tower on enceinte. Bottom: Plan of castle. Photo of Tower of Prisoners by C.J. Dub. (Wikipedia)

In 1429, Joan of Arc met the Dauphin, future Charles VII, at Chinon where he cowered from the English during the Hundred Years War. She persuaded him to let her lead a force to break the siege of Orléans and later, to follow her through enemy territory to Reims for his coronation. During her stay, Joan was quartered in the Coudray Tower.

Gisors, a key position in the strategic Vexin, dominated the Epte river valley and the approach into Normandy and its capital at Rouen. The Vexin consists of a plateau between the Isle de France and Normandy bounded to the west by the Seine and to the south by Pontoise. To the north, it extends to a point about 20km (12.4 miles) south of Rouen and Beauvais. The Epte, Andelle and Oise rivers form some of its boundaries. Robert de Belesme built a motte-and-bailey castle at the site of Gisors at the location of one built for William Rufus in 1096 when Robert Curthose left for the Crusade.[38] The huge motte had a diameter of 70m (230ft) and a height of 30m (100ft). According to Robert du Mont, abbot of Bec, Henry I surrounded the bailey with a stone wall and added towers after an existing wooden palisade had burned down. Between 1123 and 1124, Henry I built the two-level keep and possibly modified the existing chemise on top of the moat. In 1144, the castle successfully resisted its first siege when the nobles revolted against Henry I. King Stephen lost the castle to the Duke of Normandy, the Plantagenet Geoffrey V 'the Handsome'.[39] In 1145, Geoffrey, gave the castle and the Vexin region to Louis VII as repayment for his help. Henry II betrothed his son, Young Henry, to Louis' daughter, Margaret, with Gisors as part of the dowry. Since the bride and the groom were children, Louis assumed that the marriage would not be celebrated until they reached adolescence, but to his chagrin, the Pope granted permission for the wedding to take place in 1160. The Templars occupied the castle at the time. The site was important because it was on the Norman border with the French king's Royal Domain and blocked the road from Paris to Dieppe. Henry made the site more formidable with improvements from 1170 to 1177.

Gisors is supposed to be one of the first castles to have conical pointed roof towers. Henry either increased the size of or rebuilt the donjon resulting in a four level octagonal keep with pilaster buttresses and an octagonal chemise at the top of the motte for support. The entrance is on first floor of the keep. Strangely, there was no fireplace, but the third level had garderobes. Inside the chemise, there was also a chapel, a well and a kitchen. Work was done on the 800m (875 yd) curtain of the outer bailey including flanking towers. The towers were rectangular and D-shaped and Richard I (Prince Richard at the time) added the Tower of the Devil that had arrow loops on all sides at four levels. All this work was for naught since Philippe Augustus took it by treachery in 1193. In addition to other improvements, Philippe II added circular towers and the keep known as the Tower of the Prisoner (14m [45.9ft] diameter and 28m [91.8ft] high) that covered the entrance to the village and was located in the corner of the curtain wall. The lowest chamber of this three-level keep served as a prison. Each level was vaulted. In 1415, the English captured Gisors after a three-week siege during the Hundred Years War, but the French took it back in 1451. Later additions to the complex included a barbican and the adaption of sections for artillery.

Château Gaillard. Top left: Inner bailey wall with corrugated shape. Top right: Keep. Centre left: Entrance to inner bailey. Bottom: Corner tower of outer bailey with keep in background.

Château Gaillard is perched on an isolated rocky spur overlooking a bend in Seine and the village of Les Andelys in the Vexin. Its mission was to block the invasion route leading from Paris to Rouen. According to Viollet-le-Duc, the castle not only blocked the invasion route, but also served as a threat to the Île de France. Richard I built it to compensate for the loss of the Vexin and Gisors to the French by the Treaty of Issoudun (Louviers) of 1196, which gave the French control of the left bank at Vernon and Gaillon.[40] Richard seized the land from the Archbishop of Rouen in violation of the treaty. Richard completed it in the record time of two years (1196–8).[41] He spent a great deal of money on labour and materials. The walls were made of local chalk and flint bound with mortar, but the ashlars came from elsewhere. Two different types of facing stones – one pale and one dark – were set to present a striped appearance making the walls look more imposing.[42] The chalk layer made it possible to create a large number of caverns for storage in the middle bailey. Some of the castle's unique features were inspired by the fortifications Richard had seen in the Holy Land; others, such as the beak or prow of his keep, had been inspired by European fortifications, such as the castle at La Roche Guyon. In addition to the unusual keep crowned with machicoulis[43] and round curtain towers, the enceinte of the inner bailey had an unusually corrugated shape that eliminated the need for flanking towers to cover the walls.[44] This feature is thought to have made the walls more resistant to missiles by deflecting them with its curved surface. Across from the castle, on the left bank, there is an easily defended peninsula formed by the bend in the river. Château Gaillard on the right bank and an armed contingent on this peninsula allowed the English to effectively block the Seine and threaten French forces advancing along either bank. Richard constructed an octagonal fort with towers, wooden palisades and ditches on a small island across from the tip of the peninsula. The island was linked to both banks by timber bridges. At the northern end, on the right bank, another fortified position formed a bridgehead and included a village named Petit-Andelys. This position was surrounded by water with a man-made lake on its north side. Richard fortified the town of Grand-Andelys on the other side of this lake. Château Gaillard on the chalk cliffs towered 100m (328ft) above both fortified sites. The castle was situated so that an enemy force had to approach from the south on higher ground[45] and assault the outer bailey (sometimes referred to as an advanced work) before it could reach the middle bailey and the inner bailey. The deep and wide moats of the outer and middle bailey made an attack difficult. The moat between these two baileys had a fixed bridge with a sharp turn in the middle, which prevented the approach of siege engines like rams.

According to Viollet-le-Duc, there was a stockade consisting of 'three rows of piles, placed across the Seine' that included a palisaded position on the right bank below the castle to control river traffic. Further up the river on the right bank, there was another fort that also served as an anchor for the defences

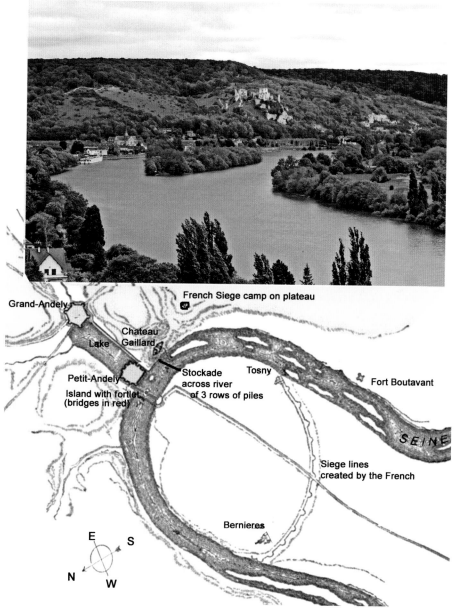

Château Gaillard. Top: View of town of Andely and Château Gaillard from down river. Bottom: Siege lines.

across the river at the neck of the peninsula. This fort, essentially a tower named Boutavant,[46] was built soon after Philippe II seized Évreux and went to war boasting that he would take Richard's 'beautiful daughter' (Château Gaillard). Before Philippe could carry out his threat, Richard defeated him at Gamaches near Eu. Richard enjoyed his time at the castle where he executed some French enemies in a less than chivalrous manner. Even though many of these positions were not made of masonry, together they formed an impressive fortress blocking the Seine. If Richard had not died in 1199, he might have converted the fortlet on the island with its bridges into a stronger position and replaced wooden defences with stone.

The death of Richard left the defence of Normandy in the hands of John, branded by history as his bumbling brother who lacked his military prowess.[47] Compared to most castles of the time, Château Gaillard deserved the title of impregnable, but when it faced its first siege in 1203 it failed to live up to expectations. The Constable of Chester, Roger de Lacy, held the fortress when the French army showed up and promptly moved against the peninsula position on the left bank in August 1203. The defenders destroyed the bridge across the Seine while Philippe Augustus ordered his men to dig a ditch between Bernières and Tonsy, using the spoil to create ramparts. Swimmers cut a path through the piles that formed a stockade across the river to allow French boats to pass through and create a pontoon bridge across the Seine by fastening them together just to the west of Petit-Andelys. A few of boats were armoured and had wooden turrets from which to bombard the little island fort. King John launched an uncoordinated two-pronged relief assault. A force led by William Marshal carried out a night attack on the French defences that stretched across the peninsula. Meanwhile, the ships John had sent up river from Rouen to attack the French pontoon bridge arrived too late to stop Marshal. Thus, the French concentrated on the English flotilla, stormed the fortlet on the island and attacked Petit-Andelys. The defenders were left with the castle. The 1,500 burghers of Petit-Andelys fled to Château Gaillard and their presence cut into the food supply needed for a long siege. In November, Roger de Lacy, his supplies dwindling, espelled a group of 500 townspeople and a similar number a little later. Both groups were allowed to pass through the French lines, but a third group became trapped between the two hostile camps since the French refused to let them pass and Roger could not afford to allow them back in. This group remained stuck beneath the castle walls and tried to survive on what little they could find to eat through the winter until Philippe showed some humanity and let the survivors pass.[48]

Philippe's army set up a siege camp on the plateau across from the south side of the castle. Like Caesar at Alesia, the French dug ditches and erected palisades to form lines of contravallation and circumvallation that included seven wooden towers. As the new year began, Philippe grew impatient and ordered his engineers to build heavy siege engines. In February 1204, he began the siege in earnest intending to smash the defences. He cleared the ground in front of the corner tower of the outer bailey that dominated the only path leading to the castle. This enabled his siege engines (belfry, battering rams and cats) to advance. From the belfry, whose height gave a slight advantage to his archers, he tried to tie down the English while other men descended into the moat with scaling ladders and clawed their way up the chalk sides to a point beneath the tower and curtain where they could mine. They eventually dug a small shaft and set it on fire bringing down part of the corner tower and a section of the curtain. Other men filled the ditch near that tower to make it easier to rush through the breach.[49] The defenders fell back to the middle bailey. Next, the French resorted to stealth, as several men scaled the cliff and climbed through the latrines on the cliff side of the middle bailey. Once inside, the intruders dropped ropes through the large windows of the chapel and adjacent structures on the apparently impregnable side of the castle and pulled up some of their comrades. Next, this small group set up a ruckus to convince the defenders that they were a sizeable force. During this commotion, either they or the defenders set a fire that consumed many of the structures in the middle bailey. Possibly the defenders had tried to smoke them out. This intrepid band of Frenchmen raced to open the bailey gate to let in the rest of the assailing force. The English took refuge in the inner bailey, but the French were able to manoeuvre their siege engines close enough to engage the main gate. The French miners tunnelled into the chalk below the wall under the cover of the stone bridge. Combined with missiles from the siege engines, the mining breached the inner bailey. Rather than retreat to the keep, the remaining 140 men of the garrison, near starvation, capitulated.[50] Thus, fell the great fortress on 6 March 1204. Normandy followed shortly after Château Gaillard.

The exact size of the garrison is unknown or the number of men lost. Possibly, the defenders may have numbered about 200 men, which would have been sufficient to man the vulnerable positions on the walls, but not enough to block gaps or counter-attack without expecting heavy losses. Thus, falling back to the next position was the logical choice before too many more men were lost. As the inner bailey was breached, only the keep, which could not accommodate 180 men for more than a short time, remained limiting its value as a last bastion. In addition, there was no well in the keep to supply the garrison with water. The apartments and garrison quarters were also in the inner bailey rather than the keep. Thus, the keep at Château Gaillard was unsuited for a last stand.

Although Philippe Augustus repaired the castle to maintain a strong position, Château Gaillard no longer played a major role in history even though it saw more action. Robert the Bruce after a temporary setback in Scotland sought refuge there in 1304. In 1419, Henry V took the castle in its second major siege and like his predecessor, he repaired and strengthened the position in 1420. It changed hands a couple more times before the Hundred Years War ended in 1453.

Chapter Seven

The Age of the Classic Castle –
Twelfth to Thirteenth Centuries

The Game of Castles Continues

The reign of King John of England began at the end of the twelfth century. Castle warfare changed little as castles became more sophisticated. Monarchs continued to exert more control be seizing castles and awarding them and associated lands to trusted noblemen. Castles of all types flowered across the continent and their sizes and shapes became increasingly complex. By the end of the century, Richard I had quickly restored the situation in England and neutralized his nemesis, Philippe II, in Normandy. When John came into power, the French king saw a new opportunity to seize Normandy. The Dukes of Anjou, Maine and Touraine did not accept John. When John raided Le Mans, his nephew Arthur I, Duke of Brittany, marched against him as Philippe approached from the east. John escaped and Philippe took Évreux. John recovered from the loss and made peace in January 1200. By 1202, they were at war again as John laid siege to the castle at Radepont (about 5km [3.1 miles] north-east of Pont de l'Arche) in July. Philippe forced John to lift the siege a week later and took the castles of Aumale and Gournay. On 30 July, John received news that his nephew, the Duke of Brittany, had besieged his mother Eleanor at Mirebeau Castle. He rushed south, surprised the besiegers and captured Arthur and 200 French knights. He imprisoned Arthur at Falaise Castle. Philippe responded by burning Tours on his way to Paris. John, known for his excessive cruelty, marched into Tours where he inflicted additional destruction, moved through Brittany to Dol and from there to the fortress of Fougères where he plundered the region. The Bretons, believing Arthur dead, invaded Anjou and took the castle at Angers. In 1202, many of the Norman lords swore loyalty to the French king. In August, John laid siege to Alençon, which had just switched sides, but his campaign ended in failure because Philippe advanced against the castles in the Vexin. First Philippe subdued the castles near Château Gaillard. In July, he again captured Gournay on the Epte. This time, he broke the dike that created a lake near the castle's moat. The resulting flood left the castle in the water. In May 1203, he seized some key positions along the Seine. including Conches and Vaudreuil. When the siege of Château Gaillard began in the autumn, John left the fortress in charge of a trusted commander and headed back to England in December. After taking Château Gaillard in March 2004, Philippe Augustus continued campaigning. In May, he seized the key Falaise Castle in Lower Normandy, defeated a Breton invasion force at Caen and completed his conquest of Normandy by seizing the capital, Rouen, in June 1204 after a siege of less than a month. John lost his territories north of the Loire. Philippe could easily have bypassed Château Gaillard and still conquered Normandy one castle at a time with similar lightning speed since he had the loyalty of the Dukes of Anjou, Maine and Touraine.

Philippe did not remain idle after taking Normandy and continued his programme of castle building and improvements. His signature contribution to military architecture was the 'Tour Philippienne'. This basic round tower lacked the sophistication of most rectangular keeps. He built them at a number of existing castles including Talbot's Tower at Falaise next to Henry I's Grand Donjon.[1] At Gisors, he built the Prisoner's Tower as a new keep and added to the defences of the enceinte. As Philippe took back most of western France, a new problem simmered in the south-west.

Château de Fougères

Fougères occupied a crossroads between Brittany, Maine, Anjou and Normandy on the eastern frontier of Brittany. It had been controlled by Breton overlords since the end of the Dark Ages. It first consisted of a wooden donjon and palisade on a high rocky outcrop that dominated its surroundings. A marshy area and a bend in the Nançon River served as defences. After a successful siege in 1166, Henry II put the wooden structures to the torch to prevent the site from blocking any future moves into Brittany. In the 1170s, the Breton baron Raoul II of Fougères rebuilt the fortifications in stone and took part in the civil war against Henry II in 1173. Early in the next century, King John passed through the town on his way to Dol during his quarrel with Arthur. Raoul III, grandson of Raoul II, strengthened the castle in late 1220s before he allied himself with King Louis IX. He built the barbican. In 1256, through marriage Fougères fell into the hands of the Lusignans of Poitou, a family that often feuded with the Plantagenets throughout the thirteenth century. The Lusignans extended the ramparts around the town and added four entrances, one at each cardinal direction. In 1314, Philip IV took the castle from the Lusignan family and gave it to the count of Alençon. In 1373, during the Hundred Years War, Bertrand du Guesclin occupied the town and in 1428, Duke John II of Alençon, sold it to the Duke of Brittany to pay his ransom. A few years before the end of the war, a mercenary group sent by the English took the castle by surprise.

The original castle occupied a formidable position at the highest point on the outcrop. Two towers formed the Réduit (Redoubt). The oldest tower, the Tour Gobelin, was built in the 1170s and a third level above the basement was added circa 1230. It was the only donjon present when King John came through. Work continued on the keep until the early thirteenth century when it reached at least three storeys with crenelated battlements. The additions are similar to those of the Mélusine Tower, indicating they date from the same period. The ashlar face begins at about 5m (16.4ft) above the base of the tower. The walls of the old keep are 3.5m (11.5ft) thick at the base and its height was about 27m (88.6ft). At each level of the tower, there are arrow loops that later had round openings for small cannons added. The great door was at second level and opened on a drawbridge that lowered into the ramparts leading to the Tour Mélusine. The third floor is octagonal with two windows and a fireplace. The top floor had a conical roof and a surrounding circular gallery with rooftop battlements.

The other tower, the Tour Mélusine, went up in the thirteenth century and was finished at the end of the next century. It is hexagonal on the interior and has walls up to 3.6m (11.8ft) thick.[2] Massive stones form the conical base creating a batter. The remainder of the structure is limestone masonry faced with ashlars. The tower is 30m (98.4ft) high and has an external diameter of 13m (42.6ft), leaving a 5.8m (19ft) wide interior. A spiral staircase gives access to the fourth level. A drawbridge spanned a small moat that led into the courtyard. A door on an upper level opened onto the ramparts that led to the Tour Surienne, which includes granite lined fireplaces and a garderobe. At the base of the tower, there is an oubliette accessed through an opening in its vaulted ceiling covered by a stone slab.[3] The rooms included arrow slits, later modified, like the Tour Gobelin. Jeanne, the baroness of Fougères, who married a member of the Lusignan family, gets credit for the construction of this tower.

The curtain walls for these two towers, which formed the Réduit, were about 3m (9.5ft) thick and 11.5m (37.7ft) high. The outer bailey, built mostly in the thirteenth century, included square towers with arrow slits on the curtain walls. This bailey covered 2 ha (4.9 acres) and included a chapel and a well. It served as a refuge for the townsfolk since the inner bailey (the Réduit) had little space. Lodgings and a palace occupied part of the south side. In the fourteenth century, the baron enlarged the old palace area. The entrance was through the twelfth-century Tour Coëtlogon, which had a drawbridge, two doors, two portcullises, arrow slits and wooden hoardings over the gate. The outer bailey (lower bailey) had the two largest towers: Tours Surienne and Raoul, which were added in 1470 and were designed for cannons. They occupied a position on the south side of the enceinte. Tour Raoul was 20m (65.5ft) in diameter and 20m (65.5ft) high; the base of its walls was 7m (22.9ft) thick and the remainder was about 5.8m (19ft) thick. These D-shaped towers had two-level basements and two floors above that housed single rooms 12m

Fougères. Top: The postern and the Gobelin Tower. Bottom left: View of the Gobelin Tower from near the main entrance. Bottom right: The Gobelin Tower with postern.

by 7m (39.3ft by 22.9ft) with positions for four cannons. At the top of the tower there was a turret surrounded by a horseshoe-shaped rampart with machicoulis.

Waters from the Nançon River, which looped around the site, were diverted around both sides of Fougères Castle to flood the nearby marshes and create several lakes forming an impressive water moat. The barbican, built in the thirteenth century, included two round flanking towers and a square gatehouse. The gatehouse, Tour Haye Saint-Hilaire, was 12m (39.3ft) high and had two levels above the ground floor. It was 7m (22.9ft) long and about 6m (19.6ft) wide and included arrow loops in the rooms of each level. A roof covered the merlons on the battlements. Arrow loops on the towers of the barbican also faced the courtyard. The entrance at ground level had two doors, two portcullises and no access to the floors above. A 5m (16.4ft)

Tour Plesguen   Tour Trémoille   Tour Haye-St.-Hilaire   Tour Guémadeuc

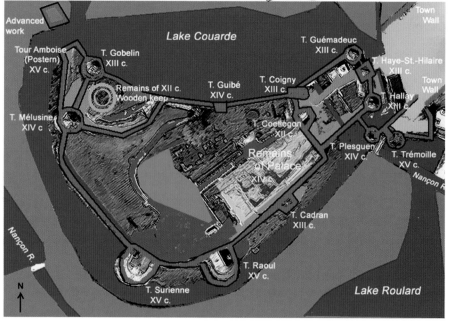

Fougères.

long curtain wall connected it to the Tour Guémadeuc, a cylindrical tower 6m (19.6ft) in diameter with arrow loops on each level, an access door at the ground level and another door on the first floor opening to the wall ramparts. The conical roof and some of the battlements appear to have been late additions. Tour Hallay, connected to the gatehouse by an 11m (36ft) long curtain wall, was similar to the Tour Guémadeuc. Its machicoulis were a late addition. The barbican controlled the sluice to the Nançon River that allowed the garrison to flood the marshes and the area around the castle. The machicoulis probably was not added to the curtain walls until the Late Middle Ages. The city wall linked to the fort's barbican. As the centuries passed, the town spilled outside these walls.

When Eleanor of Aquitaine died at the age of 80 in April 1204, Philippe Augustus began his conquest of lands south of the Loire. The barons of Aquitaine rebelled against John soon after his mother's death because they refused to accept an English ruler.[4] In May 1205 at Portchester castle, John laid out plans to retake Poitou and Anjou. He assembled a large fleet and an army bolstered with mercenaries. William Marshal, England's greatest warrior, and Archbishop Hubert refused to join him pointing out that, given the wealth and great resources of the French monarch, the operation would be great folly. John left Marshal in charge of the defence of England to counter Philippe's invasion plans. Meanwhile, Philippe marched into Poitou, but did not take La Rochelle. Chinon and Loches had remained loyal to John, but the French king seized both castles, which gave him control of Touraine. The castellan at Chinon, Hugh de Burgh, resisted until the castle fell by assault in June 1205 and he was imprisoned for over a year.[5] John achieved little in 1205, but he reinforced La Rochelle. On 8 July 2006, John landed at La Rochelle and recovered much of his lands in Aquitaine in a ruthless campaign.[6] Meanwhile, Philippe plundered the county of Thouars, but the two armies did not meet in battle and John negotiated a truce in October.

In the years that followed, John exacerbated his own difficulties despite some military successes in Ireland and Wales. He launched a castle-building programme that sparked a Welsh revolt led by Llywelyn 'the Great' in 1211. John sent an army into northern Wales to the old Norman castle of Deganwy, which Llywelyn destroyed before the English contingent could reach it. Left in an untenable position, the English withdrew and Llywelyn rebuilt the castle in 1213.[7] In 1213, the English won a major naval victory over the French. King John in collusion with his new ally, the Holy Roman Emperor, devised a plan whereby emperor would invade eastern France while he would strike in western France. In February 1214, John sailed for La Rochelle to reconquer Poitou. In June, he seized Nantes after a siege. On 17 June, Angers welcomed him and two days later,

Angers Castle. In the early thirteenth century Louis IX built the massive château was on the site of an older castle. It also served as a palace for the Dukes of Anjou. The walls are of schist and limestone and towers have a plinth. The outer walls are 3m (9.8ft) thick and extend about 500m (546.8 yds) with seventeen large circular towers 18m (59ft) in diameter and one up to 40m (131.2ft) high, but in the sixteenth century they were reduced in height and adapted for artillery. (Photo top left courtesy of Rupert Harding)

he laid siege to the powerful fortress of Roche-aux-Moines, which overlooked the Loire on the road between Angers and Nantes.[8] In July, three weeks into the siege, John received news that Philippe's son, Prince Louis, was coming to rescue the castle. Rather than engage this French force, John fled to La Rochelle where he arrived on 9 July to await the news of Emperor Otto IV's campaign. On 27 July 1214, Philippe met the Holy Roman Emperor's army of Germans, Flemish, English and Lorrainers at the Battle of Bouvines.[9] It was a decisive victory for the French. Otto lost his throne and Philippe remained firmly in control, even taking back some lost territories. Meanwhile, John retained much of Gascony, but left the continent not to return in his lifetime.

The year 1215 turned out to be disastrous for King John beginning with the Barons' Revolt and the signing of the Magna Carta on 15 June. The rebels had already seized London in May, forcing his hand. When he failed to honour the great charter in July, he faced additional difficulties. A few months later, King Philippe decided to invade England and claim its crown. In September, John went to Dover castle to await a fleet of mercenaries while his wife and son remained secure at Corfe Castle in Dorset. The barons took control of London and its fortifications.

Rochester Castle

Castles with great rectangular keeps located at London (the White Tower), Dover, Canterbury and Rochester dominated the route between the coast and the capital.[10] The first of these Norman castles featured in the revolt of 1088 instigated by Bishop Odo, William I's half-brother, who supported his eldest nephew, Robert Curthose, against William Rufus.[11] Rochester, a centre of that rebellion, was put under siege until the castle surrendered due to disease and famine.[12] Gundulf, Bishop of Rochester, who had designed the White Tower of London, supervised the construction of Rochester's curtain walls. In 1127, Archbishop William de Corbeil began the construction of the great keep, which is now the tallest remaining in England. Henry I put the castle into the custody of the Archbishop of Canterbury. When his sons revolted in the 1170s, Henry II added improvements to the keep. In 1206, John commissioned additional work on the moat, the keep and other features.

Rochester's keep consists of a ground-level basement and three floors. A cross wall divides each storey into two large halls. A well passes through each of the cross walls. The basement, mainly for storage, has a few narrow slits for light. The first floor includes the entrance through a forebuilding anteroom. Each large hall has a fireplace. There are two spiral staircases at opposite corners, but only one leads to the basement. The main floor, on the second level, has chambers in the walls and fireplaces connected to those of the first

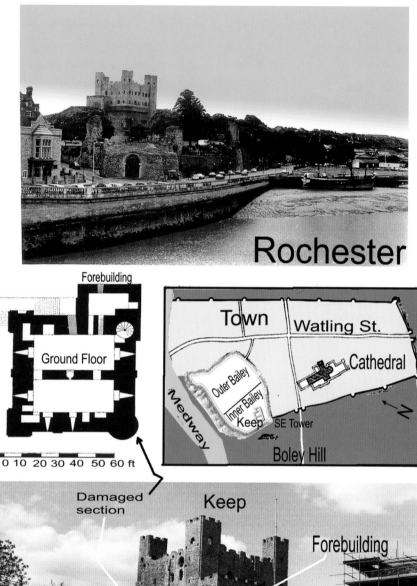

Rochester Castle. Top: View from the river. Middle: Plans. Bottom: View of keep and curtain wall.

floor. The forebuilding at this level includes the chapel. The second floor has a gallery with wall passages that look into the great halls below. The third floor, which served as the residence, has a similar layout. The top of the keep includes four turrets and a wall walk with the roof contained within, like the White Tower in London. Each side is 26m to 27m (85.3ft to 88.5ft) in length and about 31m (113ft) high with towers rising about 3.5m (12ft) above that. The walls are 3.6m (12ft) thick, but they thin out to 3.6m (10ft) near the top. The main building material was hard Kentish rag and, like the White Tower, ashlar from Caen. The stairs at the entrance to the forebuilding on the first floor included a drawbridge.

The keep occupies the south corner of the castle inside the inner bailey. The enceinte formed an irregular oval shape. Henry III added a semicircular tower to protect the south-east corner of the inner bailey. The enceinte included other towers, mostly square, now gone. On the north-east side, a drawbridge from the main gate gave access the outer bailey. The north side of the enceinte ran from the main gate to the north-west bastion. A moat protected the north, the east and south sides of the enceinte. The wall on the western side slopes down to less than 100m (109 yards) of the Medway River. A cross wall ran from east to west on the southern third of the enceinte dividing it into the inner (southern) and outer (northern) bailey. The Roman wall formed much of the enceinte. The wall built by Gundulf and later partially destroyed and modified, was from 0.6m (23.6in) to just over 1m (3.2ft) thick and a little over 6m (20ft) high. Only parts of the battlements remain today.

In the summer of 1215, after the signing of the Magna Carta, Stephen Langton, Archbishop of Canterbury, received custody of the castle. Since he was not in John's favour, the king tried to transfer control of the castle, but rebel barons seized the castle in late September before he could do so. Their force numbered 90 to 140 knights, sergeants, archers and other troops. After John arrived from Dover, as the rebels controlled London, he ordered the bridge broken to block any relief force while he besieged the castle. John took up a position on Boley Hill[13] and built five catapults to launch an around-the-clock barrage supported by his archers. The garrison resisted despite dwindling food supplies. Not content to starve the garrison out, he set his miners to tunnel beneath the south-east corner of the keep. In late November, they filled the mine with the carcasses of forty fat pigs and set them ablaze bringing down the corner of the keep. The defenders used the cross wall in the keep as a barrier and continued to fight on, but they ran out of food and surrendered on 30 November. John refrained from executing the leader, but he imprisoned the knights at the castles of Corfe and Nottingham and executed the remainder of the garrison.

Although Rochester Castle survived the war, John did not. His son, Henry III, restored the castle. A cylindrical tower replaced the keep's badly-damaged south-eastern one. He also improved the enceinte to which he added a drum tower on the south-east corner. The castle came under siege in 1264 during the Second Baron's War. Roger de Leybourne held Rochester for the king. In April, rebel forces took the town after briefly being checked crossing the Medway. They quickly broke into the bailey of the castle and the defenders retreated to the keep. The besiegers began a mine. A week later, news of the arrival of a relief force led by the king caused the lifting of the siege.

King John's Last Castle Campaign

In October, John left Dover to march on London. He followed the Roman route that passed through Canterbury. Rochester Castle, held by ninety rebel knights, blocked the strategic crossing of the Medway. On 11 October 1215, he took the town and besieged the castle. After taking the castle, John moved north to strike against the rebellious barons and retired to Nottingham Castle for Christmas. It was a secure site with its keep and the upper bailey perched high on 'Castle Rock', with cliffs 40m (130ft) high. It had a middle and outer bailey further down. Henry II had replaced the wooden keep with the stone one. John had taken refuge here before. He resumed his campaign at the beginning of the year raiding Scotland in revenge for an attack on Newcastle. During this advance to Berwick via York and during the return trip, he seized rebel castles and let his soldiers wreak havoc to assuage his anger.

The barons asked the French king to rescue them and the French arrived in late February 1216, rallying many of the barons and taking London. On May 21, Prince Louis landed in eastern Kent. King John, who had been waiting at Dover since 26 April, had just moved to Sandwich when Louis disembarked nearby. John chose to move to Winchester as Louis marched on London with a force of 1,500 knights and captured much of southern England. After he captured Winchester on 14 June, Louis advanced on Portchester Castle. John had built the small castle of Odiham between Portchester and Windsor between 1207 and 1212. It was located in a marshy area ideal for hunting. The keep was octagonal in shape, somewhat similar to Conisbrough and Orford, had an interior diameter of about 9.5m (31.1ft) and walls about 3m (9.8ft) thick. The many angles of the keep deflected missiles and reduced its vulnerability. It had two stories and a square moat with palisades. Louis was held up for fifteen days before taking Odiham whose plucky garrison of three knights and ten soldiers often sortied to harry the besiegers, but finally surrendered on 9 July.

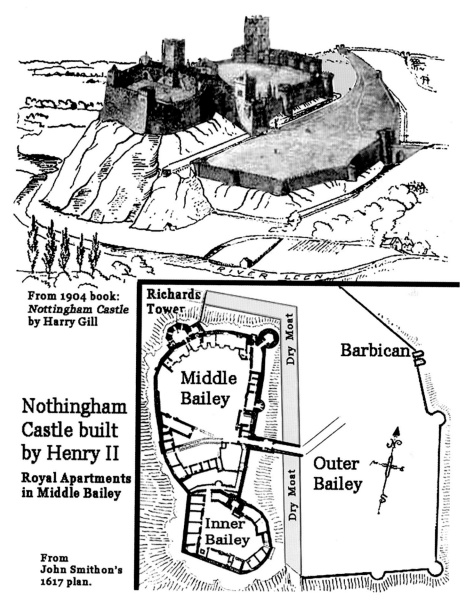

From 1904 book:
Nottingham Castle
by Harry Gill

Richards Tower

Middle Bailey

Dry Moat

Barbican

Nothingham Castle built by Henry II

Royal Apartments in Middle Bailey

Dry Moat

Outer Bailey

Inner Bailey

From John Smithon's 1617 plan.

Nottingham Castle was a motte and bailey rebuilt as a stone castle by Henry II atop Castle Hill. A middle bailey was added, followed later by an outer bailey.

After taking refuge at Corfe Castle, John decided to raid the Welsh border.[14] During this campaign, he took Shrewsbury on 4 August and inflicted much damage to the castles and lands of the rebel barons.[15] Meanwhile, Louis had Dover under siege and he had already sent the Count of Nevers to besiege Windsor Castle in June 1216. The count's siege engines relentlessly battered the walls of Windsor, but failed to cow the defenders who included sixty knights and a large garrison that comprised many mercenaries under the command of Fawkes de Breauté, a shrewd Norman as ruthless as John. In September, on his return from Wales, John tried to relieve Windsor, but withdrew after he got his Welsh archers within range of the enemy. Despite this strange behaviour, the siege ended mysteriously amid suspicions that the Count of Nevers had taken a bribe.

Windsor Castle

William the Conqueror built a motte-and-bailey castle at Windsor. The motte consisted of a chalk mound with wooden palisades. Henry II enlarged the castle and replaced the palisades with stone walls. He also strengthened the motte, which had begun to subside and cause damage. In 1194, the barons loyal to Richard put Windsor under siege trapping him within. After one month, unable to take the castle, the barons lifted the siege and John agreed to surrender all his castles to his mother Eleanor. In John's time, the castle consisted of a middle bailey with the large keep, a lower bailey west of it and an upper bailey on the east side where the construction of the royal apartments began under Henry II who also commissioned the construction of apartments in the lower bailey, which were later destroyed in a fire in 1226. Henry III later completed Windsor's wooden outer defences in stone around the lower bailey. He also created a luxurious royal palace within the castle that the Tudors used as a royal court.

Parliamentary forces imprisoned Charles I here during the English Civil War of the seventeenth century and later in the century, Charles II had much work done on the castle with more renovations taking placed in the centuries that followed. Today it remains a royal residence.

In October 1216, John fled to Newark Castle,[16] where he died a few days later. In the meantime, during the summer of 1216, Prince Louis had taken up positions on the northern approach to Dover Castle, the only practical side due to the steepness and the cliffs. The defenders of Dover put up a wooden palisade beyond the outer wall of the northern gate to protect it. Behind the palisade, a wooden bridge over a trench led to the gate. The defenders finished this work just before Louis' arrival. Hubert de Burgh commanded the garrison of 140 knights and an unknown number of archers and foot soldiers. He stocked the castle with food and weapons. Louis's army may have numbered 1,000 knights and a few thousand more men-at-arms.[17] He built siege engines including a belfry, catapults and cats. The bombardment began in July, but the English archers picked off anyone approaching from the French camp. French miners undermined and brought down a section of the palisade and French soldiers charged through the breach forcing the English to retreat through the twin-towered northern gatehouse. The French moved their siege engines closer and began to bombard

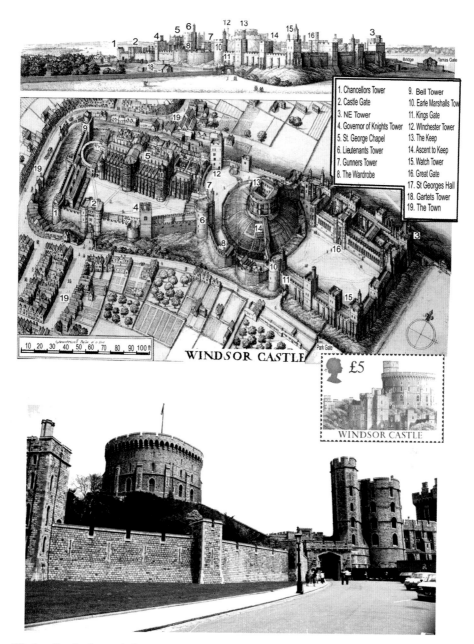

1. Chancellors Tower
2. Castle Gate
3. NE Tower
4. Governor of Knights Tower
5. St. George Chapel
6. Lieutenants Tower
7. Gunners Tower
8. The Wardrobe
9. Bell Tower
10. Earle Marshalls Tow
11. Kings Gate
12. Winchester Tower
13. The Keep
14. Ascent to Keep
15. Watch Tower
16. Great Gate
17. St Georges Hall
18. Gartets Tower
19. The Town

WINDSOR CASTLE

£5

WINDSOR CASTLE

Windsor Castle plan and photos.

the walls while English crossbowmen picked them off. Again, the French miners, protected by cats, went to work inside the ditch tunnelling towards the stone wall. Two men worked the face of each mine advancing at a rate of about 1m (3.2ft) per ten hours. They needed to tunnel into the slopes for about 50m (164ft) to get under the outer wall. In September, the miners approached the wall while

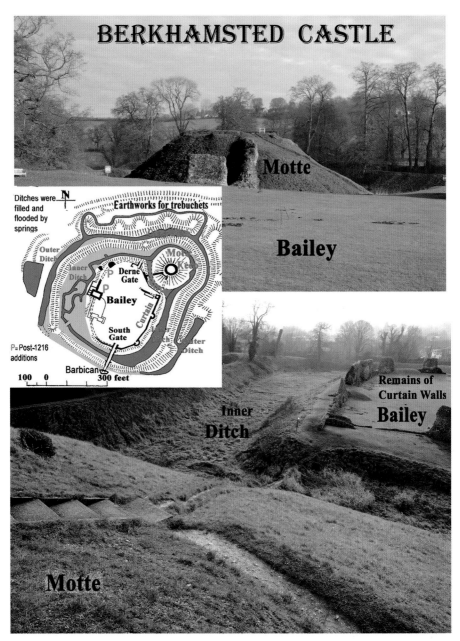

Berkhamsted Castle. Built in a valley with numerous springs during the Norman Conquest, its keep was later converted to stone. The ditches were flooded by the springs and overflowed to create a double moat. Light blue indicates additional areas that flooded. Earthworks are where Prince Louis of France installed his trebuchet during the Baron's Revolt in 1216. (Plan from HMSO) Top photo is view from the motte looking at ditch and bailey. Bottom photo is a view of the remains of the motte. (Photos courtesy of Rupert Harding)

the English worked on countermines and intercepted at least one of the French tunnels. When one of the French tunnels reached under the Northern Gate, it was greased up and set alight, causing part of the gatehouse to collapse. The French charged through the gap in the wall and engaged the defenders in vicious hand-to-hand combat. The massive French army could only get a few soldiers at a time through the gap. Again, arrows and crossbow bolts rained down on the French. The English pushed the French back through the breach and sealed it with wood and other available materials. When the news of John's death reached them in October, Louis Hubert de Burgh negotiated a truce.

As Henry III succeeded his father, Louis strove to secure additional castles in order to claim the throne for himself. Louis departed for France in February 1217 and returned in April to find that many of the barons had switched their allegiance to Henry III. He brought with him a large trebuchet and after forcing several castles like Berkhamsted[18] to capitulate by heavy bombardments, he returned to Dover. In May 1207, Louis renewed the siege of Dover in earnest after he learned that its garrison had been resupplied in violation of the truce made in October. At the same time, he sent 600 French knights and supporting troops to take Lincoln Castle. William Marshal, at the head of a relief force of only 400 knights and 500 sergeants and crossbowmen, outmanoeuvred the French as the garrison sortied from an unguarded gate catching the enemy in the town. An unusual urban engagement forced the rebels and the French to flee. Half of the combatants were taken prisoner. Louis' siege efforts at Dover came to naught and his huge trebuchet inflicted little damage. On 24 August, his fleet was defeated by the English navy at the Battle of Sandwich. Frustrated, he lifted the siege and returned France in September.

Henry III

The young Henry III's regent, Hubert de Burgh, the erstwhile commander of Dover Castle, became justiciar in 1219. His campaign to bring the barons to heel culminated with the siege of Bedford Castle. A force led by Faulk de Breauté, one of John's Norman mercenaries, had taken the castle from the rebels in 1215. In 1223, de Breauté briefly revolted against the regent and held a few castles including Bedford castle. In June 1224, Henry III surrounded Bedford Castle and the Archbishop of York excommunicated the garrison hoping to break morale, but the siege continued for eight weeks. Henry set several mangonels into action against different sides of the castle. His carpenters also built two large belfries. The bombardment began damaging the walls and an assault seized the barbican. Taking the outer bailey proved more difficult and casualties mounted. Next, his miners brought down part of the inner curtain allowing his soldiers to break into the inner bailey where they took additional losses. Finally, the king's men took on the keep, but could not force an entry. The miners tunnelled beneath the

KENILWORTH CASTLE (16th Century)

Models of Bedford and Kenilworth Castles. (Photo by Bernard Lowery)

foundation and fired the mine on 14 August. The keep remained standing, but its wall cracked causing the defenders to release their captives and surrender the next day. Henry hanged eighty of them and ordered the demolition of the castle.

Henry III faced difficulties with his barons once again when the fanatically religious mercenary Simon de Montfort, Henry's trusted lieutenant, turned on him. Henry had given him Kenilworth castle and the title of Earl of Leicester, but de Montfort was unsatisfied and led the Second Barons' Revolt in 1263.[19] He captured the king at the Battle of Lewes in 1264 and theoretically ruled England from Kenilworth Castle for about a year. Montfort was finally defeated and killed at the battle of Evesham in 1265, after which the siege began.

Kenilworth Castle grew around the great keep of Henry I. Several dammed streams formed massive water defences. The keep had walls up to 5m (17ft) thick and was about 30m (100ft) high. South-east of the castle there were 'brays' or palisades that connected with the outer bailey and the Mortimer Gatehouse with a causeway that later used as a tiltyard for jousting. Near the end, where the advanced work connected with brays, a sluice controlled the flow of water. The marshy ground west of the causeway, called the Great Mere, covered 40 ha (100 acres). The Lower Pool was on the other side of the causeway on the south-east side of the curtain of the outer bailey. A moat covered the eastern and northern outer bailey walls and the Great Mere protected the western and southern curtains. King John had built the wall of the outer bailey with many buttresses for support. There were no towers between Mortimer's Gatehouse and the north-east corner tower, which were protected by the lake. The rebels declined the king's offer to surrender, but they had prepared for the siege with a large supply of food for the 1,200 men in addition to women and children within the walls. Henry III assembled nine siege engines and had thousands of arrows and crossbow bolts for the siege, which began on 25 June 1266. The king's catapults were pelted with return fire from the castle, forcing the king to call for larger trebuchets. One of the two large belfries held 200 crossbowmen that fired into the castle from above. However, the castle catapults took out both belfries. The main assaults concentrated on the northern wall, but failed because the defenders had as many crossbowmen as their opponents did. Boats hauled from Chester took part in an assault over the lake, but they failed as well. In December, before the king could launch another massive assault, the garrison, almost out of food, surrendered and accepted the generous terms offered by the king ending the longest siege in medieval England. It had lasted 172 days. Henry's son, Edward I, took part in the siege and it is thought that the water defences inspired the design for his castles in Wales.

Crusade in Languedoc

The region of Languedoc loosely stretches from the Rhône to the Garonne Rivers. It is bounded in the north by the Dordogne, which stretches as far south as the Pyrenees. The land of the Basques, Gascony, borders it on the west. Its actual border shifted during the High Middle Ages as the English advanced from Aquitaine and the French and Aragonese kings vied for domination of the region. Some of the key urban centres were Nîmes in the east, Rodez and Cahors in the north, Foix and Perpignan in the south and Narbonne, Béziers and Montpellier

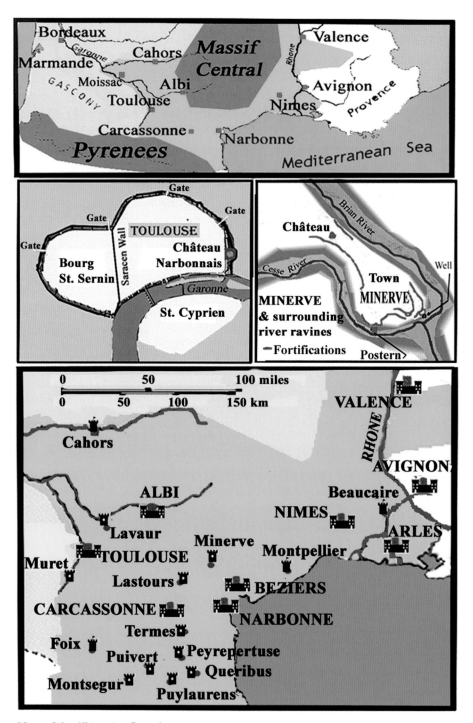

Maps of the Albigensian Crusade.

near the coast. In the central area are Carcassonne and Toulouse, the capital, occupying the main east–west route. The territory varies from a coastal plain to mountainous and hilly regions between the Pyrenees and the Massif Central. The region was the crossroads between Aquitaine and the Mediterranean and a gateway into Aragon. The major cities were fortified. Many of the towns built in the eleventh and twelfth centuries were laid out in a pattern called 'circulade', in which homes were placed in concentric circles around a church or possibly a fort. The Visigoths occupied the area of the former Roman province of Septimania for several centuries of the Dark Ages. In 725, the Muslim governor of Iberia invaded the region, took Carcassonne after a siege and enslaved much of the population. In 759, the Frankish forces of Pepin the Short drove the Arabs from the region. During the twelfth century, when compared to France and England, the region was relatively liberal. The courts of the counts and viscounts filled with traveling troubadours and the nobles allowed various minorities like Cathars and Jews to flourish. In the eleventh century and until its demise, the county of

Carcassonne. Castle gate and towers with hoardings.

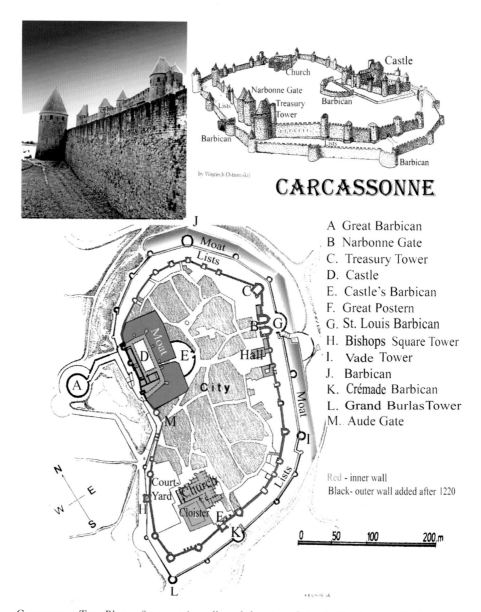

Carcassonne. Top: Photo of concentric walls and drawing of the fortifications by W. Ostrowski. Bottom: Plan of fortifications from Viollet-le-Duc.

Toulouse was under the Raymondine dynasty. The Trencavel family became a major factor first as viscounts of Albi and as viscounts of Carcassonne, Nîmes, Narbonne and Béziers in the twelfth century. The region had about 500 castles, but half of their lords gave no feudal service according to archaeologist Aubrey Burl.[20] The noblemen of the region were fiercely independent and challenged each other for domination while remaining relatively free from dominance of the kings of France, England and Aragon.

Carcassonne. Top: The Narbonne Gate. Middle: View of castle and walls from the ruins of the Great Barbican. Bottom: View of Carcassonne with the Narbonne Gate on the far right-hand side.

In the twelfth century, the spread of the nonconformist Cathar form of Christianity in the region alarmed Innocent III, elected Pope at the end of the century, who decided to stop its expansion. However, papal legates failed to bring the Cathars back into the fold. In 1208, a knight killed the Pope's legate and

Count Raymond VI of Toulouse was blamed and excommunicated by Innocent III who branded the Cathars heretics. Thus began the Albigensian Crusade.[21] Many of the Crusaders came from the north including a large group of ribauds, militia-like groups of light infantry who in fact mere scavengers who followed the army looking to plunder. Philippe Augustus, who had other reservations at the time, sent a number of lesser nobles such as Simon de Montfort to join the leaders of the crusade that included the Duke of Burgundy and the Count of Nevers. Each of these lords brought their own retinue, archers, crossbowmen and men-at-arms that formed a polyglot organization similar to other crusades. After the defeat at Hattin in 1187, which resulted in the loss of Jerusalem, followed by the failure of the Third Crusade, the Church and the Crusaders were thirsty for revenge against anyone. A number of the knights of the region supported the Cathars and even converted to their faith. Raymond VI pleaded for forgiveness and in 1209 joined the crusade, which became as violent as and more ruthless than the crusades in the Holy Land had been.

The fortified cities involved included Toulouse, Carcassonne, Béziers and Narbonne and smaller defended cities where the Cathars lived. When most of these urban centres fell to the Crusaders, the Cathars sought refuge in several mountain castles whose location alone defied besiegers.

Carcassonne, the most famous of these cities, occupied a key position in the centre of the east-west corridor between the Pyrenees and the Massif Central in a region known as the Midi-Pyrenees. Defended since ancient times when it was an oppidium (hilltop fort) under the Celts, the Romans had turned it into a major fortified city. The Visigoths and their successors repaired and improved its walls and towers throughout the Dark Ages and into the twelfth century. The Romans began construction similar to their other sites with a foundation of a few layers of large stones covered by mortar and above that a concrete core made of stones, gravel and similar materials bound by a mortar made of one-third lime and two-thirds sand between two masonry walls. The walls rose to about 8m (27ft) in height. Several of the Roman D-shaped towers were modified. During the High Middle Ages, before the crusade, two small towns adjacent to the wall, Saint-Michel and Saint-Vincent, became bourgs with their own walls and towers linked to the city wall. One was on the north-east side and the other on the south-east side.[22]

In the summer of 1209, the Crusaders, about 20,000 men strong, emerged from the Rhône valley and targeted the fortified city of Béziers. The papal legate, Arnaud Amaury and the Crusaders met with Viscount Raymond Roger Trencavel at Montpellier. The viscount attempted to negotiate, but Arnaud's demands were too steep. Trencavel returned to Béziers on 21 July, prepared the city for a siege and rode off to prepare other sites as well. The Crusaders arrived the next day and ordered all Catholics to leave the city. No detailed information is available about the defences of Béziers besides the fact that it had tall walls and stood on an escarpment located next to the River Orb. Depending on the source, these impressive walls protected 9,000 to 20,000 people, including women and children. In the Crusader army, not everyone was a soldier either, so the forces were evenly matched. On 27 July, a hot summer day, the ribauds were bathing in the nearby river when the defenders launched a sortie. The ribauds routed the raiders and pursued them inside the city walls before the gates could close, plundered and slaughtered mercilessly and put Béziers to the torch.

Word of the massacre spread rapidly and Narbonne opened its gates to the Crusaders without a fight. The Crusaders marched on to Carcassonne and put it under siege on 1 August. Raymond Roger handled the defence. When he decided to make a sortie, his entourage convinced him that it was a bad idea, considering what had happened at Béziers. Each section of the city walls was under the command of a nobleman who lived nearby with his family. Each of the sections included one to two towers. Supposedly, 4,000 people sheltered in the city, half of whom actually defended it. The two adjacent boroughs with lower walls and towers served as outworks. Like most outworks, their purpose was to keep the enemy siege engines out of range of the city walls. The main problem for the defenders was that the hot dry summer had left their water supply low.

Sapping or mining under the walls led to the fall and destruction of the two boroughs. The more weakly defended of the two fell on the third day followed by the second one the next day. According to some chroniclers, Trencavel himself evacuated and set fire to them. The Crusaders were unable to bring their siege engines within range of the city walls.[23] They could only move the smaller ones close so that an attack on the walls failed. The city's water supply dwindled when the Crusaders cut them off from the Aude River.[24] The number of people sheltered in the city had increased greatly as peasants from the surrounding area took refuge. Soon the refugees cut into the water supply as well as the food supply. About this time, King Pedro II of Aragon arrived and asked permission from Arnaud Amaury to enter the city and negotiate since he was Trencavel's overlord. Raymond Roger declined the less-than-generous terms offered by the papal legate. He asked for Pedro's backing, but the king, who had only a small force with him, declined to help and departed. The Crusaders filled in sections of the dry moat with faggots and other materials and renewed their attack on the walls. They met a hail of missiles and retreated. If they had reached the towers, they would have been pelted with a variety of projectiles from the hoardings Raymond-Roger had erected. Finally, on 15 August Raymond-Roger entered the enemy camp to negotiate, but he was tricked and was taken hostage after surrendering the city. The victors forced the citizens to depart without their possessions. They held the viscount prisoner until his death in November. His family fled to the protection of the Count of Foix. Simon de Montfort became viscount of Carcassonne and the crusading army dispersed since many of the knights had completed their forty days of feudal service.[25] The leaders of the crusade went home and Arnaud Armory and a few remaining lords elected Simon de Montfort's to command the remaining contingent of 30 knights and about 500 soldiers.

In the autumn of 1209, Simon de Montfort moved part of his small force out of Carcassonne. Several fortified towns surrendered without a fight. In some cases, the burghers fled in terror after having heard of the events of that summer. Montfort did not have enough men to garrison them all. In key towns like Montréal, located just west of Carcassonne, he had to leave a priest in charge. Peter-Roger of Cabaret (the region north of Carcassonne), who had been at Carcassonne, retreated to his mountain top castle of Cabaret at Lastours, where he decided to make a stand. Montfort laid siege to his three castles. The small castle of Cabaret was a five-sided keep with an adjacent hall and quarters only about 7m by 14m (22.9ft by 45.9ft), surrounded by a chemise. It was located on a rocky spur about 300m (984ft) above the village of Lastours. At the time, there were two other castles held by Peter-Roger located higher up on the site: Surdespoine and Quertinheux.[26] Steep surrounding sides made access difficult. Construction had ended only one decade or so before the crusade. Montfort's siege failed and Peter-Roger surrendered the castle in 1211 after negotiations that allowed him to leave the area unscathed.

After the autumn of 1209, problems flared up throughout the region. Failure to take Lastours had been a serious setback for Simon de Montfort who could not do much more until he got reinforcements at the end of the winter. In March,

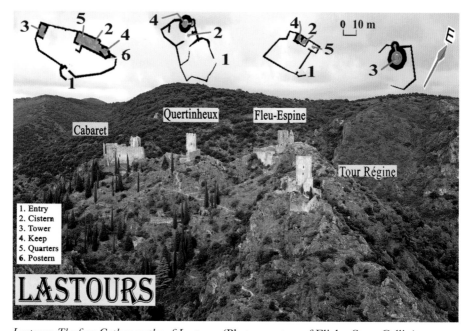

Lastours. The four Cathar castles of Lastours. (Photo courtesy of Flickr: Steve Collis.)

with the arrival of hundreds of knights, he was ready to move. A new terror campaign was launched. The Crusaders reached Bram, one of many fortified villages of the 'circulade' type. It fell after three days of resistance and Montfort ordered the hundred defenders blinded and mutilated as an example to others. In July, Montfort's 7,000 Crusaders laid siege to the fortified town of Minerve, which, like Lastours and Termes, sheltered Cathars and served as a base for raids against the Crusaders. The town occupied an elevated position on top of a high rock spur created by the confluence of two rivers that had cut into the limestone plateau creating deep gorges with cliff sides up to 90m (295.2ft) high. Curtain walls on top of these cliffs surrounded the town making it unassailable from all sides but one. That one side – the 30m (98.4ft) wide base of the spur – was blocked by a castle. On the south-west side, a postern led down to the gorge and on the south-east side a path led to bottom of the ravine where defences covered the only well available to augment the water supply of the town's cisterns. Montfort divided his little army into four parts, each with a siege engine three of which were mangonels and the fourth a trebuchet named Malevoisine (Bad Neighbour).[27] He used Malevoisine to batter the water supply. The catapults, at the same elevation as the town on the other side of the gorges, smashed holes in the high walls. Weeks of bombardment demoralized the defenders. The Crusaders also tried to take the well by assault. Finally, on 17 July 1210, seven weeks into the siege, the defenders launched a nighttime sortie down across the ravine and across the Briant River and climbed the other side to set the poorly-guarded Malevoisine on fire. Unfortunately, the crew put out the fire before the machine incurred serious damage. With their food supply almost gone and the well virtually destroyed, the 200-man garrison surrendered later that week. The Crusaders spared the villagers but they burned 180 Cathars alive.

The next major stronghold to be attacked that summer was the castle of Termes that stood about 500m (1,640.2ft) above the village of the same name. Its outer wall was 8m to 10m (26.2ft to 32.5ft) high and included a well-protected entrance with two circular towers and a central keep. The siege began in August 1210 and ended four months later. Montfort received major reinforcements in September, which allowed him to maintain a tight siege. The battered castle was almost out of water and morale was collapsing as many of the defenders slipped away. Supposedly, this caused Peter-Roger to negotiate the surrender of Cabaret in March 1211.

Montfort's campaign of terror continued against those who defied him, as he burned 300 more Cathars and hanged 80 knights. In the spring of 1211, Simon de Montfort moved against Lavaur, which was held by Geralda de Lavaur. The town occupied a position above the Agout River with cliffs on one side and thick walls protecting the other sides. The attackers tried several times to fill the moat with brush as their siege towers moved closer to the walls. Meanwhile, sappers undermined the walls, but the defenders countermined trying to block their efforts. When the six-week siege ended on 3 May, the Crusaders beat and abused Geralda, threw her down a well and stoned her to death.

In May, Simon de Montfort marched on the mountaintop fortress of Puylaurens only to find that its defenders had fled. In June, only a few places continued to resist and he prepared to put Toulouse under siege. This effort was half hearted and the city defences too strong. The city on the right bank of the Garonne was protected by walls from the Roman era that were up to 2.5m (8.2ft) thick and 5m (16.4ft) high with towers spaced about 40m (43.7 yds) apart. A bourgh on its western side had its own twelfth-century wall with towers. The bourgh on the southern bank of the river was not defended. By the end of June, Montfort broke off the siege and spent the next months involved in operations to maintain control of the region.

In 1212 and 1213, Simon de Montfort spent much time taking back castles and towns he had lost. He was no less vicious toward those who resisted than he had been in previous years. One of these castles, Hautpoul, was so difficult to approach that his siege engines could not reach it, but he still managed to capture it. Raymond VI of Toulouse first took shelter on the mountaintop castle of Puylaurens then fled to Toulouse. Meanwhile, Montfort's conquests continued and the strong castle of Penne d'Agenis capitulated after an eight-week siege. Other towns fell, including Moissac, which had only its walls for protection and no natural defences. After four weeks of bombardments and assaults, the town surrendered in September and the victors executed several hundred of Raymond's mercenaries.

Despite the warnings of the Pope, King Pedro II of Aragon entered the region to challenge the Crusader army. A major battle took place at Muret in September 1213. Count Raymond and the Count of Foix attacked the town and its fortress, held by only thirty French knights, on 12 September. Simon de Montfort's came to the rescue with 900 cavalry (including 240 knights) and 700 foot soldiers. They engaged and defeated King Pedro's 3,000 cavalry while most of Raymond's 20,000 to 30,000 militiamen were attacking Muret. When they learned of Pedro's defeat and death, Raymond's men began to flee but many were slaughtered. According to the chroniclers, fewer than a dozen Crusaders died, but their opponents lost over two-thirds of their men. Raymond and the remnants of his army fled to Toulouse. Many towns of Languedoc closed their gates to the Crusaders.

Count Raymond found a new ally in King John who landed at La Rochelle in 1214 and took Simon de Montfort's castle. However, John's efforts failed to weaken the French king. More volunteers came to renew the crusade and Montfort continued his campaign against whoever resisted and harboured heretics. In 1215, it appeared that Montfort had things well under control when he was joined by Prince Louis and they entered Toulouse on 11 November. The Church stripped Raymond VI of his lands and Montfort received the title of Count of Toulouse and Duke of Narbonne after dismantling key parts Narbonne's defences.[28]

In 1216, Raymond VI and his son went to Provence where many of the towns were in revolt against the king of France. Raymond VI delegated the siege of the castle of Beaucaire on the Rhône to his son, Raymond VII, while he went to Aragon to recruit troops. The citizens of the town of Beaucaire welcomed the young Raymond VII with open arms when he launched a thirteen-week siege of the castle. Simon de Montfort, who had been in Paris at the time, assembled an army and besieged Raymond's troops in the town, but he was unable to relieve the defenders of the château. The garrison, starving and already eating its horses, finally surrendered on 24 August. Montfort suffered his first major defeat. He proceeded to Toulouse, which had turned against him, entered it at the head of a large force and started setting fires to spread panic, but the populace resisted and barricaded the streets while fighting the flames. Bishop Fulk tried to mediate the next day. The city was to pay compensation, he decreed. However, this led to more difficulties as the citizens sent for Count Raymond VI, then in Aragon, to come to their aid. While Montfort was engaged with Adhemar of Poitiers east of the Rhône, Raymond VI returned in September 1217. Soon Toulouse was in revolt and Montfort had to respond. He built siege engines and surrounded the city before beginning a bombardment. The siege began in October 1217 and lasted through the winter as more Crusaders joined the fight. The constant hostilities did not break the defenders. In the summer of 1218, Montfort resorted to cats to try to breach the ditch and breach the walls, but the defenders smashed them with their siege engines. Finally, according to the chronicler William of Puylaurens, Montfort 'went into the cat and a stone thrown from an enemy mangonel fell on his head; he died at once'. A few weeks later, on 25 July, the siege was lifted.

Fortresses on the Rhône: Beaucaire and Avignon

The Beaucaire fortress stands on cliffs over 40m (120ft) above the Rhône on a site the Romans had used to guard the main trade route. It was the birthplace of Raymond VII and the property of the Counts of Toulouse that faced the border with Provence. The Roman works were replaced with towers and walls, but it is not precisely known what it looked like in 1216. The castle's well-known triangular keep with two vaulted levels is about 20m (68ft) high and its battlements rise 70m (230ft) above the river. According to Aubrey Burl (*God's Heretics*), it was built during the siege of 1216. However, archaeological evidence indicates that construction took place after 1226 when the site became a royal fortress. The present keep was built in three stages and it was finished with the addition of machicoulis. The curtain walls, up to 10m (32.8ft) high, were on top of the cliff and surrounded the castle. The castle is divided into an upper and a lower bailey and triangular donjon is on the eastern cliff side where they meet. A châtelet (small fortification) on

Beaucaire. Photos of its unusual triangular-shaped keep and plan.

the eastern side below the main wall was accessible only by a steep path. Four large circular towers – only one of which remains – occupied the corners and a barbican stood at the south-eastern entrance. The living quarters and hall with loopholes occupied the walls in the upper bailey (south-east). Beaucaire experienced no major battle besides the siege of 1216. In the seventeenth

1. St. Andre Fortress   2. Tour de Philippe

Avignon and Fort St. André.

century, during the reign of Louis XIII, it was partially destroyed to eliminate potential threats to the king's control. In 1400, across the river from Beaucaire, construction began on a castle at Tarascon similar to Paris' Bastille.

Further up the river from Beaucaire is Avignon, where papal councils excommunicated Raymond VI during the Albigensian Crusade. The city became autonomous from the Holy Roman Empire. When Prince Louis (Louis VIII, the Lion) inherited the throne of France, he launched a crusade in 1224 and he advanced down the Rhône in 1226 and sought permission to cross at Avignon. While part of his army was crossing there, it was attacked by villains who fled behind the walls of the city, which sparked a three-month long retaliatory siege that started in June and ended early in September. The

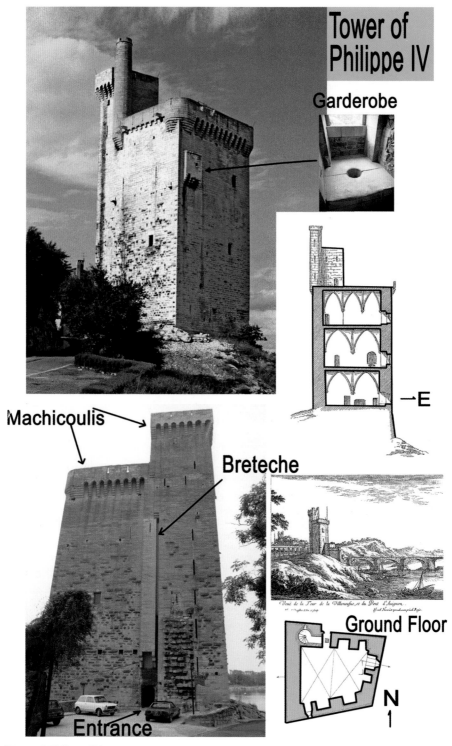

Tower of Philippe IV.

King lost up to 3,000 men to disease and the city officials agreed to surrender and pay a stiff penalty. Louis destroyed the city fortifications. In 1234, the leaders of the city began rebuilding the curtains and thirty-nine towers 30m to 40m (32.8 yds to 43.7 yds) beyond the ruins. The walls, which were finished in 1248, covered 4.3km (2.7 miles). A large 4m (13.1ft) deep moat was fed water from nearby rivers. Early in the next century, Pope Clement V took up residence there making it the seat of the papacy for most of the century. In 1355, work began on a new set of 8m (26.2ft) high walls and eight gates. The walls included thirty-five high towers and fifty intermediate ones, three of which were semicircular and the rest of which were square or rectangular and open on the inside.[29] By the end of the fourteenth century, machicoulis were added to the towers and walls. In the 1400, a polygonal tower completed the complex. The famous Palace of the Popes was built during the same century and it became the main strongpoint in the city.

Across the Rhône from Avignon, at Villeneuve-lès-Avignon, the two-storey Tower of Philippe the Fair (King Philippe IV) was completed in 1302. Another level was added to it at mid-century. A gatehouse, a tower and other fortifications formed a defensive complex at the end of the bridge that crossed the Rhône. A short distance to the north of this complex stood the Benedictine abbey of Saint-André, which Philippe IV surrounded with fortifications during the first half of the fourteenth century that became known as Fort Saint André. The fort stands out for the two large gatehouse towers.

In May 1219, Prince Louis, back in France from his English adventure, left Paris to renew the crusade. He besieged the town of Marmande with 600 knights and 10,000 foot soldiers, including archers. The town surrendered, the garrison was disarmed and the civilians were massacred. In 1220, Louis marched on Toulouse and put it under siege that ended in failure after forty-five days. In 1223, Count Raymond's son and the Count of Foix began to recover their lost lands. The violence continued unabated as strongholds changed hands. By 1223, Simon de Montfort, Raymond VI (Count of Toulouse), Raymond Roger (Count of Foix), Innocent III and King Philippe II, the principal leaders of both sides in the conflict, were dead. Amaury de Montfort, Simon's son,[30] and Raymond VII (Count of Toulouse) and Roger-Bernard II, the new Count of Foix, became the principal antagonists and continued the struggle. In 1224, Amaury de Montfort was besieged in Carcassonne, capitulated and left the region ending the crusade.

Amaury de Montfort convinced Louis VIII, son of Philippe II, to launch a new crusade in May 1224. He began be overrunning most of the lands north of the Garonne. As the king's army approached, the Count of Toulouse and others who had fought the Crusaders now offered to join their cause and the king prepared to return to Paris, but died in November 1226. Soon treachery was afoot and Raymond of Toulouse was in trouble and was excommunicated.

When Louis VIII laid siege to Avignon in 1226, the city surrendered after three months and the Crusaders tore down its walls. The cities of Languedoc did not resist after that. For many years, fortified towns and castles that were briefly reconquered became centres of resistance more than once. Local garrisons often gave up rather than suffer cruel punishment for resisting. They allowed the Crusaders to burn alive the Cathars who did not renounce their faith. In many cases, the garrisons included mercenaries, but more often the townspeople, including women, joined the fight simply as a matter of survival. Only a few holdouts remained after Louis' crusade, usually in isolated towns or castles out of the mainstream.

In 1240, a revolt was sparked when Raymond Trencavel returned from Aragon to take back Carcassonne, which he considered his birthright. The king's seneschal,[31] William des Ormes, who held Carcassonne, prepared for the siege by adding the hoardings on the towers. The count's castle, built in 1120, still served as a last line of defence. However, after the city had become a royal possession in 1226, work began on a set of outer walls. The townspeople of St. Vincent allowed Raymond's men to use their homes for mining operations. In mid-September, after Ormes led a successful sortie, he wrote to Blanche of Castile, mother of King Louis IX, that the rebels constantly attacked since the beginning of the siege and that his crossbowmen and perrièrs inflicted many casualties. The rebels, he wrote, moved a mangonel within range of a barbican, but his own machine installed on that position forced them to abandon their weapon. Next, he reported, they mined the barbican of the Narbonnaise Gate, but his men built a stone wall so they could hold half of the barbican. The rebels' mines opened breaches in the walls in five places and the defenders had to plug the gaps by erecting palisades in the lists and countermine. The inner wall was still at the back of the defenders. The rebels launched an assault on 30 September and again on 6 October, but they failed both times. On 11 October, word came that King Louis IX (St. Louis) had sent a relief army.[32] Trencavel called off the siege and returned to Aragon. The rebels fled, leaving a path of destruction.[33]

Extensive work on the city walls under Philippe III (reigned 1270–85) resulted in the unusual drawbridge at the St. Louis Barbican of the main entrance, the large circular Vade Tower, the Aude Barbican that led to the river and additional barbicans. Most of the towers of the outer wall were open in the rear, which allowed the defenders on the inner wall to dominate the outer wall if it was captured by the enemy. No stone machicoulis were added to the walls and towers. The seneschal also removed the bourgs.

King Louis IX purchased the castle of Peyrepertuse in 1239 from one of his father's vassals. During Raymond Trencavel's revolt, the former owner, William of Peyrepertuse, received the castle with some of his former lands. When the

French besieged the castle, William surrendered on 16 November. A besieger could only plan to starve out the garrison since the castle was at an elevation of 800m (2,624.6ft) on a large rocky ridge. After the return of the castle to the Crown, the king ordered more work to be done.

As the rebellious lords of Languedoc were silenced, the remaining Cathars sought sanctuary in isolated towns and castles, but they could not go unnoticed indefinitely. A number of them took refuge at the castle of Montségur. The castle, which rested on top of a large limestone mountain with difficult access in an isolated location, served as a religious centre for the remaining Cathars. In 1242, a raid from this site on the town of Avignonet resulted in the deaths of two inquisitors, which provoked a response. Hugh of Arcis, the seneschal

Montségur. Top: Map and photo of castle. Bottom: Photo of keep and monument.

in Carcassonne assembled an army that is said to have numbered as many as 10,000 men, but was probably half that size and had several hundred knights. The château of Montségur stood at an elevation of about 1,200m (3,000ft), with the village at the base of the steep sided mountain. Raymond of Pereill had built

Puylaurens and Peyrepertuse.

it as a refuge for the Cathars and rebuilt a new castle on the ruins of one from the previous century.[34] He had the castle well stocked with weapons and supplies. Despite its small size, it had a good water supply. During the rebellion of 1240, a number of Cathars had sought refuge here and built huts around its walls. The Cathars and the garrison of about a hundred soldiers built a series of wooden palisades to block the approaches to its two entrances. Supposedly, they built a barbican at the base of the mountain. The castle had a small courtyard and high walls that were 1.5m to 2m (4.9ft to 6.5ft) thick and connected with its square keep/chapel. The walls may have been 15m to 20m (49.2ft to 65.6ft) high. The garrison may have lived in some large caverns near or below the castle.

The French set up their camp at the Col du Tremblement, at an altitude of 1,000m (32,80ft), which put them about 200m (655ft) below the château and 100m (328ft) above the village that they also occupied.[35] From this distance and height, the catapults could not damage the defences. For five months, the besiegers could not even keep the defenders isolated from outside support and reinforcements. Supplies continued to reach the castle, albeit only in small numbers and quantities. The siege was beginning to last longer than most of the crusade. Finally, in October a group of Gascon mercenaries with mountain climbing skills managed to scamper 80m (262ft) up a cliff known as the Roc de la Tour, by a tower on the north-east side of the mountain. This position was supposed to be about 600m (656 yds) from the castle. In November, the Gascons hauled up the pieces of a trebuchet brought by the Bishop of Albi and started bombarding the lines of palisades the defenders had placed below the castle.[36] In December, an engineer slipped into the castle through the loose encirclement and constructed a siege weapon for the defenders so they could return fire. At the end of December, despite the winter conditions or perhaps because of them, the Crusaders managed to capture the Tour de L'Est, a circular barbican about 400m (437 yds) from Roc de La Tour, putting them closer to the northern entrance to the castle.[37] The defenders launched a violent but unsuccessful counter-attack. Meanwhile, two Cathars smuggled out their people's treasure. In January, the French forces reached the walls of the castle, but the defenders drove them back. The bombardment continued ceaselessly and a sortie failed to drive the besiegers away from the 'eastern barbican' (probably the Tour de l'Est). At the end of February, the leaders of the resistance decided it was time to negotiate.

Hugh of Arcis agreed to the terms and allowed the defending soldiers and the Cathars who met the demands of the church to live. Most of the Cathars, however, refused to submit to the Church and they were burned at the stake. Montségur was rebuilt on the same foundations and was probably very similar to the original.

Although a few isolated Cathar strongholds remained, it was deemed not worth the effort to go after them. One of these refuges was Quéribus, a formidable fortress surrounded with cliffs, built on three levels, with the keep at the top.

Queribus Castle: Two views and a plan of the castle, which was on the highest peak in the area. Here the remaining Cathars took refuge after the fall of Montségur in 1244. Most of the Cathars escaped when a French army arrived in 1255, ending the crusade.

When the seneschal of Carcassonne besieged it in 1255, its small leaderless garrison surrendered without a fight. Quéribus became one of the 'Five Sons of Carcassonne' together with the castles of Aguilar, Peyrepertuse, Termes and Puylaurens, forbidding sentinels on the frontier with Spain until 1659.

St. Louis' Fortified Port

Before he went on crusade to the Holy Land, King Louis IX (reigned 1226–70), known as St. Louis, built a fortified port at Aigues Mortes ('Dead Waters') in the Rhône Delta. Although he was troubled by the issue of the Cathars, he was ready to enter upon a real crusade. Louis did not want to use Italian ports and ships to reach the Holy Land as past Crusaders had done. Marseille was controlled by his brother Charles of Anjou (King of Naples, Agde, Count of Toulouse and Montpellier and King of Aragon). To address these concerns, Louis decided to build a port about 33km (21 miles) in a salt marsh south-west of Nîmes where older fortifications had existed since Roman times. He launched his project in 1240 when he got possession of the town and the lands around it and built a road through the marshes. Next, Louis erected the Carbonnière Tower, which straddled the road and served as a watchtower as well as a toll station. His keep, the Constance Tower, rose from the site of the Carolingian Malafère Tower in the town. Work on the enceinte did not begin until 1272 when King Philippe III, the Bold, talked the leaders of the Republic of Genoa into helping finance its construction. After some difficulties and delays, the enceinte was completed during the next century.

The Constance Tower was the first structure built and completed in 1254. It is Philpienne style tower with a diameter of about 20m (65.7ft), a height of over 33m (108.2ft) and 6m (19.6ft) thick walls. The tower consists of two large vaulted halls and a small basement. The walls are pierced with arrow loops, which are very long and whose function seems to be a light source. The keep has a moat and a drawbridge. The guardroom is on the first floor opposite a postern. Each well-defended entrance includes a portcullis with murder holes. If the enemy reached the hall of the first floor, the defenders could fire down upon them from a gallery above, below the second level.

The rectangular town enceinte is about 1.7km (1 mile) long. Its wall is 2.5m (8.2ft) thick and 11m (36ft) high. It has circular towers on three corners and the Constance Tower on the fourth. The walls include five main entrances between two large semicircular towers. Rectangular towers defend the four secondary entrances. Each tower included portcullis. The gateways and tower walls have bretèches, some of which were probably garderobes since they do not project over any opening. Some towers have tall bartizans that may have been additions from a later period. A moat encircled the enceinte.

Louis departed on his first crusade from Aigues Mortes in 1248, before his tower was completed. That crusade ended in disaster in 1250 when he was captured in Egypt. In 1270, he launched another unsuccessful crusade that culminated in his death in Tunis on 25 August.

1.Tower of Constance 2.Carbonnière Tower

Aigues Mortes. Top. Carbonnière Tower blocking access road to the port and entrance gate of town.
Middle: Plan of town and photo of section of town walls. Bottom: Tower of Constance and map.

Chapter Eight

From Wales to Italy –
Twelfth to Fifteenth Centuries

The Welsh Wilderness

Although the Romans conquered Wales in the first century AD, they left few traces of their occupation. They found and extracted large deposits of gold, copper and lead, but showed little interest in colonizing the heavily-forested, mountainous regions of northern Wales. The Cambrian Mountains that dominate most of central and northern part of Wales present difficult terrain, even though they have few peaks over 914m (3,000ft). The less mountainous north-east includes hills and moorlands. The more inviting southern part of Wales, which includes a low mountain range, rolling hills and some plains, is good for agriculture and was the only area the Romans attempted to colonize. They tried to control the remainder of Wales with about twenty forts. During the Dark Ages and after the Anglo-Saxon invasions of England, several Welsh kingdoms emerged. The Anglo-Saxon kingdoms of Mercia, Northumbria and Wessex were in conflict with the Welsh kingdoms of Powys, Gwent and Gwynedd. Along the border between these two distinct linguistic and cultural regions, King Offa of Mercia built Offa's Dyke in the eighth century.

The only walled town the Romans established in Wales was Caerwent (Roman Isca), in the kingdom of Gwent. Archaeologists estimate the walls of Caerwent may have been up to 10m (32ft) high and included several hollow polygonal towers. Nearby there are remains of an eleventh-century Norman motte without its wooden donjon. The Normans may have built it and other castles for Edward the Confessor to control Welsh raids in the 1050s.

In 1067, the Norman William FitzOsbern, Earl of Hereford, built Chepstow Castle on a ridge with a cliff that overlooks the main crossing of the Wye River. It had a large rectangular keep consisting of a basement and two additional levels. King William confiscated the castle from FitzOsbern's son Roger when he rebelled against him in 1075. The Welsh captured the castle several times during the twelfth century. In 1189, William Marshal obtained the castle through marriage and updated it. He added a lower bailey with a twin-towered gatehouse among other features. Roger Bigo, his son-in-law, inherited the castle in 1270 and added Marten's Tower, which was 12.8m (41.9ft) in diameter and 19.2m (62.9ft) high and had impressive spurs.

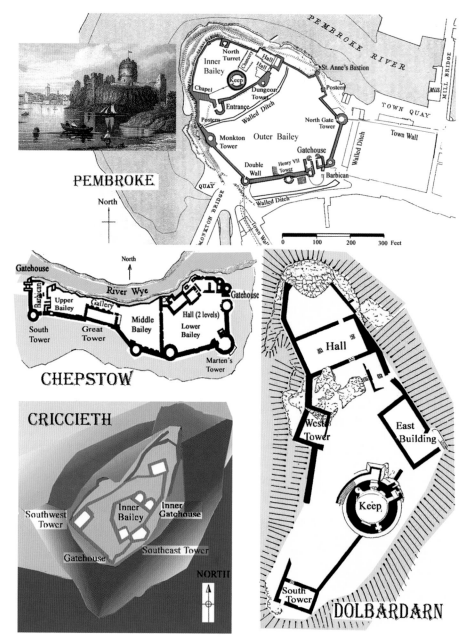

Welsh Castles: Plans of Pembroke (with old illustration), Chepstow, Criccieth and Dolbardarn.

In the twelfth century, Chepstow served as a base for the conquest of southern Wales. From other locations on the south coast such as Cardiff, Swansea and Pembroke, the Normans established additional castles to secure their hold. In 1091, Robert Fitzhamon, Lord of Gloucester, conquered Glamorgan and built a motte-and-bailey castle with a wooden keep within the walls of the old Roman fort at Cardiff. During the twelfth century, the donjon was replaced with a polygonal stone shell keep with a gate tower.

In 1093, Arnulf de Montgomery built a wooden keep with palisades on a rocky promontory projecting into the Cleddau River. This became Pembroke Castle. It held out against two sieges before William Marshal rebuilt it in stone with a

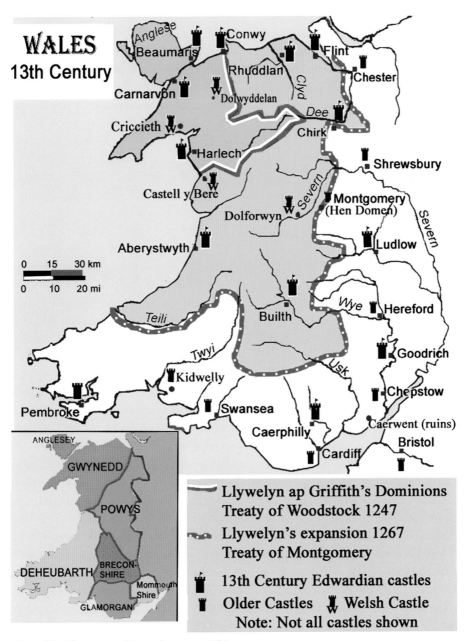

Map of fortifications in thirteenth-century Wales.

cylindrical tower keep between 1190 and 1220. The massive keep of limestone ashlars has a 6m (19ft) thick plinth and a diameter of 16m (53ft). It is 24m (80ft) high and has a unique stone dome. In time of war, hoardings that consisted of two platforms around the dome were installed on the battlements. The basement has no loopholes for light, the first floor has two narrow ones and the remaining two floors have several in addition to a window. A narrow forebuilding includes the stairs and between it and the keep, a drawbridge allows access to the keep. Montgomery also rebuilt the inner bailey, strengthening it with a 0.45m (19in) thick stone wall. The impressive gatehouse, added by William's son Gilbert in about 1250, includes two towers with three portcullises, murder holes, other defensive features and a barbican. The town walls connected with the castle walls of the outer bailey on both sides of the promontory so a land assault must come through the town.

At Swansea, also on the south coast, Henry de Beaumont built a timber castle in 1107. When the Welsh attacked in 1116, they only succeeded in destroying its outer defences. In 1192, the castle withstood a ten-week siege by Rhys ap Gruffydd, the Prince of Deheubarth. Robert FitzHamon later defeated Rhys. Under Llywelyn the Great in 1217, the Welsh finally took the castle after several attempts, but, in agreement with Henry III, returned it in 1220 to the English who rebuilt it in stone. In the next century, the castle lost its military importance.

In 1106, Bishop Roger of Salisbury constructed the earth-and-timber castle of Kidwelly. During the Welsh revolt of 1136, Gwellian, the wife of Griffith ap Rhys, Prince of Deheubarth, died while leading the attack on Kidwelly while her husband was away enlisting help from other Welsh princes. Later, in 1159, Kidwelly fell to Rhys ap Gruffydd. The Welsh took it again in 1159, 1190 and 1215. In 1220, the Chaworth family received the castle and held it during the revolt of Llywelyn the Great in 1231. Patrick de Chaworth (1250–83) rebuilt the castle with local stone forming a D-shaped enclosure. In the 1270s, Payn de Chaworth added a quadrangular inner bailey and an apron wall. In the 1390s, the height of three of the inner bailey towers was raised and work began on a massive gatehouse that was rebuilt after Owain Glyndwr's revolt in the early 1400s.

In the north in the 1070s, Roger de Montgomery built Hen Domen, a large motte-and-bailey castle with wood structures on the Severn at a place he called Montgomery. After Roger died, his son Hugh lost it to Cadwgan ap Bleddyn, the Prince of Pows in 1095. The Welsh took control of the area in 1215 and allowed the castle to fall into decay. Between 1223 and 1227, Hubert de Burgh, who reoccupied the town selected another location to build a new stone castle on a rocky outcrop overlooking the town. It included two D-shaped towers as part of a gatehouse with the private chambers on the upper two levels, a high curtain walls and a well tower. Llywelyn the Great attacked it in 1228, but failed to take it. After this siege, the castle was expanded with the addition of a middle and outer bailey. The middle bailey also had a double-tower gatehouse and with a drawbridge. It was separated from the inner bailey by a large moat. A dry moat surrounded most of it. The outer bailey had lower walls and covered the other two baileys except the sides that faced a steep slope. The town walls were a short distance away. In 1233, the Welsh launched another fruitless attack. In 1402, Owain Glyndwr attacked and sacked the walled town, but was unable to take the castle.

Before the arrival of the Normans, the Welsh leaders may have used older fortifications rather than building their own. In 1170, Iorwerth, the father of Llywelyn the Great, built Dolwddelan, one of the earliest Welsh castles, on a rocky knoll high above the Lledr Valley to control the road from Conwy. Added protection was provided by ditches cut in the rock and steep slopes. Llywelyn was born here. After capturing the site, the English built the West Tower, a large two-floor rectangule and a curtain wall about 1.8m (6ft) thick to connect the two towers. In 1283, Edward added to its defences. Centuries later, during the restoration process in the Victorian Age, the height of the keep was increased to double its original size.

Around 1230, Llwelyn the Great built Criccieth Castle on a headland between two beaches that overlooked the town of the same name and his grandson continued the work. In 1282, Edward I captured the castle, repaired and improved it. The work continued under Edward II. They added the Engine Tower in the outer bailey which supposedly had mangonels mounted on it. They built a massive twin-towered gatehouse designed to replace the castle keep on the outer bailey. In 1294 during Welsh rebellion, the English withstood a siege of several months. When Owain Glyndwr revolted in 1400, the castle, held by six men-at-arms and fifty archers, surrendered when French warships sent to support Owain cut off supplies by sea. The castle was set on fire and its walls were razed.

Llywelyn also built several other castles including Dolbadarn Castle in a key mountain pass west of Dolwyddelan. This castle has a large circular stone keep 12.2m (40ft) in diameter and 15.2m (50ft) high and two rectangular curtain towers. It fell to Edward I in 1284. Llywelyn built Castell y Bere between Criccieth and Harlech on top of a rock outcrop. It includes a round tower, two larger D-shaped towers (one at each end) and a square tower between them, making it the largest castle in Wales. Edward captured and destroyed it in 1294.

After Llywelyn ap Griffith reconquered his old territories in 1257, King Henry III conceded him control over them by the Treaty of Montgomery in 1267. Llywelyn built Castle Dolforwyn in this region on a steep rocky ridge overlooking the Severn Valley. Work on the castle took place between 1273 and 1277 without a licence from the English king. It consisted of a large rectangular keep on the west side and a large circular tower on the eastern end linked by curtain walls forming a rectangular enclosure made of two wards divided by a ditch cut in the rock. The walls included a D-shaped tower on the north side and two entrances. When Roger Mortimer and Henry de Lacy besieged the castle in

1277, the defenders surrendered after a couple of weeks when their water supply ran out. Roger Mortimer took over the castle and improved it.

The Norman Gilbert de Clare constructed a castle at Aberystwyth, which was handed over to Rhys ap Griffith, ruler of Deheubarth, by King Henry II in 1171. In 1207, Rhys' successors, fearing Llywelyn the Great, destroyed the castle, but they rebuilt it later. In 1215, Llywelyn took the castle from them and it continued to change hands until King Edward I built his own castle there, which fell to Owain Glyndwr in 1404 and was recaptured three years later.

Most Welsh castles had walls of slate or a similar stone called siltstone. In some Welsh castles sandstone was used. D-shaped towers were a common feature in Welsh castles and often built with dry stone. The ready availability of construction materials made castle-building in Wales easy. About two-thirds of the country consists of slate, shale, sandstone and limestone, which are good for castle construction. There are also large coal deposits to fuel the smiths' furnaces. Although slate and shale have the same appearance, shale is softer and can be crushed and mixed to make various types of clay and cement. Although roof tiles were sometimes made of shale, slate was preferred for castles and churches because it offered better protection against fire. In 1287, the first slate roof was installed in northern Wales on the towers of Conwy Castle.

Wales, the Last Celtic Bastion South of Scotland

The Anglo-Saxon invasion of Britain swallowed up most of Roman Britain, but the Celtic people of Wales resisted. The legendary King Arthur, if he actually existed, would have been the last of the Britons to resist. The Anglo-Saxon kingdoms of Mercia, Northumbria and Wessex tried to conquer the Welsh lands, but had little success. Offa's Dyke served to block Welsh raiders in the Dark Ages. In the eleventh century, a unified Britain under the crown of England tried to make further incursions into Wales. The threat increased as William the Conqueror took the English crown and began to expand into Wales, relying on motte-and-bailey castles. The coastal lowlands and plains of southern Wales presented the easiest target.

The mountainous central and northern region with only three good invasion routes formed the bastion of Welsh resistance. In the north, the Normans coming from their base in Chester used the Dee River Valley to penetrate this bastion. To the south, they came out of Shrewsbury following the Severn River Valley. The southernmost approach into the central region was from Hereford along the Wye River Valley. From Chepstow Castle in south-east Wales and later other locations on the south coast, Norman knights on horseback easily defeated the Welsh infantry and bowmen. Robert Fitzhamon, Lord of Gloucester, allied with a Welsh prince to defeat a rival.[1]

After his conquest of Glamorgan (southern Wales) in 1091, he established a motte-and-bailey castle with a wooden keep within the walls of the old Roman fort. Arnulf de Montgomery established Pembroke Castle in 1093 on a rocky promontory. Initially, the Normans had the advantage because the Welsh had little knowledge of castle warfare. They besieged Pembroke and almost starved the defenders into surrendering. In 1116, the Welsh had a little more success attacking a timber castle at Swansea, on the south coast, where they destroyed the outer defences, but failed to take the stronghold.

Bernard de Neufmarché built a castle at Brecon. He defeated and killed the King of Deheubarth and conquered Brycheiniog between 1088 and 1095. He took possession of the upper valleys of the Wye and Usk. The Welsh in the region revolted in 1095, driving the Normans back into their castles.

Roger de Montgomery moved up the Severn from Shrewsbury and built Hen Domen – a motte-and-bailey castle with a wooden keep – at a site he named Montgomery. When Roger died, his son Hugh held the castle but he lost it in 1095 to Cadwgan ap Bleddyn, the Prince of Powis.

In the end of the eleventh century, the Normans made major inroads into Wales and secured their positions with timber and turf castles. In the twelfth century, they consolidated their positions by converting timber castles to stone as the Welsh obtained more experience in castle warfare.

Griffith ap Conan (1055–1137), Prince of North Wales, helped keep Gwynedd (former kingdom in north-west Wales) free of Normans and drove them from Anglesey where he killed Robert de Rhuddlan in 1093. Robert had allied himself with Griffith ap Cynan when the latter tried to recover the crown of Gwynedd from another Welsh leader in 1075. Griffith was defeated and fled to Ireland, but Robert seized the territory east of the Conwy River and secured his territory with many castles. Griffith came back and defeated his rival to become King of Gwynedd. The Normans, supposedly led by Robert, captured and imprisoned him at Chester. He later escaped, supposedly killed Robert during the Welsh revolt of 1093 and he took back his throne.

The princes of Powys also fought the Normans, mainly the Montgomery family, driving them from the Severn valley, defeating them in battle and storming their castles. The sons of Bleddyn in the east followed the examples of Griffith ap Cynan in the north and Griffith ap Rhys (1081–1137) in the south. The Welsh were finally able to defeat Norman armies and take Norman castles. Griffith ap Rhys came to terms with King Henry I, but in 1136, he joined the sons of Griffith ap Cynan in a rebellion against the Normans. His wife died leading an attack of Kidwelly in 1136. Shortly afterward, Griffith ap Rhys won a decisive victory over the Normans at Crug Mawr (Cardigan), but died suddenly the next year.

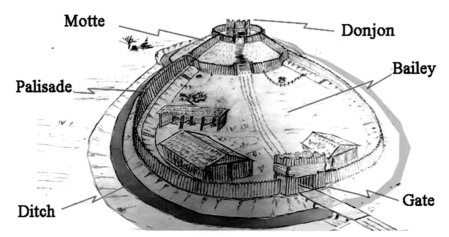

Example of Motte & Bailey with small wooden Donjon on the Motte.   Drawing by W. Ostrowski

Model of Norman Motte & Bailey Castle at Hen Domen. Photo by Peter Scholefield. Courtesy of Old Bell Museum, Montgomery, Powys, Wales.

Drawing of a motte-and-bailey castle by W. Ostrowski. Bottom: Timber donjon of Hen Domen by permission of the Old Bell Museum, Montgomery, Powys, Wales.

Owain Gwynedd (1100–70) followed his father, Griffith ap Conan, in 1137 as king of Gwynedd. The sons of Griffith ap Rees and Bleddyn succeeded their fathers, ushering in a period of military success for the Welsh until the end of the century. The reign of Stephen, marked by conflict among the English barons, gave the Welsh an opportunity. Owain Gwynedd pushed his territory all the way east to Rhuddlan. The other Welsh rulers also expanded their areas of control. Several princes forged alliances to fight the Normans. Finally, King Henry II took action against Wales advancing in the north to Rhuddlan in 1157, but he was routed at Coleshill. Henry was badly beaten again in 1165 at Berwyn and struck a compromise with Rhys ap Griffith (1132–97) of Deheubarth, to maintain control of the south. The situation in south remained stable until Henry died in 1189. Rhys ap Griffith laid siege to Swansea for ten weeks in 1192, but failed to take it. In 1196, he captured several castles and defeated Roger de Mortimer at the Battle of Radnor, but he died the next year.

Prince Llywelyn ap Iorwerth (1172–1240), also known as 'the Great', became Prince of Gwynedd in 1195 and after King John removed his rival in 1208, he became Prince of Pows. When John invaded Wales in 1211, Llywelyn rallied the Welsh. Later, he joined the Barons' Revolt as he expanded his control over both north and south Wales. In 1228, he attacked the stone castle built in 1223 by Hubert de Burgh at Montgomery, but failed to take it. Llywelyn captured several English castles while William Marshal had his hands full containing him. He secured his borders and attacked Montgomery Castle once more in 1233 but failed again.

When Llywelyn the Great died in 1240, his younger son Dafydd[2] (1212–46) succeeded him and was the first person to take the title of Prince of Wales. Since Dafydd's mother was the daughter of King John, his uncle, King Henry III, let him assume the title, but he invaded Gynedd in 1241 forcing Dafydd to submit. Henry held Dafydd's older brother Griffith as hostage, possibly intending to use him as a rival. However, Griffith fell to his death trying to escape from the Tower of London. In 1245, Dafydd and other Welsh princes struck back, this time defeating Henry. Dafydd died in 1246, but his two sons, Owain and Llywelyn ap Griffith (1223–82) divided Gwynedd and continued the war until the Treaty of Woodstock of 1247 that gave Henry the territories east of Conwy. In 1255, Llywelyn ap Griffith defeated his two brothers (the younger of whom had just come of age) and became the sole ruler. He expanded his territory and he assumed the title of Prince of Wales.[3] In 1265, Llywelyn went on the offensive, just as King Henry III regained power in England. The next year, the Welsh defeated Roger Mortimer, which led to the Treaty of Montgomery in 1267 marking the high water-mark of Llywelyn's power. In 1272, Henry III's son, Edward I, ascended the throne.

In 1277, after Llywelyn failed to pay homage to him, Edward launched his first Welsh campaign. In July, he led an army of 15,500 (including 9,000 Welshmen) into Gwynedd. Llywelyn surrendered without a battle in November. Edward recovered most of the territory lost to Llywelyn after the 1260s. Edward skilfully used Welsh princes as allies. In 1282, the second Welsh campaign began after Llywelyn's brother Dafydd – an erstwhile ally of Edward – Llywelyn and other Welsh princes attacked the English. Edward launched a three-pronged invasion with Roger Mortimer operating from the vicinity of Shrewsbury, the Earl of Gloucester moving from the south and the king striking from the north. Despite some setbacks and the loss of Roger Mortimer, the English ambushed and killed Llywelyn near Builth in December 1282. Edward renewed his offensive in January 1283 and took Dolwyddelan Castle in the heart of Gwynedd's mountainous region known as Snowdonia after the highest mountain. Meanwhile, the Earl of Pembroke[4] advanced from the south and took Castell y Bere on 25 April. The campaign ended in June 1283 when Dafydd was captured and executed at Shrewsbury. England finally dominated Wales. The Statute of Rhuddlan divided the conquered lands into six shires under the rule of English administrators.[5] In 1293, the Welsh rebelled after the English tried to recruit men for a war in Gascony. Madog ap Llywelyn rose in Anglesey as a new leader and struck at the incomplete castle of Caernarfon, which he took by surprise. His men put Harlech under siege while he took on Conwy. In 1294, Edward tried to crush this revolt, but Madog put him under siege at Conwy during a severe winter. In February 1295, the first supply ship reached Edward and Madog lifted the siege. Edward went on to ravage Anglesey and crush the rebellion. In 1301, the king proclaimed his son Prince of Wales. From 1297 to 1305, Edward had his hands full with the revolt of William Wallace in Scotland and he died in Scotland, but Wales was largely subdued. The last great Welsh Revolt came in 1400 under Owain Glyndowr.

Game of Castles: Edward's Iron Ring

During the thirteenth century, the English began to improve their castles in Wales, replacing many of the old motte-and-bailey castles or expanding them. After Edward I began his wars of conquest against the Welsh in 1277, more dramatic changes took place with the creation of 'Edwardian' castles. To secure their hold over the Welsh, the English used the castles along the coast, which they could supply by sea. Edward intended his new castles to keep the Welsh hemmed in and prevent further uprisings. Two prominent features of his new castles, also seen in some earlier castles, were their size and shape, which were meant to leave the enemy in awe and possibly discourage attacks. In some cases, the builders

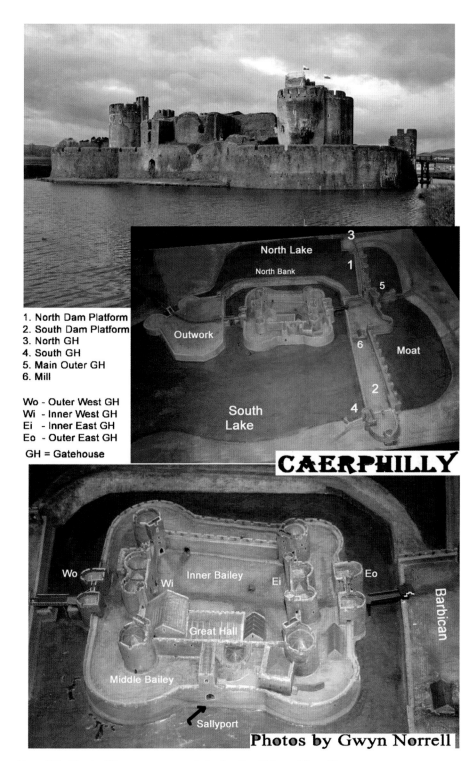

1. North Dam Platform
2. South Dam Platform
3. North GH
4. South GH
5. Main Outer GH
6. Mill

Wo - Outer West GH
Wi - Inner West GH
Ei - Inner East GH
Eo - Outer East GH

GH = Gatehouse

Caerphilly Castle. (Photos courtesy of the family of Gwyn Norrell) achieved these psychological effects by adding turrets to towers to emphasize their height. In addition, they whitewashed the walls to make them stand out. Sometimes, bands of coloured stone gave the structures an awe-inspiring and majestic appearance.

Before Edward began raising his ring of castles, Gilbert de Clare, Earl of Gloucester, began work in the south on one of the first and most impressive concentric castles in Britain as part of his campaign to subdue Glamorgan. Construction on Caerphilly Castle started in April 1268. Llywelyn ap Griffith prevented the work from going forward by launching a raid on 11 October 1270 and burning down what had been built.[6] Gilbert resumed the work in June 1271 while the Welsh prince continued to harry him. During the 1270s, Gilbert's men finished most of the work at great expense. The exact date of completion is unknown. Two artificial lakes left the castle on a cluster of islands. The dams that form the two lakes consist of earth excavated from the large ditch in front of them. The southern section of the dam had battlements along a platform. The similarly fortified northern platform is narrower. At the end of each platform, there is a well-protected postern. In the centre between the two platforms, there is a barbican with a large gatehouse and a pair of drawbridges. Another drawbridge allows access to the central island with the castle. According to historian Allen Brown, these are 'the most elaborate water defences in all Britain' occupying 12 ha (30 acres).[7] The castle on the central island consists of two sets of walls. One wall forms the outer bailey and includes a low wall with two towers that cover the drawbridge between the island and the barbican. At the west end, a second set of towers forms a hornwork that guards another drawbridge leading to the second island. The walls of the inner bailey are high and include four round corner towers and two large gatehouses. Since there is no keep, the constable lived in the large eastern gatehouse. The western gatehouse is smaller, but has facilities as well. The Great Hall and other facilities are located against the walls of the inner bailey. On the south side, a special water postern gives access to the lake.

This great castle played no significant role in the Welsh wars of independence. In January 1316, when the Welsh of Glamorgan revolted, 10,000 men attacked Caerphilly Castle. Despite being lightly manned, the castle stopped them. In March, a relief force of 130 men-at-arms and 2,000 infantry from Cardiff relieved the castle. In May 1321, the barons of Wales, the Marcher Lords, rose with 800 men-at-arms, 500 light cavalry and 10,000 infantry, against Hugh le Despenser, lord of Glamorgan, when he encroached on their lands. They took the town and the castle of Cardiff and went on to capture Caerphilly and several other castles. They seized nine castles in ten days. Hugh le Despenser and his father were exiled and his lands were confiscated by the Crown.[8] In late October 1326, King Edward II fled to Wales from his French wife Queen Isabela and her lover, Roger Mortimer who had invaded England. Edward II set up his command post at Caerphilly and prepared it for an attack. However, he fled westward early in November leaving a large part of his treasury at Caerphilly. He was captured in mid-November and the queen had him murdered in September of the next year. Meanwhile, Caerphilly remained under siege defended by 5 knights, about 140 troops and 400 Welsh foot soldiers. While Edward was held prisoner at Kenilworth, he sent orders for the castle not to surrender to the queen. However, Isabela's commander offered to pardon the well-armed and well-supplied garrison, they surrendered in March 1327. A dispute between the barons and the king in 1329 again brought Caerphilly briefly under siege. After this, the castle lost both military and political importance and fell into oblivion. There are claims that Owain Glyndwr captured the castle in 1403 but lost it the next year. Caerphilly's concentric design served as a model for some of Edward I's Welsh castles.

In 1277, Edward initiated a construction programme in Wales that involved modernizing existing royal border castles like Chester, Shrewsbury and Montgomery and some of the captured Welsh castles, especially those in Gwynedd, including Criccieth. The castles of the marcher lords underwent some work between 1277 and the end of the century. Edward's renovations were done at Rhuddlan (1277–82), Flint (1277–86), Holt (1277–1311), Builth (1277–82) and Aberystwyth (1277–89).[9] The marcher lords refurbished Chirk and Denbigh in 1283. Edward intended to isolate the Welsh stronghold of Snowdonia by creating an iron ring around it.

Work began on Flint, the first new castle, in 1277 on a rocky platform that dominated a ford in the River Dee. It was situated one-day's march down the old Roman road from Chester and a day's march from Rhuddlan. First, almost 1,000 men excavated ditches and worked on the earthworks. Next, Master James of St. George came to supervise the construction.[10] The curtain walls with three large round projecting corner towers rose around an almost square courtyard. In 1281, construction began on a huge circular keep outside the south-east corner, in a location similar to the Philippienne tower at Aigues Mortes. It was not finished until 1286. It was surrounded by a 6m (20ft) deep moat that surrounded the castle. It was filled with water from the tidal river. In 1281, a square tower that served as the entrance was completed. Drawbridges gave access to the entrance and the tower. A fortified town for English settlers was established next to the castle, a policy Edward followed at the other new castles to consolidate his hold over Wales. Labourers and specialists such as masons, carpenters, quarrymen, etc. were brought, some forcibly, from all over England to build Edward's castles in Wales.

Construction on Rhuddlan Castle began in September 1277; Master James took over in the 1280s. Like in most of Edward's castles, local stone was used wherever possible. If the local material was not good enough for quoins for corners, openings and arrow loops, it was brought from another source. At

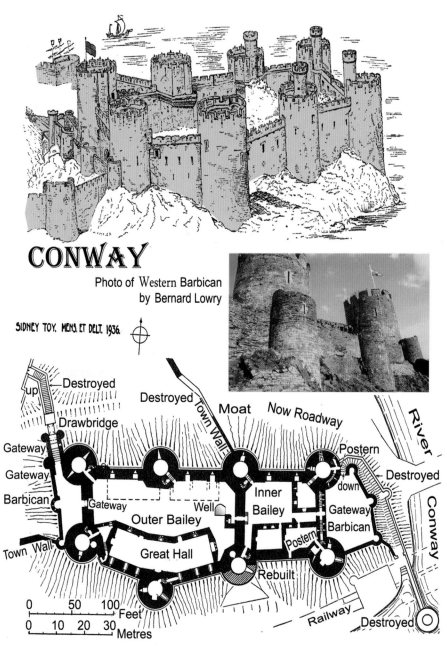

Conwy Castle. Photo of western barbican courtesy of Bernard Lowry. Plan from Sidney Toy's Castles.

Rhuddlan, purple sandstone was used on the lower courses and yellow sandstone on the upper layers, but colour did not matter since the completed castle was whitewashed. Rhuddlan is a concentric castle with a lozenge or diamond-shaped inner bailey. It has two corner towers and two large double-towered gatehouses in opposite corners. At this time, huge gatehouses started to replace keeps. The outer bailey walls are low, have four gates and used to be protected by a 4.6m (15ft) deep and 15m (50ft) wide moat on three sides. The fourth side looms over steep terrain that slopes down to the river where there is a fortified dock and a river gate. The nearby town was surrounded with a wooden palisade.

After Daffydd's War (Edward's second Welsh campaign), Edward built three additional castles to close his Iron Ring. Due to their remote locations, they required access from the sea. Edward needed increasing numbers of workers and more funds derived from taxes for the project. The new round of castle-building started in 1283 at Conwy (1283–90), Caernarfon (1283–1301) and Harlech (1283–90) and Master James was assigned the design of all three. He built them on solid rock to prevent mining. The garrison of Conwy Castle was supposed to include thirty soldiers – half of whom were crossbowmen – a mason, a carpenter, an engineer, a blacksmith and a chaplain. The site selected for the castle is a rocky outcrop above the Conwy River next to the sea, an ideal position to prevent enemy mining. The stone came from the construction site; the red sandstone was quarried from the riverbank. Although it was not a concentric castle, it was the most expensive of the Edwardian castles in Wales. The castle has high curtain walls and eight large projecting round towers 12.2m (40ft) to 21m (69ft) high and capable of operating independently. The curtains form a rough rectangle except where it bends out on the south side of the outer bailey, which forms the western two-thirds of the castle. The walls separating the inner bailey from the outer bailey served as the last line of defence. There is no keep, nor gatehouses and the east and west gates are situated between two towers, each of which has a barbican. The east gate leads down to the river. The walls and towers have 142 arrow slits designed for longbows. The west end used to connect to the town wall. The other end of the town wall joined the north-west tower of the inner bailey. The town wall was 1.3km (0.8 miles) long and had 21 towers and about 500 arrow slits.

In 1294 during Madog's revolt, the Welsh quickly took Caernarfon, which brought Edward back to Wales. He reached Conwy in December leaving most of his army on the east bank of the river. After Christmas, he took a small force to pursue the rebels, but he was ambushed and had to take refuge in the castle where he was put under siege for several weeks when Wales experienced one of its worst winter storms. The rising river made it impossible for his army to come to the rescue and no ships could reach him. As supplies dwindled, the weather turned and the first ships reached the castle dock in February. Madog had to lift the siege and retreat.

Due to its location, workers, supplies and materials brought to Caernarfon (1283–1301) by sea. It was built on the site of a wooden motte-and-bailey. It was possible to shift workers between Conwy and Harlech. Most of the work was completed by 1291. The layout of Caernarfon is similar to Conwy's with no keep or concentric walls and a cross wall between the inner and outer bailey. It

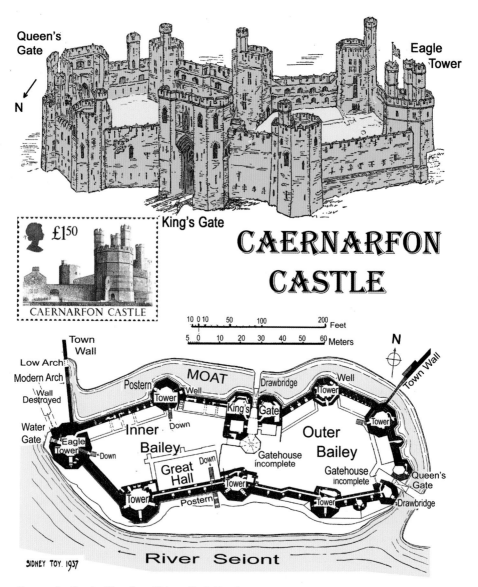

Caernarfon Castle. Plan from Sidney Toy's Castles.

includes two gates leading into the outer bailey with two large double-towered gatehouses. The King's Gate, centrally located in the north wall, has five doors, six portcullises and a drawbridge. On the west end, a water gate is accessed from the large Eagle Tower, which includes four turrets. The walls have six additional large towers, as well as the gate towers. Unlike Conwy, they were polygonal. The large towers included living quarters. The castle is surrounded in part by a wet moat and in part by the Seiont River.

In September 1294, Madog's rebellion crossed from Anglesey and his men raced into the fortified town at Caernarfon when the gates were open for market day. They used siege ladders to climb an unfinished section of castle walls on the side facing the town. Instead of 10m (30ft) high, this section rose only 4m (12ft) above the bottom of the ditch. The rebels quickly overwhelmed and slaughtered the garrison. After the rebels were defeated, the castle was completed. Arrow loops of an unusual type were added to the north wall and King's Tower. They consist of an exterior loop with three embrasures on the interior that allow three crossbowmen to fire at the same time through one loophole.[11] Owain Glyndwr's men attacked the castle three times between 1401 and 1404 but failed to take it.

Harlech (1283–90), one of the strongest Edwardian castles, commanded the area around it from a high rocky outcrop overlooking the sea. Records show that over 800 men participated in its construction. Master James was appointed as the first constable of this masterpiece. Built of sandstone, it has a large gatehouse that served as a keep. The inner walls of this concentric castle are 3.6m (12ft) thick and 12m (35ft) high. The inner bailey, with four large corner towers and a massive gatehouse, is roughly square. It used to house all the facilities. The outer bailey is not very wide and includes a low wall dominated by the inner walls and projecting towers. Beyond the outer ward on the south and east side (the gatehouse was on the east side), there is a ditch up to 15m (45ft) wide. The west and north sides loom over a steep slope. Another wall runs to the water gate. The dock is located about 61m (200ft) below the castle, at the base of the cliff.

As in the other large Edwardian castles, the garrison was small and consisted of about thirty soldiers – including ten crossbowmen – a blacksmith, carpenters, a mason and a chaplain. During Madog's Revolt, Harlech, Criccieth and Aberystwyth castles were put under siege from 1294 until 1295 when reinforcements arrived by sea from Conwy after that castle was relieved in February 1295. After the siege, new defences were added to protect access to the water gates. During the revolt of 1400, the Welsh besieged Harlech again, this time with the support of the French fleet, which blockaded it from the sea forcing it to surrender after one year. The English retook the castle in 1409.

After capturing Madog, Edward crushed the centre of the revolt in Anglesey where he built the castle of Beaumaris (1295–1330s) on the site from which he could block the channel between the island and the mainland. Beaumaris Castle is located on low and level land. Master James was again in charge of construction. The inner bailey is almost square and has four large circular projecting corner towers, one large projecting D-shaped tower in the middle of the east and west curtains and two large gatehouses on the north and south walls respectively. The one on the south wall includes a barbican. The walls of the inner bailey are about 5m (15ft) thick and 11m (36ft) high. The outer bailey has lower walls, twelve small towers and two gatehouses. The wet moat is about 15m (45ft) wide. The

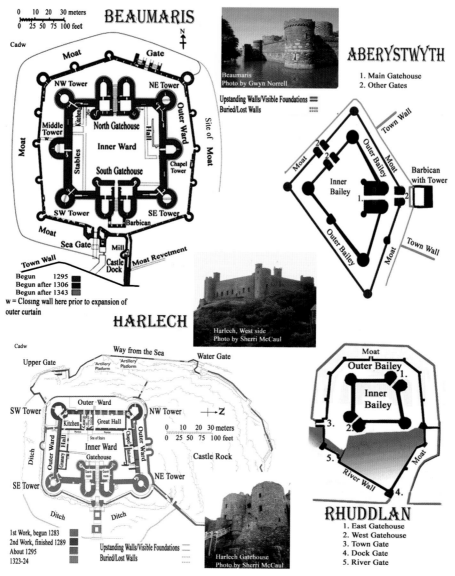

Plans of Beaumaris, Harlech from CADW (Welsh National Environmental Protection) and plans of Rhuddlan and Aberystwyth and photo of Beaumaris by Gwyn Norrell. Photos of Harlech by Sherri McCaul.

gatehouses and towers were never completed. Edward died before it was finished and the castle never served in any of the medieval conflicts.

Thus, the completed Edwardian castles only served in two local Welsh uprisings. The first happened in 1294 in protest against conscription for service in a foreign war and against taxes and the second in 1400. The castles were part of a massive and expensive construction project designed for large garrisons, but often held by no more than thirty soldiers. Although they were among the finest and strongest castles built in England, they saw little action after the revolt of 1400.

Land of Fortifications and Conflict

Political unity disintegrated on the Italian peninsula during the Dark Ages as it became a battleground after the fall of the Western Roman Empire as forces of Byzantines, Germanic groups and even Saracens ravaged the region. By the eleventh century, the Normans exerted influence in the southern part of the peninsula as the Pope struggled to restore order. At the end of the Dark Ages, the Holy Roman Empire, centred in modern-day Germany, seemed to offer security but the emperors soon challenged the power of the Pope. While Byzantium engaged the Normans and others in the southern part of the peninsula early in the High Middle Ages, many of the towns and cities of central and northern Italy sought autonomy or independence. The Lombard League, led by the Republic of Milan formed with Papal support in 1164, served as a barrier against the interference of Holy Roman Emperor Frederick Barbarossa in northern Italy.

A century earlier, political and religious policies produced a split between Pope Gregory VII and Emperor Henry IV over investiture. As a result, Henry invaded Italy and Gregory excommunicated him until he did penance in 1077. Henry invaded the peninsula again in 1080. In the spring of 1081, he initiated a siege of Rome's that lasted on an off for three years. Tuscans, Normans and Roman militiamen defended the city walls. After forty days, Henry pulled his troops back. He returned the following spring to resume the siege. This time, he breached the walls, but was unable to exploit his advantage and withdrew from Rome in 1082. He had to deal with Countess Matilda of Tuscany, a supporter of Gregory, who engaged his forces in the Apennines and the Po valley relying on her many castles. Matilda had controlled Lombardy, Romagna and Tuscany and turned most of her lands over to the Pope in 1080. At the end of 1082, Henry put Rome under siege again and remained for seven months. Meanwhile, Pope Gregory tried to enlist the support of Robert Guiscard, the Norman conqueror of southern Italy.

In 1083, Henry IV tried to take the Vatican and a fortress next to St. Peter's, but he failed. This area was not protected by the Aurelian Wall, but by the Leonine Wall built by Pope Leo IV in the ninth century to enclose the Vatican and Leonine City on the west bank of the Tiber. As support for Gregory VII began to wane, he only maintained his position with gold sent by Robert Guiscard. The defenders began to show the strain of the long siege. On 2 June 1083, Henry's Milanese and Saxon troops scaled the walls and took Leonine City with the future leader of the First Crusade, Godfrey of Bouillon, leading the way. A vicious fight ensued around the Basilica of St. Peter where the defenders took refuge. Henry's German troops, disregarding sanctuary laws, slaughtered them anyway. Pope Gregory, who had escaped to the fortress of Castel Sant'Angelo, formerly Hadrian's Tomb, watched the unholy emperor enter St. Peter's accompanied by the anti-Pope, Clement III. Since Henry held Leonine and the Romans still held the city, the belligerents decided to negotiate. Henry tore down the walls of Leonine and built a fort for his own garrison. Henry headed for Tuscany to take care of the margraves who remained loyal to Gregory VII and continued to resist. When he returned to Leonine at Christmas, he learned that his garrison had succumbed to disease and that the Romans had torn down his fort. Declaring this a violation of his treaty with Gregory, he resumed the conflict and took Rome on 21 March 1084. Gregory's nephew turned the former temple of Septizonium on the Palatine hill into a fortress. Henry besieged it as if it were a castle and virtually destroyed it before the defenders surrendered. The siege of Rome continued, as Henry had to eliminate or starve into submission each of its strongpoints. Gregory sent for Robert Guiscard who marched on Rome with an army of 6,000 cavalry and 30,000 infantry. When Guiscard's cavalry appeared on 21 May, Henry realized it was more than he could handle and withdrew, but not before bringing down the towers of the Capitol and the Leonine Walls. The Romans still held barricades and barred his men from the city when Guiscard arrived on 24 May. It was a hollow victory for Rome and the Pope since Robert's troops included Calabrians and even Saracen mercenaries from Sicily who came to plunder. The Romans took up arms against the men who violated their city and turned against Gregory, forcing him to flee to a castle in Salerno. Although Rome survived the siege, there were no winners. Henry IV returned to Italy in 1090 and this time he was defeated by Matilda whose victory led Milan, Cremona, Lodi and other cities to break away from the Empire.

Rome and the Holy Roman Empire continued to be at odds throughout the twelfth century. The cities of northern and central Italy wanted independence and alternately allied themselves and fought with the Empire, Rome and each other. Frederick Barbarossa attempt to dominate the Lombard League was defeated at the Battle of Legnano in 1176. The Italian city-states had a variety of political systems ranging from democratically elected governments to tyrannies and their allegiance split between the Guelphs who supported the Pope and the Ghibellines who favoured the Empire. The peninsula had an abundance of castles and other types of fortifications. Italian military engineers were among the best of the period.

Northern and central Italy consisted mostly of city-states at war with each other or involved in wars with the Holy Roman Empire. By the latter part of the twelfth century, prominent families vied for power within each city-state. As a result, most of the aristocracy moved into the cities for safety and built private tower houses much higher than the defensive towers on city walls. Since the cities continued to depend on their walls for protection, these towers were best suited for defence against rival families within the walls. Another reason for building these residential towers was that real estate was at a premium in these crowded urban centres.

San Gimignano in Tuscany is one of the few fortified towns where many tower houses remain. It is located on the main pilgrimage route from France to Rome. During the thirteenth and fourteenth centuries, family and political rivalries between the Guelphs and Ghibellines were rife in this town. As a result, seventy-two towers were built before the Renaissance. The town fell under the jurisdiction of the Bishop of Volterra who controlled about a dozen castles early in the twelfth century. In 1129, as San Gimignano tried to gain some freedom from the bishop's control, it fought with the nearby town of Casaglia and tried to take its castle. After 1170, San Gimignano broke free of another Bishop of Volterra, but went through external and internal conflicts for years. The Guelph faction dominated the town. As the city expanded, a new walled borough grew up beyond its original walls. As its power increased, it took control of more of the bishop's castles. In the thirteenth century, the city was contested between Ghibelline Siena and Guelph Florence.

The town of Semifonte, which lay midway between Siena and Florence, was controlled by the Ghibellines. The Florentines besieged it in 1202, breached its walls and levelled the fortifications and the town. In 1204, the war brought the destruction of the castle of Fosci and moved on to the gates of Siena. As the regional fighting continued for years, San Gimignano sided with the Bishop of Volterra. However, the bishop turned against it in 1227, only to find himself besieged in his castle of Gambassi, north of Volterra and San Gimignano. The siege failed and the conflict ended in 1235, but the next year, San Gimignano joined Florence in a war against Pistoia. The rest of the century was not much different as many conflicts similar to those that involved San Gimignano flared around the peninsula. Castles and walled cities played a major role in a confusing and complex history.

San Gimignano's first ring of walls, built in the late tenth century, enclosed a castle and extended 1,108m (0.68 miles). By the end of the twelfth century, the second ring with eight gates enclosed the present town. This wall was 2,175m (1.69 miles) in length. In 1252, riots damaged sections of this wall near two of its gates, but ten years later the townspeople restored the defences. The town's first tower, Rognosa built circa 1200, is 51m (167ft) high. It served as a court and a prison. It was followed by the tower of the Commune (Big Tower) next to the Palace of the Podesta (chief magistrate), 54m (177ft) high and built between 1300 and 1311. The town's noble families also erected towers for their own protection. These residences provided a minimum of comfort but they were supposed to be fireproof and impregnable and served as symbols of power and wealth for the families that built them. In 1255, a city ordinance prohibited the construction of towers higher than Rognosa, but the Salvucci family soon violated the rule.

San Gimignano. View of the town and some of its towers.

Tarquinia in Latium, south of San Gimignano, also retains a number of its medieval tower houses. In many ways, it is typical of Italian towns, which included city walls, a castle and tower houses. Like other towns north of Rome, it went through the violent period that lasted from the eleventh to fourteenth century. In 1245, it weathered a major siege by Emperor Frederick II, but it surrendered in 1355 to the Orsinis, a Guelph Roman family.

Frederick II, born in Italy, became King of Sicily and later Holy Roman Emperor and took part in a crusade. Unlike many of his contemporaries, he was

Frederick II's Castel del Monte and a model. (Photos by Gabriela Mundo)

well educated. Like other emperors, he found himself at odds with the Pope and was involved in conflicts in the peninsula where we spent most of his time. He relied on castle-building to strengthen his power and seems to have favoured the region of Apulia and Basilicata (Lucania) in southern Italy, where he had over 100 castles. In 1240, he built Castel del Monte on a hill at an elevation of 540m (1,771ft), in a location where it is constantly exposed to the sun. It is thought that he did this because of his interest in astronomy and the sciences. The castle is octagonal with a diameter of 56m (183.7ft) and includes eight octagonal towers, three of which have staircases. The castle walls are 16.5m (54.1ft) high and the tower walls are 3.1m (10.1ft) high. The castle consists of two levels 25m (82ft) high with eight rooms each. Three ground-floor doors open on the courtyard. The castle does not seem to have had a military function because it has no drawbridges, murder holes or even battlements. However, the battlements may have been removed and there may have been defensive wall around it.

Lerici. Top: View of tower and walls. Right: View of tower. Left: Plans.

The stonework is impressive and the interior includes the type of stonework commonly found in luxurious palaces. Most historians believe it was a hunting lodge since Frederick's son, Manfred the King of Sicily, used it for that purpose.

In 1238, Frederick laid siege to the city of Brescia because if it fell – he reasoned – Milan would follow suit. He used a large array of siege engines and employed sappers for the purpose. He hired the Spanish engineer Calamandrino, one of the best of his time, to design his siege engines. However, when Calamandrino was captured in a raid, he agreed to help the Brescians improve their fortifications and develop weapons to match those he had built for the emperor. Since the siege was getting nowhere, Frederick, in desperation, tied prisoners to his rams and belfries to discourage return fire. The town's leaders responded by placing prisoners in the path of the approaching battering rams. After a night raid on his camp left a great number of casualties, Frederick lifted the siege and pulled back to Cremona. The revolt in Lombardy only worsened as Genoa joined Milan.

Some Italian cities, like Lerici, were oriented towards the sea and were much coveted for their ports. Such was the case of Lerici where Pisa wanted to establish a foothold. In 1241, Pisa, a Ghibelline republic, sent forty ships to join Fredrick's fleet to confront the Genoese navy. At the Battle of Giglio, Frederick II and his allies defeated the Genoese. The victory allowed the Pisans to move into Lerici where they expanded the castle that the Genoese had begun to build in 1152 on a rocky promontory in the harbour. They turned the original tower into a pentagonal one and added a chemise. In 1254, defeated by Genoa, Pisa was required to evacuate Lerici and its castle, but did not do so until 1256. The town remained a bone of contention between the Guelphs and Ghibellines and Genoa and Pisa until 1426 when Aragon took ownership. The Aragonese retained control over Lerici only until 1479 when Florence got involved.

Italian City States and Title Confusion

Compared to other western European regions, medieval Italy was a land of political confusion. After the formal creation of the Holy Roman Empire in the tenth century, numerous disputes arose between the Pope and the Emperors over secular and non-secular matters. Theoretically, the Emperor controlled both the German people and the Latin population of Italy. Whenever relations between the Pope and the Emperor soured, the Emperor was not crowned and he was referred to as 'King of the Germans' who lived in 'Germany'. Although the Germans were often divided, the Italians were a tangled web of historic confusion. The Normans who invaded the southern part of the peninsula gave the region some measure of stability, neutralized the Saracens in Sicily in the eleventh century and ended Byzantine control not long after that. Frederick II, from the German House of Hohenstaufen, first became King of Sicily and later Holy Roman Emperor. To the north of Rome, the Italians challenged imperial authority from the time of Henry IV in the eleventh century and long afterwards.

In 1076 Countess Matilda of Tuscany (1046–1115) ruled over much of northern and central Italy, including Tuscany, Emilia-Romagna and Lombardy. After her death, many of the towns and cities she had controlled sought autonomy or full independence. In 1164, the anti-imperialist Lombard League formed to check the authority of Emperor Frederick Barbarossa.

Verona was important to imperial interests because it was located at the end of the main invasion route from the north through the Brenner Pass. In the thirteenth century, it was ruled by the tyrant Ezzelino da Romano (1194–1259). He supported Frederick II and opposed the Lombard cities and the powerful Este family, members of the Guelph (pro-Pope) faction, which had taken control of Ferrara in 1184 and held sway over several towns in the lower Po valley. When the Estes defeated Ezzelino, the Scaliger family, who were also Ghibellines (pro-Empire), took over Verona where they remained a major power until 1329. Their control extended eastward to Padua, Treviso, westward to Brescia and the lakes around it, Parma and Lucca and a strip of territory between these last two cities.

The Guelph faction, which opposed Frederick II, controlled Milan, the main city of the Lombard League. In 1277, the Visconti family held sway over Milan and more than a dozen other major cities in northern Italy. However, they often changed sides. Other cities, like Mantua, also changed alliances, but they were also divided into city factions, which led to internecine wars. Tyrants ruled many of the Italian cities. In central Italy, the aristocratic Roman Orsini family expanded Rome's control in the eleventh and twelfth centuries in support of the Pope, but another powerful Roman family, the Colonnas, was Ghibelline.

Venice and Genoa, both well fortified, acted independently and became naval powers transporting Crusaders to the Holy Land. They became veritable empires with colonies in the Mediterranean and the Black Sea. A few prominent families like the Dorias and the Spinolas dominated Genoa from the tenth century on. Both families tended to be Ghibellines and supported Frederick Barbarossa in exchange for commercial rights in the German lands to the north. In Florence, the Medici banking family rose to power in the fourteenth century.

All these cities required fortifications to protect themselves from rivals, both far and near and most of the major families built castles and tower houses for their own protection. During this period, the siege was more common than traditional battles.

Verona bridge and Castelvecchio (Old Castle): Two aerial photos from US Southern European Task Force (SETAF) courtesy of Col. Adrian Traas.

Between 1354 and 1357 Cangrande II della Scala built the Castelvecchio (Old Castle) in Verona, probably on the site of a Roman fort. He incorporated part of the city walls into this castle. The waters of the Adige River once filled the surrounding moat. The castle includes six towers, the tallest of which is the keep, which is similar to the tower houses of the era. It also included a bridge with

Castelvecchio, Verona: Exterior and interior views of the walls and towers, and Scalaga statue.

three great arches and red-brick towers built in 1355, destroyed in the Second World War but rebuilt after it. One of the castle's rectangular towers defended one end of the bridge. A second tower with two drawbridges defended the other end. The Scaliger family built a network of castles to control the key route north and to protect their base in Verona. One of these strongholds, Scaliger Castle, at Sirmione on Lake Garda was more than a mere castle; it was a fortified port on the lake. Its construction began in 1277 at the entrance to a peninsula. Two drawbridges over the surrounding moat allow access to the castle. One of them lowers over the water barrier that separates the peninsula from the mainland and the other opens toward the town gate with another drawbridge.

It is difficult to follow the development and history of medieval fortifications in Italy, especially north of Rome, because it involves numerous city-states often at war with each other, the Holy Roman Empire and the Papacy, not to mention family rivalries within cities. In many cases, the victors razed their opponents' fortifications and rebuilt on the ruins. The Italian peninsula represented a bridge between Northern Europe and the Near East as its cities traded and developed local industries not commonly found in feudal Europe.

The castles at Vulci and Assisi exemplify the complex history of Italian fortifications. The castle of Vulci stood on the border of the Papal States and Tuscany. It was first a ninth-century fortified Benedictine Abbey defending the ancient Etruscan bridge across the Fiora River from Saracen raids. In the twelfth century, the abbey became a castle with a trapezoidal shape, four cylindrical towers and a keep. Two sides of the castle face the gorge of the Fiora River. A wet moat protected the castle's eastern section and part of the northern side. Improvements such as the machicoulis on the keep were added during the Late Middle Ages. Two Ghibelline families, the Aldorandeschi and the Di Vico, contested control of the castle. The Templars may have used the castle in the thirteenth century as a reception centre for pilgrims.

Two castles defended the city of Assisi. Rocca Maggiore castle stands in a commanding position at the top of a hill; Rocca Minore is further down the hill. Rocca Maggiore was built in 1174 on the site of older fortifications by Archbishop Cristiano di Magonza (Christian of Mainz), a representative of the Pope and the emperor, who had taken Assisi after a siege in 1173. It is claimed that it was the childhood home of Frederick II. Konrad von Urslinger, Count of Assisi and Duke of Spoleto, provoked the ire of the townspeople who revolted against him in 1198 and tore down the castle. In 1353, Cardinal Gil Álvarez Carrillo de Albornoz, appointed as legate by Pope Innocent VI residing in Avignon, was given the mission to reconquer and rebuild the Papal States. He built the Rocca Minore in 1360 and rebuilt Rocca Maggiore in 1367. He used the remaining section of the western part of the outer walls and some of the interior positions. A long wall that may have had an interior passage connected the two castles. In 1392, the city council of Perugia, put the condottiere Biordo Michelotti in control of the

Vulci Castle. Views of the castle and the Etruscan bridge.

city to avoid being absorbed into the Papal States. By 1394, Michelotti expanded Perugia's control to Assisi where he strengthened the castle and increased the height of the keep. In 1458, the lord of Assisi built a wall connecting the castle to the town. A long wall, with an interior passage, connects the Rocca Maggiore to a large lookout tower. Two sixteenth-century popes made further additions, including a round tower near the gate.

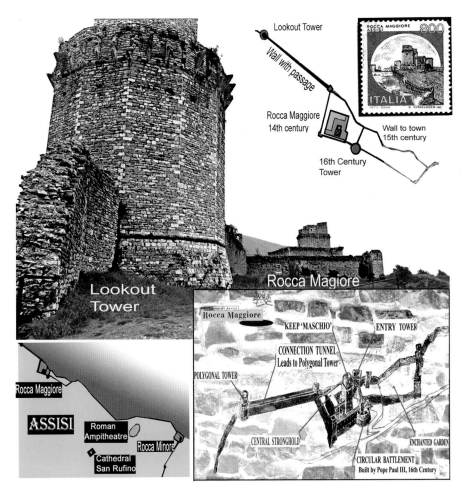

Assisi Castle. Top: Lookout tower with castle in background. Bottom: Plans.

The fortress of Gradara also reflects a long and mixed history of construction. Located on top of a hill between the Marche and Romagna 13km (8 miles) north of the city of Pesaro and 25km (15.5 miles) south of Rimini, it offered the de Griffo family of the early thirteen century a dominant position. The brothers Pietro and Rodolfo Griffo are credited with the construction of the castle's main tower on top of a 142m (465.8ft) hill. Late in the century, various contenders took control of this donjon. In 1299, Malatesta da Verucchio, a member the Guelph faction of Rimini, took the city and the Pope made him lord of Gradara. His son Pandolfo completed the construction between 1307 and 1324. The square keep built by the de Griffo family became part of the castle, which includes three polygonal towers. According to local historians, it was one of the first castles to have machicoulis along its towers and walls. The keep with three polygonal corner towers and high curtain walls served as a palace. A lower set of walls with a

Gradara Castle. Top: View of town wall and entrance. Middle: Exterior and interior view of gate of outer bailey (Left: castle tower can be seen in background of exterior view). Bottom: Plan and view of tower on town wall.

rectangular tower forms an upper bailey. A second set of walls, almost 1km (0.62 miles) long, which connects the upper bailey to the lower bailey and encloses the old town, has similar wall towers and a large polygonal corner tower. When it was finished, the fortress included seventeen towers and three drawbridges over its dry moats built between the thirteen and fourteenth centuries. Cardinal Albornoz defeated the Malatestas in 1353 and took most of their territory, but he allowed them to remain in control of Gradara, Rimini and a few other cities. The Malatesta family was involved with a murder, adultery and a love affair that Dante immortalized in the *Divine Comedy*. In 1424, during the long blood feud with the Montefeltro family, the inept Galeazzo Malatesta allowed troops of Filippo Maria Visconti, Duke of Milan, to enter the castle. They took the opportunity to seize him and imprison him in the castle. When Filippo became aware of the situation, he removed the captain of the offending troops and returned the castle to its rightful owner. The Pope recruited Sigismondo Malatesta to defend his interests when Francesco Sforza and the Duke of Montefeltro contracted an alliance. In October 1446, Sforza laid siege to Gradara with a large army and siege engines and kept heavy pressure on the castle for forty days. Finally, a blizzard forced Sforza to lift the siege. In 1463, the combined forces of Montefeltros and Sforzas put Gradara under siege. The Pope turned against Malatesta because he was a ruthless tyrant and excommunicated him, which incited the population against him. In February 1464, the Pope granted Gradara to the Sforzas. However, the townspeople were opposed to Sforza rule until Giovanni Sforza won their favour and restored the fortress.

The hostilities between the Malatestas, the Montefeltros and the Papacy caused difficulties for another commune that emerged as a republic and retains its independence to this day. San Marino began as a settlement and stronghold on Mount Titano about 750m (2,460.6ft) above sea level. According to local history, a mason from an Adriatic island founded the town in the tenth century and built walls for its small religious community. The stone of the mountain provided excellent material for building the fortifications. The first 'fortress' was the Guaita Tower, which included a pentagonal keep with curtain walls and towers. This castle occupies a narrow shelf on a ridge and it is linked to the first church in the village. The Guaita Tower, the largest of the three towers of San Marino, reached its most advanced state in the fifteenth century. From this castle, a set of walls surrounded the approachable sections of the town.

The second tower, Cesta, which occupies the site of an ancient Roman fortification, was built in the thirteenth century. It is also pentagonal and it is surrounded by a curtain wall. Later, in the sixteenth century, a wall running from this castle, along the ridge, to the city wall was built. All the defences of this face the slope to the south-west and the approach to the city. Not far from the rear of the wall is the cliff side of the ridge. Finally, the Montale Tower, which stands

The Three Towers of San Marino. Top: The second tower, Cesta, located on the highest summit of Monte Titano. Bottom left: View of the third tower, Montale, from Cesta. Bottom right: The first tower, Guaita, the oldest of the three.

The Three Towers of San Marino: Plan and photo with view of Guaita from Cesta.

alone, was erected in the fourteenth century. Supposedly, it was built because the threat from the Malatesta family had increased.

The Republic of San Marino aligned itself with the Counts of Montefeltro at this time and both parties agreed to let Cardinal Albornoz control the San Marino fortress. However, this did not happen until the defeat of the Malatestas. The city's fortifications were completed by the end of the fourteenth century. During the fifteenth century, the ruler of Rimini, the duke of Urbino, the king of Naples and the Pope were involved in a war with Sigismondo Pandolfo Malatesta. In the 1440s, Sigismondo set out on a surprise night attack on San Marino, but the troops from Urbino sent a warning. In 1449, Malatesta tried to bribe some citizens of San Marino, but that did not work either. In 1461, the leaders of San Marino were offered all the castles they could conquer in Malatesta's territory. When the war ended in 1463, the troops of San Marino occupied the castles of Fiorentino, Montegiardino, Servalle and Faetano; this was the last time the

The medieval walls of Florence. The remaining section located south of Arno includes square towers with battering (part of the sixth set of walls). Photo of the only entrance gate with no towers.
(Photos courtesy of Martyn Gregg)

Medieval town of Sermoneta and Castello Caetani. (Photos by Gabriella Mundo)

Bracciano and Tivoli: Top: Castle Orsini-Odescalchi at Bracciano, Italy built between 1470 and 1485 by the Orsini family on site of an earlier castle. Built on a trapezoidal plan, it has six large towers. It played a role in Renaissance politics. Bottom: Rocca Pia at the hilltop town of Tivoli built in 1461 by Pope Pius II to control a riotous population. Supposedly built in a single year, it has four corner towers (two large towers – the tallest is 36.5m [119.7ft] high).

Castel Sant'Angelo. Top: View across the Tiber: Bottom left: Seventeenth-century model. Bottom right: drawing showing post-medieval additions, including bastions, for the age of artillery.

Republic expanded. In 1503, Cesare Borgia, son of the Pope, occupied San Marino, but the city shortly won back its freedom. As the fortress of Mount Titano faded into obsolescence, a much more modern fortress appeared nearby at San Leo.

Many Italian cities and towns, unlike those in other parts of Europe, grew rapidly during the Middle Ages thanks to their political independence. The constant strife between factions required them also to build and maintain walls. Florence exemplifies this trend. It was founded by the Romans in the first century BC and its population grew to 10,000 during the next two centuries. However, by the sixth century, its Roman walls became too difficult to defend because the population had dropped to 1,000. The town built a second wall to enclose the

Ferrara, Castello Estense was begun in 1385 by Marquis Nicholas II d'Este for his protection after a revolt of the townspeople. It evolved into a Renaissance palace. The Tower of Lions existed before work began. In 1476, the castle became the residence of the court.

smaller settlement. By the tenth century, the city had grown again and required a third wall. Construction on a fourth wall began in 1078 to accommodate a population of 20,000 people. Expansion had gone in all directions beyond the third wall and across the Arno, but the new wall did not include that area south of the river. A new wall that included both sides of the river and other areas of expansion was begun in the 1170s. However, the section south of the river was only protected by palisades and adding defences to the walls of buildings. Finally, in 1284, a new wall came to protect the entire city; it took just under fifty years to complete and included many projecting square towers about 35m (114.8ft) high and sixteen gates, one of which had towers. These walls enclosed some uninhabited areas to accommodate further expansion. Their height was reduced when artillery appeared at the beginning of the Italian Renaissance.

Many of the small villages and hamlets occupied hilltops or mountaintops and had been fortified for centuries. The village of Sermoneta, in Latium, had a large stone keep over 42m (137.7ft) high and a small tower built by the Annibaldi family in the mid-twelfth century. Count Pietro Caetani purchased the castle and territory in 1297 from the Annibaldi and turned it into a massive fortress with five sets of encircling walls, some up to 3m (9.8ft) thick, moats and drawbridges. Pope Alexander VI, of the Borgia family, took the fortress from the Caetani family and completed the work. Also in Latium, the castle of Bracciano, built by the Orsini family, is on a hill that dominates the area and overlooks Lake Bracciano. It replaced an earlier castle built by the di Vico family in the eleventh century, which was taken over by the Orsinis in the 1230s. The castle became a possession of the Pope later in the next century. The Orsinis regained it in the fifteenth century, started renovating it in 1470 and completed the work in 1486. Cesare Borgia and his father failed twice to take Bracciano Castle in the sixteenth century. The castle includes six large towers, five of which are round and one of which dates back to the twelfth century. Its courtyard is triangular, but the castle is an irregular trapezoid. Today, it is one of the largest castles in Italy.

Not all Italian castles occupied elevated positions, however. Castel Sant'Angelo stands next to the River Tiber. It was built on Hadrian's Tomb; added towers and encircling walls turned it into a very strong fortress and a refuge for the Popes. Este Castle at Ferrara, also known as Castello di San Michele, was built in the centre of the city on level ground. After a tax revolt in 1385, Niccolò II d'Este concluded that his palace was not strong enough to protect him from the people's wrath and decided to build a brick castle. He added curtain walls and three new towers to an existing tower. The castle was connected to his palace by a passageway. The castle includes a wet moat with three entrances with drawbridges that have ravelins in front of them. The castle underwent extensive modifications during the sixteenth century.

Conclusion

The Western Roman Empire became Latin Europe and expanded beyond the Italian peninsula to encompass and absorb much of Celtic Europe and the western edge of Germanic Europe from the Frisian coast to the Alps. Their fortification-building skills and their road system allowed the Romans to dominate and control successfully the region for several centuries. However, considerable population movements on the eastern borders finally brought about the slow collapse of the Roman Empire, initiating the era known as the Dark Ages. During this first half of the Middle Ages, little of great significance happened in the development of fortifications. The stones from many Roman-era walls were quarried for the construction of other structures such as churches. The most significant development in the West at the end of this era was the development of the motte-and-bailey castle with a wooden donjon or keep that eventually became built in stone in the tenth and eleventh centuries.

When the Byzantines tried to recapture the Italian peninsula in the sixth century, fortified cities played a major role in the wars that ensued. When the Moors invaded Iberia in the eighth century and the Norsemen struck coastal regions of Western Europe during the next, fortifications had to become more effective. Castle-building entered its heyday during the transition into the High Middle Ages when it reinforced the feudal system in some areas. Influence of the Near East showed up in Christian Europe when the Crusaders returned home from the wars in the Holy Land. The rocky relations between the Plantagenet rulers of England and the Capetians of France further affected castle building in Western Europe. In Italy, the Holy Roman Emperors and the Popes fought over control of the fragmented peninsula where fortified cities played a more important role than individual castles did. During this time, the English kings expanded their control into Wales by securing the region with great castles.

In this volume, we described the way the Romans built fortifications as small as legionary forts and as large as the great walls of Rome. We have examined only a sample of the thousands of wooden and stone castles and fortifications in the former lands of the Western Roman Empire, concentrating on some of the most significant structures. In the next volume, *Castle to Fortress*, we start with the Reconquista in Iberia and the fortifications built during that era. In addition, we cover the last great war in feudal Europe, the Hundred Years War between England and France when battles were few and sieges were many. This war ended with the introduction of the cannon, which brought about drastic changes to fortifications, many of which began in the Italian peninsula, the cradle of the Renaissance. The end of the Middle Ages and the introduction of the cannon brought an end to the age of castles and a return to forts and fortresses. Due to changes in design, many castles were modified or abandoned. The Renaissance fort and fortress marked the beginning of a trend in military architecture that would last for centuries.

Town Wall

Remains of Castle

Viollet le Duc 1856

Photo of model by
Drew Hammond

Coucy: Built by Enguerrand III in the 1220s, the donjon at a width of 35m (114.8ft) and a height of 55m (180.4ft), was one of the largest in France. Top left: Model of Coucy. Top right: The keep of Coucy destroyed by the Germans in the First World War. Centre left: Remains of the Coucy town wall. Bottom left: Remains of Coucy Castle. (Photo top left courtesy of Drew Hammond)

Appendix I

Table of Monarchs

Castile & Leon* *Aragon***	France	England	Wales (Kingdom of Gwnedd)	Holy Roman Empire
Sancho III* 1000–35**	Henry I 1031–60	**Edward the Confessor** 1042–66	Gruffydd (Griffith) 1039–63	Conrad II 1024–39
				Henry III 1039–56
Fernando I 1035–65 *Ramiro I 1035–63*	Philippe I 1060–1108	Harold II 1066	Bleddyn ap Cyfyn 1063–75	**Henry IV** 1056–1105
Alfonso VI 1065–1109 *Sancho I Ramirez 1063–94* *Pedro I 1094–1104*		**William I** 1066–87	Trahaern 1075–81	
Urraca 1109–1126 *Alfonso I 1104–34*		William II 1087–1100	Gruffydd ap Cynan 1081–1137	
Alfonso VII 1126–57 *Ramiro II 1134–7*	Louis VI 1108–37	**Henry I** 1100–35		Henry V 1106–25
Sancho III 1157–8				Lothair III 1125–37
Ramon Berenguer IV 1137–62	Louis VII 1137–80	Stephen 1135–54	**Owan Gwynedd** 1137–70	Conrad III 1138–52
Alfonso VIII 1158–1214 (Fernando II 1157–88) *Alfonso II 1162–96*		**Henry II** 1154–89	Dafydd ab Owain Gwynedd 1170–94	**Fredrick I** 1152–90

Castile & Leon* *Aragon***	France	England	Wales (Kingdom of Gwnedd)	Holy Roman Empire
Enrique I 1214–1217 (Alfonso IX 1188–1230) *Pedro II* 1196—1213	**Philippe II, Augustus** 1180–1223	**Richard I** 1189–99	**Llywelyn the Great** 1194–1240	Henry VI 1190–7
		John 1199–1216		Philip 1198– 1208
Fernando III 1217–52 *Jaime I* 1213–76	Louis VIII 1223–6	**Henry III** 1216–72	Dafydd ap Llywelyn 1240–6	Otto IV 1198–1215 **Fredrick II** 1212–50
	St. Louis IX 1226–70			Conrad IV 1250–4
Pedro III 1276–85	Philippe III 1270–85	**Edward I** 1272–1307	**Llywelyn ap Gruffydd** 1246–82	Richard 1257–72 **Rudolf**
Alfonso III 1285–91	Philippe IV 1285–1314		Sons of the English king become Prince of Wales	1273–91 Adolf 1292–8 Albert I 1298–1308
Jaime II 1291–1327	Louis X 1314–16	Edward II 1307–27	beginning with Edward I's son: Prince Edward 1301–7	Henry VII 1308–13
	Philippe V 1316–22			Ludwig 1314–47
Alfonso IV 1327–36	Charles IV 1322–8	**Edward III** 1327–77		Charles IV 1346–78
Alfonso XI 1325–50	Philippe VI 1328–50			
Pedro I 1350–69 *Pedro IV* 1336–87	Jean II 1350–64			
Enrique II 1369–79 *Juan I* 1379–90	Charles V 1364–80	Richard II 1377–99		Vacalav 1378–1410
Enrique III 1390–1406 *Martin I* 1396–1410	Charles VI 1380–1422	Henry IV 1399–1413		Rupert III 1400–11
Ferdinand I 1412–16	**Charles VII** 1422–61	**Henry V** 1413–22		Sigismund 1410–37
Juan II 1406–54 *Alfonso V* 1416–58		Henry VI 1422–71		Albert II 1437–9

Castile & Leon* *Aragon***	France	England	Wales (Kingdom of Gwnedd)	Holy Roman Empire
Enrique IV 1454–74 *Juan II* 1458–79	Louis XI 1461–83	Edward IV 1442–83		Frederick III 1440–93
Isabela I 1474–1504 *Ferdinand II* 1479–1516	**Charles VIII** 1483–98 Louis XII 1498–1515	Edward V 1483 Richard III 1483–5 Henry VII 1485–1509		Maximilian I 1493–1519 Charles V 1519–55
Charles I 1516–55	**Francis I** 1515–47	**Henry VIII** 1509–47		

*Kings of only Leon, when Castile and Leon not united, in (parenthesis).
**Kings of Aragon *italicized*
***Sancho III of Navarre ruled Navarre, Leon, Castile and Aragon.

Notes

Chapter 1

1. Hellenistic civilization likewise borrowed and improved upon what had come from Greek and Middle Eastern cultures.
2. The turf formed the ramparts topped by a palisade of sharpened stakes. The troops used leather tents. Other facilities in the camp, which were laid out in specified positions, were also sheltered in leather tents.
3. The defences along the Rhine and the frontier of Raetia are often referred to as the Limes Germanicus. Those along the remainder of the European frontier have other designations: the Danubian Limes (including 420km [260.9 miles] of the Pannonian Limes running from Vienna to Belgrade), the Limes Moesiae between Black Sea and Danube, the Limes Transalutanus in Dacia (Romania), etc.
4. Mommsen, *Provinces of the Roman Empire*, pp. 128–9.
5. Parts of modern Switzerland, Austria and Bavaria.
6. Tacitus' description catalogues most of the elements of siege warfare of this period. These methods, which were centuries old, persisted well into the modern era although they were most popular during the Middle Ages and the Renaissance. See Tacitus, *The Histories*, Vol. I and II, Kindle e-book locations 5567–5584.
7. Sergeant, *The Franks*, Kindle ebook location 458.
8. This work does not cover the positions of the Roman Empire in Africa and Asia, which were significantly different because of the terrain, nor is the front along the Danube covered in detail since this work's topic is Western Europe.
9. According to some sources, the term vallum refers to a ditch; many others suggests that the term referred to the rampart and associated ditch. However, the etymology of the term suggests that the term originally referred to a curtain wall made of posts and eventually referred to all ramparts, including those made of stone.
10. Eight men was the smallest military unit. It was considered a tent group since a tent held eight men.
11. The height is not known, but Hugh Elton points out that the tower at Dover had four storeys and was between 13m and 24m (42.6ft and 78.7ft) high.
12. Hugh Elton gives different figures for the Late Empire claiming the ditches were 2–4m (6.5–13.1ft) deep (averaging 3m [9.8ft] depth) and 5–15m (16.4–49.2ft) wide (averaging 10m [32.8ft]). Elton, *Warfare in Roman Europe*, p. 161.
13. Not all historians agree on the height and width of the walls since most are estimates based on archaeological work.
14. Elton, *Warfare in Roman Europe*, p. 163, believes they were probably similar to city walls at 8m to 10m (26.2ft to 32.8ft) high at rampart-walk level to require the use of scaling ladders.
15. Bishop, *Handbook to Roman Legionary Fortresses*, Kindle e-book locations 655–656.

16. Vexillation fortress is a term used by British archaeologists to avoid confusion with regular legionary fortresses.

17. Eighty men formed a unit called a 'century'. A century consisted of ten contubernia (tent groups) consisting of eight men each. A cohort consisted of six centuries totaling 480 men. A legion had ten cohorts, the 1st Cohort usually being double the strength of the others. A legion also included an attached cavalry unit or 'ala' of 120 men. The term ala derives from wing meaning they protected the flanks in battle. A legate, a former tribune or a member of the senatorial class was appointed to command a legion until Gallienus abolished the office and replaced it with that of prefect, member of the equestrian class. Septimus Severus had begun appointing prefects to command legions over a century before. The senior tribune was his second-in-command and also came from the senatorial class. A camp prefect was the third-in-command in charge of maintaining the camp and selecting the site and construction of fortifications. He had also served as a tribune. There were five other tribunes from the equestrian (knight) class of citizens. The tribunes had separate quarters. The senior centurion commanded the First Cohort. Each legion had up to sixty centurions, each in command of a century. Unlike the tribunes, the centurions were professional soldiers and would be considered the lowest-ranking officers.

18. The marching camps had open gates – simple openings in the ramparts. One method of defending it was to place a mound a few metres in front of the opening. A second method, called a clavicular, was to extend the rampart so it curved in front of or behind the open gateway.

19. Similar fortifications were used in the Roman provinces of Africa and Asia, but they are not part of this study. Differences in terrain and vegetation in those areas required a different approach to choosing the site and building defensive positions.

20. Johnson, *Late Roman Fortifications*, p. 150.

21. Playing-card shape refers to rectangular with rounded corners. Many archaeologists and historians use the term to describe the basic layout of Roman forts according to the *Concise Oxford Dictionary of Archaeology* by Timothy Darvill (Oxford Univ. Press, 2002).

22. Breeze, *Frontiers of Imperial Rome*, Kindle e-book location 2352.

23. They would have looked like the castles of the High Middle Ages rather than those of an earlier period. Breeze, *Frontiers of Imperial Rome*, Kindle e-book locations 1314–1315.

24. The Juthungi were a Germanic tribe, also known as the Semmoni and part of the Suevi, a confederation that included the Marcomanni and other tribes.

25. Diocletian is better known for his persecution of the Christians before he abdicated in 305.

26. Zosimus, *History of Zosimus*, Kindle e-book locations 1005–1012.

27. Ammianus, *The Later Roman Empire* AD *354-378*, Kindle e-book locations 9057–9071.

28. Elton, *Warfare in Roman Europe*, pp. 155–6.

Chapter 2

1. Eboracum (York), built sometime after AD 71. By the end of the century, the troops began converting it into a stone fortress. It was 470m x 425m (513.9 yds x 464.7 yds) covering 20 ha (50 acres).

2. Deva (Chester) was a timber fortress built between AD 78 and 88 and after the end of the century converted to stone. It was 590m x 410m (645.2 yds x 448.3 yds) covering 24.3 ha (60.7 acres).

3. Parker, *The Roman Legions*, p. 160.

4. Today the wall is located as close as 1km (0.6 miles) from the border with Scotland and is now entirely in England.

5. The reader should remember that the measurements of these fortifications will vary between sources since they are based mostly on archaeological data, which also include many estimates and assumptions. Even when it comes to historical dates, historians often have no records of actual dates including in the case of invasions.

6. The term 'berm' usually refers to a mound or raised section. However, the scholars describing the Roman 'walls' apply this term to a level strip between the ditch and the wall. In the feature known as the 'Vallum' south of Hadrian's Wall there was an actual berm (mound-like structure) running north of the ditch and south of the ditch parallel to the ditch.

7. Since records are few, it is difficult to determine who made these decisions. It was probably not the emperor and possibly came from the governor since he was the highest official on the island and exercised command over the legions and auxiliary troops on the island.

8. There is substantial disagreement on this subject. In addition, archaeological research can often yield different results about the ruins especially when the excavations were done on a site at different times.

9. There are some questions concerning the barracks. Most standard barrack blocks held eighty soldiers. The ones for the cavalry held fewer. Most forts had mixed garrisons, which leads to disagreements concerning the size of the garrison. In addition, some forts were modified between the second and fourth centuries when the garrisons also changed in size and type. Thus, all numbers presented are only rough estimates and do not apply to a specific time.

10. Dere Street was a military road built by Agricola for his invasion of the north.

11. Although he reigned during a period of peace, Antoninus expanded Rome's territory in north-west Dacia and built a new wall there.

12. These berms, here and on other fortifications like Hadrian's Wall, were apparently made wide enough for the troops on the parapets to have a good angle for hurling javelins at the enemy inside the V-shaped ditch.

13. In Hadrian's Wall, they were made of stone.

14. Fields, *Rome's Northern Frontier*, pp. 33–43.

15. If more troops were needed it would seem pulling back to the Hadrian Wall would not make sense since it was a much longer defensive line than the Antonine Wall. Possibly tribes between the walls were hostile, requiring additional troops.

16. Septimus Severus also defeated another rival, Pescennius Niger, governor of Syria, whose legions proclaimed him emperor, in 194. He defeated Albinus in Gaul in 197, but found himself at war with the Parthians that same year and returned to Rome in 202.

17. This was a critical time for both the Eastern and Western Roman Empires since in 378 Emperor Valens died in battle when his army was defeated at Adrianople. Magnus Maximus had helped Theodosius I (son of his former commander) become emperor in the East. Gratian in 383 was in Raetia engaging the Alamanni, but he quickly

marched into Gaul, but most of his troops defected to the pretender at Paris. Gratian was assassinated as he fled to Lyon. In 387 Magnus Maximus marched on Rome and Valentinian II fled. Theodosius marched into Italy and the usurper gave up.

18. He was neither the first nor the last emperor to be given this title, since even some of Hadrian and Probus' coins use it, but he was one of the few who really deserved it since the empire was on the verge of collapsing at the time.

19. The importance of Rome had declined over the years as most emperors resided in other cities. However, Rome was still considered the seat of power where the Senate remained. As a matter of fact, most of the emperors of the third century were not even born in Rome and some were not true Romans. Aurelian was born in Moesia in the northern part of the Balkans.

20. William Burr, *Ancient and Modern Engineering*, pp. 28–9.

21. The next emperor, Carus (282–3), crushed another wave of Germanic invaders over the Danube before he had to engage the Persians against whom he was successful. He was found dead in his tent either struck down by lightning or a disease, having ruled less than a year later. Some historians like Michael Grant, however, suspect foul play. The next two emperors, who ruled between AD 283 and 284, were also assassinated.

22. Assuming it took three years to complete Hadrian's Wall, it probably took one year for one legion to build about 20km (12.4 miles) of wall, including milecastles if no work was done during the winter months. Thus, we can estimate that it took about three years to complete the circuit of Rome's walls with a workforce no larger than one legion.

23. A Roman consul whose tomb was built circa 14 BC.

24. Tufa is a type of limestone common in Italy. It is relatively soft (softer than travertine) and easy to cut into blocks, but it has a rough surface which cannot be made smooth. Large blocks were used in fortifications, gates and towers and on the lower section of the concrete wall to form a plinth.

25. Pozzolana was a volcanic ash the Romans mixed with lime to create a resistant cement, which, mixed with pieces of tufa, formed a strong concrete mixture. Pieces of lower quality travertine may also have been used in the concrete core, but travertine smoothed up better than tufa and was later used on gates. Good-quality travertine was used on many public buildings and temples.

26. Most of the construction details come from Ian Richmond's *The City Wall of Imperial Rome*, which is often quoted by other sources.

27. In *The City Wall of Imperial Rome*, Ian Richmond mentions, in addition to posterns, several wickets (small gates or doorways).

28. The metal springs of the ballista had an estimated lifespan of about a decade, so the weapon could be expensive to maintain in large numbers.

29. If those forces totaled 12,000 men, that would give about 650 men per kilometre (0.6 miles) or 65 men per 100m (109 yds), which should have been sufficient. To build a legionary fortress that averaged about a 2km (1.2 miles) perimeter a 6,000-man legion could place 300 men per 100m. An enemy force would need far more men to engage of a city the size of Rome in a siege.

30. By this time, Rome was only the symbolic centre of the empire, since other cities served as capitals. The population supported Maxentius because of its privileged status and because it rebelled against being subjected to new taxes.

31. In 412 Jovinus, a Gallo-Roman senator, claimed the title of emperor at Mainz after the pretender Constantine had been eliminated at Arles. He was taken out in 414. Meanwhile, Honorius had to allow the Burgundians to occupy the left bank of the Rhine and become federates with their capital at Worms.

32. The regent played one general off the other. This rivalry allowed the Vandals to take over North Africa. The general in her favour who defeated Aetius, also died in that battle and thus Aetius' services were needed again the next year.

33. Gregory of Tours, *History of the Franks*, p. 117.

34. Details from Stephen Johnson's *Roman Imperial Fortifications*, pp. 13–25.

35. Cologne had been established as a colony and fortified in the first century.

36. Some cities like Trier and Metz did not resist and allowed their people to be slaughtered.

Chapter 3

1. Alcok, in *Was this Camelot?*, used remaining data, allowing for copying errors accumulated over the years, to calculate that the battle was fought in either 490, 499 or 518.

2. Author of the twelfth-century *History of the Kings of Britain*.

3. It is impossible to tell if these Saxon sites or the Franks' military camps qualified as forts, fortresses or simply a fortified camp, because the original manuscripts were not clear on the subject. In addition, later translators often used the terms interchangeably. It is doubtful that either the Saxons or Franks built anything more complex than earthen defences with wooden palisades.

4. Oman, *The Dark Ages*, Kindle e-book location 271.

5. Odovacar received generous terms. Soon after, he was assassinated.

6. Enrico Cirelli's article 'Ravenna – Rise of a Late Antique Capital' gives details on Ravenna and Roman improvements in northern Italy.

7. The Gothic Wars (535–54) began when another Byzantine army attacked the Ostrogoths in Dalmatia in 535.

8. Isauria was in the Taurus Mountains of southern Anatolia. The troops from this region were skilled in this kind of work.

9. Bury, like Procopius, seems to estimate 100,000 Goths or more.

10. Prokopios, *The Wars of Justinian*, pp. 300–1.

11. No dates are well established for any of these events, but the arrival of the Franks at Tortona must have been after May 539.

12. Before this setback, Totila had already used his fleet to occupy Sardinia and Corsica.

13. Narses' army, according to Procopius, had 1,500 cavalry on the left flank and on each side of the battle front 4000. Behind each group of archers were Byzantine troops, while the centre was made of Heruli and Lombards on foot. The archers were dismounted.

14. Historians generally refer to the old walled Roman cities as fortresses during the Dark Ages for lack of a better definition. Roman forts and entrenched camps used by the Franks are often called castrum (plural castra). Some cities, walled or not, included a castrum.

15. Gregory probably exaggerated their size, especially the width of the walls.

16. The Arian Christians were considered heretical by Catholics. Many Germanic groups were Arian early in the Dark Ages.

17. Carcassonne and Narbonne, eastward to Beziers and the Rhône River and south to the Pyrenees, formed a region known as Septimania taken over by the Visigoths in 462. They also referred to it as Gallia Narbonensis.

18. Current research still questions what the Visigoths actually did. According to some historians, they added new fortifications, but according to others, they simply maintained or restored the existing Roman defences. They are not noted as great builders.

19. Early in his reign, Euric (466–84) had engaged in wars with the Suebi for control of the north-west part of Iberia. In 471, he conquered the Roman province of Tarraconensis (Catalonia and the Ebro valley) pushing Rome out of the peninsula. His control extended to the Rhône – including Arles and Marseilles – and the Loire River.

20. Two Roman gates still remain; Porte de France and Porte Augustus with an inscription from 16 BC on the latter. The city was served by an aqueduct that included the Pont du Gard.

21. Porta Palatina in Turin is one of the remaining examples of a gateway built in the time of Augustus. It was more of a monument than a defensive feature to demonstrate the glory of Rome. This was common during the period of the early Principate of the first and second century AD.

22. The most recent information comes from: Sarantis and Christie, *War and Warfare in Late Antiquity*.

23. Pérez García, Victor Lluís. 'Late Roman and Visigothic Fortifications in Conventus Tarraconensis (Hispania)'.

24. This was after the removal of Romulus Augustulus by Odoacer and the time of the Ostrogoth takeover in Italy.

25. Leovigild was the last Arian king of the Visigoths.

Chapter 4

1. There is no consensus among historians that the trebuchet was in use in Europe at this time. It consisted of a long lever that was pulled down with ropes by several men pulling and suddenly released to hurl heavy projectiles.

2. The ladders were most likely built on site since the height of the walls had to be estimated to make sure the ladders would reach the top. Often the ladders sported hooks that held them to the walls.

3. The term tortoise is derived from the Latin 'testudo', a Roman defensive formation that used interlocking shields to provide overhead cover from missile attack. The Franks also used this formation to approach walls.

4. Timothy Reuter estimates that armies operating for any length of time during the Carolingian era could not number more than 2,000 to 3,000 men since logistical support for larger forces would have been difficult and foraging would not have sustained them during a siege (Maurice Keen, *Medieval Warfare*, p. 30).

5. Ceuta in Africa and Gibraltar in Europe form the ancient Pillars of Hercules.

6. According to Joseph Callaghan, Tarik's force consisted mostly of about 12,000 Berbers (*History of Medieval Spain*, p. 95).

7. Tarik launched a terror campaign to break the will of the Visigoths. He ordered his men to burn the flesh of some of the dead and allowed some prisoners to escape to spread the rumour that the Muslims were flesh eaters.

8. In *Mahometan Empire,* James Murphy does not specify exactly what was taking place in the mobile tower that Ibn El-Athir in *Annales* refers to as a 'debabba'. They may have been digging against the base of the tower or actually mining, something the Germanic groups did not do at the time.

9. Bachrach, *Early Carolingian Warfare*, p. 208.

10. Meanwhile, Charles Martel, Mayor of the Palace of Austrasia, defeated Neustria's king at Vichy in 717 and chased him to Paris. The next year, he invaded Saxony. In 719, Raganfred, mayor of the palace of Neustria, joined forces with Eudo of Aquitaine, but Charles defeated them at Soissons. Charles launched a series of campaigns in Saxony in 720 and in Alemannia and Bavaria in 725. Eudo of Aquitaine requested help during the siege of Toulouse in 720, but Charles delayed taking action because he was still involved in fighting the Saxons in the East.

11. Eudo's troops formed only a small portion of Charles Martel's army, but they were less disciplined than the Frankish troops, which consisted mostly of infantry. The Frankish army took up a position where the terrain protected its flanks thus preventing the Saracens from executing their favourite tactic of turning the flanks. Each army is estimated at about 15,000 to 20,000 men. Another key factor in these wars were the old Roman roads, which served both sides and remained the key line of communications in Western Europe.

12. Charles Martel introduced the use of archers who played an important role in siege warfare when bows became more effective. The Franks relied on a solid phalanx as an infantry formation, which, unlike the Greek phalanx, consisted of men closely packed together rather than lines of men wielding spears.

13. Eudo, already in his late 70s or early 80s, took back Aquitaine and died in 735. He was succeeded by his son Hunoald, who was followed by his son Waiffre in 745. Charlemagne took control of Aquitaine in the late 770s.

14. It is also possible that his troops lacked the necessary skills and that scaling ladders and rams were not sufficient to take the formidable defences of the city. However, Peter Purton claims in *Early Medieval Sieges* that Charles' army came fully equipped with siege machinery.

15. Encircling defences, also known as circumvallation, were not a new method in siege warfare. One of the most famous examples was Julius Caesar's at Alesia in 52 BC. He also built a wall of contravallation to protect the rear of his wall of circumvallation from a relief force. In most cases, the siege works were not actual walls, but could take a variety of shapes, such earthen positions, palisades and such.

16. It is not clear how the city's defences were linked to the coast or how much the coastline has changed since then.

17. The 'Do Nothing' Merovingian king, Theuderic IV, died in 737 and the Pope, under pressure from the Lombards who threatened Rome, asked Charles Martel for help in exchange for recognition of his domination of the kingdom of the Franks. At his death in October 741, Charles divided his kingdom among his sons: Pippin, Carloman and Gripho. Two of the brothers disinherited Gripho, who fled to Laon and surrendered after a short siege in 742. In 743, Gripho fled to Saxony and then to Bavaria after the fortress of Seeburg surrendered to his brothers. Pippin and Carloman put Childeric III, the last Merovingian, on the throne in 743 after leaving it vacant for years. Duke Hunoald of Aquitaine quickly took an oath of loyalty when the Franks invaded his land in 745. In 747 Carloman entered the monastic life. Childeric III, deposed in 751,

was sent to a monastery and Pope Zachary acknowledged Pippin the Short as the first Carolingian king of the Franks. The Frankish army seemed virtually unstoppable, thanks to the heavy cavalry created by Charles Martel, but the Arabs remained a major problem.

18. As Lombard king from 749 to 756 he took Ravenna in 751 and other lands of the Pope.

19. The Abbasids overthrew the Umayyads in 750 and took over the Caliphate ruling the Islamic world. They even attempted to negotiate with Charlemagne to fight the Umayyads.

20. Ansemundus joined forces with Pippin and was killed outside Narbonne.

21. Bourbon is a town south-east of Bourges in central France. It is about half-way between Bourges and Clermont

22. Chantelle is north of Clermont. It is between Bourbon and Clermont.

23. Clermont-Farrand was the main city in the Auvergne. The region was located in the Massif Central that formed a major barrier in north-east Aquitaine and included Bourbon and Chantelle. The Massif borders the northern frontier of Septimania.

24. Located about midway between Poitiers and Angers and about midway between Bourges and the coast it was a town with a well-sited old Roman fort only described as possibly the strongest position in Aquitania.

25. See Bernard Bachrach's *Early Carolingian Warfare* or the more difficult to obtain *Chronicle of Fredegar* for additional details. This was Pippin's best-documented siege and demonstrated the skills of the Franks in siege warfare.

26. As previously mentioned, there is no consensus among historians that the Franks were able to raise such a large force. The number could be closer to about 5,000 or less for extended operations.

27. The Franks and the Anglo-Saxons put the responsibility of maintaining roads and bridges on the shoulders of communities and even the Church. However, this did not prevent some roads from deteriorating since the locals did not employ Roman road-building methods.

28. Not much is known of Fredega Continuator. The actual name of this chronicler is unknown and it may refer to several chroniclers since this work mainly covers the previous century.

29. According to some accounts, it was not the son of Waiffre but rather his father who returned from exile at a monastery.

30. Greek Fire helped defeat the Umayyad army this time.

31. Byzantium financed their campaign to destroy the Gepids in 567, which revealed Byzantium's inability to maintain is frontiers or to clean out the remaining Ostrogoth strongholds in the Italian Peninsula. Narses was recalled in 566.

32. The location of this fortress was either near Parma on the north bank of the Po or at Lake Como.

33. The last Exarch (Byzantine governor), who administered Imperial control of Italy and Dalmatia from Ravenna, was killed and Byzantine control over northern Italy and Rome was broken. This eventually led to the creation of the Papal States after Charlemagne dealt with the Lombards later in the century.

34. His cavalry did not consist of the heavily-armed knights that appeared at the end of the Dark Ages. There is no consensus among historians about how much of the Frankish army actually consisted of cavalry, especially before the mass use of the stirrup in the ninth century.

35. The Vikings fought mostly on foot. However, the Norsemen allowed to settle in Normandy in the ninth century created the feudal armoured knight and the tactics associated with him.

36. Little information is available on Tortosa (Dortosa) although some claim it was one of the strongest fortresses in Spain. This port city was a centre of wealth. Roman legionary veterans established it in 1 BC. It probably had a Roman wall maintained in good condition. The Muslims took it between AD 713 and 718. New fortifications were built in the High Middle Ages and no traces of the old defences survive today. No adequate plans have been published.

37. The 'March' or 'Mark' referred to the frontiers or borderlands between realms. These were disputed areas administered by a count, marquis or margrave, depending on the country.

38. Lothair retained the title of Holy Roman Emperor and the central section (northern Italy, Provence, Burgundy, Alsace-Lorraine, the Low Countries) of the Empire. Louis the German held the lands east of the Rhine known as East Francia. Louis the Stammerer (877–9) took over West Francia when his father, Charles the Bald, died. Louis the Stammerer's son replaced him as Louis III (879–82) and his brother Carloman II replaced him in 882.In 884, on the death of Carloman, Charles the Fat, King of East Francia since 882, was given West Francia and reunited Charlemagne's old empire for a short time until he was removed in 888.

39. The Swedish Vikings are associated mostly with going east through Slavic lands to Byzantinum.

40. These raiders are believed to have been Norwegian Vikings operating out of Ireland.

41. There is no extant description of this fortress.

42. His account can be found in Gwyn Jones' *A History of the Vikings* and Charles Stanton's *Medieval Maritime Warfare*.

43. Various sources may have conflated this raid with the activities of the Viking Hastein who supposedly did the same thing and sailed into the Mediterranean in 859.

44. The *Anglo-Saxon Chronicle* lists the numbers of Viking ships used in their operations, but it probably exaggerated the size of their forces, which varied. However, chroniclers seem to agree that the average ship carried eighty men. During the ninth century, most Viking fleets averaged thirty to fifty ships. Some raiding parties numbered only a few ships while others are claimed to have consisted of 100 or more. See Sawyer's *Vikings* for a complete list or any edition of the *Anglo-Saxon Chronicle*.

45. Some consider this the Ragnar Lodbrok of legend. Losses come from the eleventh-century *The Annals of Xanten*.

46. In *Medieval Maritime Warfare*, Charles Stanton references these attacks from the *Annals of St-Bertin* (Kindle e-book location 5023). In *The Vikings and their Enemies* Philip Line mentions that Frankish illustrations show archers in the defence of Paris in 857 (Kindle e-book location 3121).

47. Hedeby was at the head of the Sliefjord and that fjord alone was about the same length as the Danewirke.

48. The stone wall is a more impressive work, but it is beyond the scope of this book. The dating for sections of the wall has been pushed back during archaeological research in the twenty-first century.

49. Recent archaeological discoveries indicate that the dyke may have been built as early as the fourth century, during the Roman occupation. Its measurements vary widely and they are mostly based on estimates.

50. The *Burghal Hidage*, compiled in the tenth century by Alfred's son, listed thirty-three burhs and their defence requirements. The largest burhs were located at Chichester, Cricklade, Exeter, Malmesbury, Oxford, Sashes, Southark, Wallingford, Wareham, Warwick, Wilton, Winchester and Worchester. Their walls varied from 1,000m (0.6 miles) to a little over 3,000m (1.9 miles) in length. Over sixty burhs were built during the ninth and tenth centuries. The Vikings of Danelaw had fewer than a dozen fortified towns, which included York, Lincoln, Nottingham, Derby, Leicester, Stamford, Thetford and Northampton. Most were probably older fortified sites. York served as the capital. After the Battle of Tettenhall in 910 the Danes were left leaderless. In 919, Ragnald – a Norwegian Viking from Ireland – seized York, but he was driven out in 927 by a Saxon king. Northumbria became a battleground between the Irish Vikings, the Scots and the Saxons until 944, when the Saxons gained the upper hand. Eric Bloodaxe, exiled from Norway, retook York in 948 until he was driven out by the English.

51. The *Anglo-Saxon Chronicle* and other sources give various names to the large Viking army that assembled in the ninth century. Some refer to it as the Great Heathen Army.

52. See Bernard Scholz's *Carolingian Chronicles* for a translation.

53. Fronsac is located on a tributary of the Garonne north-east of Bordeaux. Today the 'castle' Charles built has been identified as a fortified camp, most likely turf-and-timber, on a mound.

54. Nicholas Hooper and Matthew Bennett claim that despite massive undefended Carolingian palaces, 'town walls seem to have been non-existent in the earlier ninth century, the old Roman walls having been used as quarries' and that Paris was the exception. Reims and Laon had no defences or wooden walls like Le Mans and Tours and were burned by the Vikings in 882 (*Cambridge Illustrated Atlas of Warfare; The Middle Ages*, p. 33).

55. Abbo was a Benedictine monk at the Abbey Germain-des-Prés located on the Left Bank on the outskirts of the Paris.

56. According to Stewart Baldwin (http://www.rootsweb.ancestry.com/~medieval/danking.htm) Sigfred III was king of the Danes from 873–87 (dates vary). He became a Christian in 882, but this may have been another Sigfred and not him.

57. Some sources put these events in 866.

58. Between 859 and 862 Hastein raided the Mediterranean from Spain to southern France to North Africa. He wintered at the mouth of the Rhône and attacked Arles and further north. He tried to take Rome using a ruse having his men claim he was dead and wanted a Christian burial. They took him into the city in a coffin and at the burial site he popped out of the coffin and stabbed the bishop as his men took the city by surprise. Soon he discovered he had made a mistake. The city he had taken was Luni and not Rome. He was defeated off of Iberia and moved overland to take Pamplona. Returning to the Atlantic, he later he took Angers and participated in raids in Francia and England

59. Peter Sawyer associates Charles defence of the Upper Seine and Upper Loire successful enough to result in the Vikings to go unchecked, ravaging the regions of the Lower Seine and Lower Loire and then turning toward England in the 860s with their 'Great Army' (*Kings and Vikings*, pp. 90–1).

60. An English translation of the section on the siege of Paris in the *Annals of St. Vaast* can be found in James Robinson's *Readings in European History*, pp. 163–9.

61. Some sources believe there may have been some type of tower or turret on the bridges in addition to the tower at each end of the bridge. There may have been some type of castra with the tower on the right bank.

62. Some remains of the stone foundations of the Roman walls have been excavated, which only indicates they were close to the shoreline but does not give any clue as to their size.

63. Sawyer, *Kings and Vikings*, p. 88.

64. A Roman legionary fortress averaged from 10 ha to 15 ha (25 acres to 37.5 acres) and comfortably held up to 6,000 men. Timothy Reuter estimates that the largest towns in northern Europe had populations of no more than 15,000 to 20,000 (Keen, *Medieval Warfare*, p. 30). Paris probably numbered fewer than 15,000 inhabitants. It is doubtful that the island held more than 11,000 civilians and troops at the time since that would be one person for about every $9m^2$. Habitable space would have been smaller if one accounts for roads, streets, buildings, storage facilities, etc. In addition, sufficient food would be needed requiring storage and even gardens. Thus, including civilians and soldiers it is probable that there were no more than 6,000 people in Paris during the eight-month siege. Based on Reuter's numbers and the fact that there were few Viking settlements, mostly villages, it is also unlikely that the invasion force consisted of more than 5,000 to 10,000 men collected from many villages especially since not every able bodied man could be taken from each village.

65. Based on what we know of Rome, we can assume that Roman city walls did not reach a maximum height and that there were fewer towers along river frontage since the Romans assumed that the river itself provided enough protection.

66. Jim Bradbury claims that the work on this fortified bridge began in 870, but was incomplete at the time of the siege (*Medieval Siege*, p. 45).

67. Dass, *Viking Attacks on Paris*, p. 33.

68. All sources agree the lower part of the tower was of stone and this may have been the foundation and first level. It also could have been the first two levels, but we do not know how high it was.

69. Charles Stanton in *Medieval Maritime Warfare* quotes medievalist Carroll Gilmore who calculated not more than 5,000 to 8,000 men with each ship carrying only about 26 men (Kindle e-book location 5593).

70. Some sources claim February, but Abbo's dates are not clear. In fact, his account is not very reliable, so it is best to summarize some of the things he relates.

71. A Roman formation consisting of the closely-grouped troops holding shields over their heads to protect themselves from enemy missiles

72. Jim Bradbury claims there were three (*Medieval Sieges*, p. 45).

73. Charles the Simple was crowned at Reims and became Odo's rival and took over West Francia on his death in 898.

Chapter 5

1. Hugh was a direct descendant of Robert the Strong, the brother of Odo the Count of Paris. Robert had revolted against Charles the Bald in 859 and afterwards fought against the Bretons and Vikings in the 860s.

2. There is no conclusive proof as to whether Rollo was of Norwegian or Danish decent.

3. Known as William the Bastard (c. 1027–87), he was the only son of Duke Robert I (Robert the Devil) and illegitimate. He was born in the castle at Falaise.

4. William's force consisted mainly of adventurers from Brittany, Flanders, Aquitaine and other regions on the promise of sharing the spoils. Thus, his small army of archers, foot soldiers and cavalrymen may be considered a professional mercenary force, which offered an advantage over typical feudal levies of the time.

5. William the Conqueror was succeeded by his son William II 'Rufus' in 1087 who was followed by Henry I in 1100, another of William I's sons. Then in 1135 came Stephen, a child of William I's daughter, who engaged in a nineteen-year civil war with the daughter of Henry I, Matilda. Upon his death in 1154 he was replaced by Henry II, son of the Plantagenet count of Anjou who was married to Matilda. Henry married the ex-wife of the French king, Eleanor of Aquitaine, who came with her lands.

6. Otto's father Henry the Fowler (Heinrich der Finkler), had been elected king of East Francia in 919 when the last Carolingian king died. Otto succeeded him in 936. He was crowned Holy Roman Emperor by the Pope in 962 thus founding the Holy Roman Empire or First Reich.

7. No description of the castle is given and it is not the famous thirteenth-century Scaliger Castle at Sirmione.

8. At this battle, the Papal forces numbered over 6,000 men and the Normans about 3,500 (about 3,000 Norman cavalry and allied infantry). This was the first time the various Norman bands assembled into a large force. In 1074, Pope Gregory VII excommunicated Robert Guiscard for raiding Papal lands, but in 1084, he came to the pope's aid and forced Holy Roman Emperor Heinrich IV from Rome.

9. The term castrum/castra is easily translated into castle and often used in the Middle Ages, but the Roman term did not refer to a privately-owned fort or fortress.

10. Regis Faucon and Yves Lescroart point out that after 1091, the seigneur (feudal noble) had the right to fortify his manor house against attack. The seigneurial enclosure 'Constructed with or without outbuildings, the logis originally consisted of a simple square wooden tower standing on an earth motte encircled by ditches and light defences. The outer bailey, generally not as well defended, enclosed outhouses, garrets, cowsheds, stables and a cider press, all of which were usually centred on the dovecote. This arrangement developed fully during the 15th century…' (Faucon and Lescroart, *Manor Houses in Normandy*, p. 17).

11. Hill, *Charles the Bald's Edict of Pîtres*, p. 154.

12. Davis, 'English Licenses to Crenellate: 1199-1567', pp. 228–30. Kings, counts and dukes in Europe often licensed the construction of fortifications.

13. In the twelfth century, the fiefs of the Count of Champagne provided 2,300 knights, but he was only required to send ten to the king (Beeler, *Warfare in Feudal Europe*, p. 37).

14. Kings, duke, counts and lesser noblemen often had to depend on mercenaries or paid soldiers to garrison their castles and perform other duties. These soldiers for hire often included landless noblemen and actual professionals without class distinction.

15. Maiden Castle goes back to the Bronze Age and in the fifth century BC it was enlarged and was in use during the Roman occupation.

16. The French term donjon refers the keep. The term keep was not applied until after the Middle Ages, but is generally used when describing medieval castles.

17. This castle was only discovered in the late 1960s when the site was being bulldozed (Brown, *Castles from the Air*, pp. 32–3).

18. Fulk III was known as 'the Black' for his reputation for savagery and ruthlessness, although he was also supposed to be very pious. He supported the Capetian dynasty and was a bitter enemy of Odo II (Eudes II) of Blois. Fulk's first victory was in 992 over Duke Conan I of Brittany who later died in battle. Fulk went on to fight Count Hugh III of Maine and Odo II of Blois, who opposed King Hugh Capet.

19. If the soil layer was thin and the subsoils were not silts or clays or the bedrock was close to the surface and consisted of limestone, sandstone, granite etc., revetments might not be needed.

20. A word derived from Norman French for a walled enclosure.

21. Simpler ringworks that consisted of a moat and palisade enclosing an area with structures could also be considered a castle if it included the residence of the owner.

22. After the medieval era, in the sixteenth century, it became known as a 'keep' in England.

23. Americans refer to the ground floor as the first floor, while the British refer to the first floor as the floor above the ground floor.

24. Goodall, *The English Castle 1066-1650*, p. 51.

25. This information comes from Malcolm Hislop's *Castle Builders*, a comprehensive study of mottes and other features of mainly English motte-and-bailey castles as well as other types of castles based on archaeological and historic evidence mainly in England.

26. William the Conqueror had built a fort on the site in 1070 and it appears a Saxon burh existed there before that. Late-twentieth century archaeological work uncovered the remains of this massive motte and bailey.

27. Galleried battlements extending over the wall, like hoardings on a stone wall, allowed the defender to control the base of the wall by dropping rocks and missiles on the assailants. Some still refer to these galleries as hoardings, although they are not exactly the same as on stone fortifications where they were only temporary structures. On wooden fortifications they were part the wall. The archaeology of the site reveals the foundation post holes showing the trace of an indented approach to the gate, but the height of towers and gate towers and the existence of overhanging battlements can only be left to conjecture.

28. Higham and Barker, *Timber Castles*, p. 199.

29. Until recently Loches was dated almost a century after Fulk Nerra, but now he is credited with its construction.

30. Bisson, 'Feudalism in Twelfth-Century Catalonia', p. 174.

31. Beeler, *Warfare in Feudal Europe*, pp. 155–6.

32. Talus, plinth, batter and spur are generally the same feature, but talus specifically refers to the sloping effect. The terms are often used interchangeably. Batter actually refers to thickening the base of the wall or tower. When it is steeply sloped it is called a plinth. A more curved slope is known as talus. See Glossary.

33. Some historians claim it is a myth and the stairs did not turn this way to give the defender the advantage.

34. In *The Castle Explorer's Guide*, Frank Bottomley defines a solar as a well-lit parlour on any level facing south or a room for the lord with windows located in an inaccessible side of the keep. In *How to Read Castles*, Hislop also defines it as a private room on an upper floor.

35. Colchester Castle has a similar design, but a larger floor plan. It is now partially in ruins and its upper levels are gone. In *The English Castle* (p. 81), John Goodall reports

that excavations at Ivry la Bataille began in the late 1960s, revealing the remains of a great tower similar in layout to the White Tower and Colchester, except that the chapel was on the north-east corner. The structure at Ivry appears to date from the end of the tenth century.

36. According to legend, this area included an isolated cell known as 'Little Ease' which was too small to stand or lie in comfortably.

37. Terms like keep, great tower and donjon are used interchangeably like a number of others terms referring to castles, although most were not used in the medieval era. Often they are used in this way to create more colourful prose.

38. In English, the term machicoulis applies to the bretèche as well as to the machicolations, whereas in French it does not.

39. Malcolm Hislop claims the use of ashlar became widespread in Europe by 1100 (*How to Read Castles*, p. 54).

40. This technique dates back to Ancient Greece.

Chapter 6

1. Robert rose up against his father with backing of the French king. William died during the siege of Mantes.

2. The castle was probably a motte and bailey on a hill above the town. Robert was imprisoned for the remainder of his life and died at Cardiff Castle in 1134. A powerful nobleman, Robert II de Belèsme, joined Robert at Tinchebray and fled when the army was defeated. He held territory south of Normandy including forty castles (most probably motte-and-bailey). He held castles between Alençon and Domfront. In 1110–12, another revolt, this time of Norman barons, threatened Henry I. Robert II was sent to negotiate and he was made a prisoner for the rest of his life. According to Ordericus Vitalius, Robert II was an evil and brutal man, but his views may have been biased. Vitalius may have confused Robert II with Robert I de Belèsme who seems to have lived at the time of the events that inspired the legend of Robert the Devil.

3. Matilda was married to the Holy Roman Emperor, which earned her the nickname of Empress Maude. After his death she married Geoffrey Plantagenet, Count of Anjou.

4. Only his sons John and Richard were still alive in 1189.

5. Richard was already experienced in siege warfare. See section on Castle Warfare below.

6. The castle probably consisted of a keep, several towers on the enceinte, but little is left other than a circular keep built after the death of Richard. The castle controlled the road from Limoges-Perigueux that led to Bordeaux.

7. Bradbury, *Medieval Sieges*, p. 71.

8. Bradbury details Geoffrey's sieges beginning in 1136 with the attacks on Le Sap and Falaise in 1138, which ended in failure. However, Geoffrey also won several victories that included Fontaine in 1140, Avranches and Coutances in 1141, Verneuil and Vaudreuil in 1143, Rouen in 1144 and Arques in 1145 (Bradbury, *Medieval Sieges*, p. 73.)

9. These castles are not worth naming since like many others little to no descriptions remain. In addition, many of the castles that fell during the numerous sieges are seldom described since detailed records are not available and many were rebuilt with different features and configurations.

10. Another example of a castle destroyed and rebuilt.

11. Located north of Saintes and south-east of Rochefort, the castle of Pons was rebuilt as a large tower in 1187 and was later modified into its present form.
12. Mclynn, *Richard & John*, p.56.
13. Young Henry, in league with the French king, held Limoges. Young Henry went on the offensive when the siege lifted and died of a fever in June 1183.
14. The Byzantines invented Greek Fire; its exact ingredients are unknown. It is also not known how close the formula used in the West was to the original. It was an ancient version of modern napalm. Water made it burn even more fiercely.
15. His allies had already put the castle under siege.
16. Fréteval, north of Tours, included one of the first large round donjons built in about 1100.
17. The castle at Dieppe, built in 1188 by Henry II and Richard, was destroyed by Philippe in 1195. The town walls were not built until about 1350.
18. The Vexin was a county about 20km (12.4 miles) from Rouen.
19. Henry made Becket, a commoner and his friend, Chancellor. Becket helped him control England with the creation of an early civil service and a restoration of law and order. To weaken control of the church, Henry had Beckett, not a cleric, made Archbishop of Canterbury. As the saying goes Becket 'found God'.
20. Conan IV's daughter married Geoffrey, Henry's son and then Henry forced Conan to abdicate in favor of Geoffrey. Henry acted as his son's regent until the he came of age.
21. Henry gave his sons no holdings from which to acquire funds and this led to their resentment.
22. Years earlier William II of England had built a timber and turf ringwork at Carlisle on the site of an old Roman fort behind Hadrian's Wall and destroyed by the Danes in the ninth century. An earthwork with three gates protected the town. In 1122 Henry I had the castle rebuilt in stone with a keep. The Scots had captured the town, but soon lost it in 1157 and then Henry II had a gatehouse added and divided the castle into two wards.
23. Charles Oman wrote that there were thirty royal castles by 1100 either inside or adjacent to town walls including the Tower of London, Cambridge, Chester, Colchester, Exeter, Cloucester, Hereford, Lincoln, Old Sarum, Winchester, Worchester, Chester and York dominating population centers. Others were at strategic points like Dover, Portchester, Scarborough and Orford. Oman noted the kings attempted to acquire a private castles built at strategic points. On the other hand, the baronial castles built to control a vassal's fief, often were located in not easily accessible sites making them more difficult to conquer (Oman, *Castles*, pp. 11–12).
24. Goodall, *The English Castle*, pp. 137–8.
25. A keep was built in the fifteenth century.
26. The castle twice resisted two sieges in the 1173 and 1174 and claims to be the only Northumberland castle to resist the Scots. The 7.3m x 6.1m (20ft x 24ft) keep was 3m (10ft) thick and received another story in the next century with a barbican added early in the fourteenth century.
27. The castle's claim to fame is not from this war, but from being featured as Hogwarts in the Harry Potter films.
28. One of the two 24m (80ft) high lighthouses still remains.

29. Little is known about Maurice's background, only that he was a skilled and well-paid engineer.
30. By comparison, Henry's construction of Orford castle cost 23 per cent that of Dover while his son Richard a decade later spent almost 20 per cent more for Château Gaillard which he had built in a record time of about two to three years. Henry's keep at Newcastle cost about 16 per cent of the bill for the keep at Dover (which alone was about two-thirds the cost of Dover Castle).
31. The forebuilding now has a roof.
32. Goodall points out that Maurice's' smaller keep at Newcastle was similar with the arrangement of the forebuilding and the water supply (Goodall, *English Castle*, p. 141).
33. The keep went through many alterations, including the mounting of guns on the roof in the Late Middle Ages.
34. Today it has been replaced with a flat roof level with the battlements.
35. This tower may not have been built until the 1190s.
36. Most of the tower names are relatively recent such as the Tour du Moulin which in modern times had a windmill on top, the Boissy Tower from the sixteenth-century governors and the Dogs Tower which was located next to the kennels.
37. Philip was heavily in debt to the Templars and confiscated their property in France.
38. Suger, abbot of St. Denis, wrote there was a wooden keep, but French historian Yves Burand claimed there is no proof.
39. Geoffrey Plantagenet became Count of Anjou when his father left for the Holy Land. He married Matilda, daughter of King Henry I, in 1128. In 1135 she invaded England to challenge Stephen for the throne while her husband began the conquest of Normandy. Their son became Henry II of England, but in 1151 was Duke of Normandy.
40. By the treaty, Richard agreed that Les Andelys, property of the Archbishopric of Rouen, would not be fortified and neither king would claim sovereignty over it. Richard broke the agreement three months later and began construction of his new castle. The archbishop's protest and order of interdiction were overridden by the Pope who took King Richard's side. As compensation, Richard gave the archbishop the castle of Louviers and the town of Dieppe (Scudamore, *Normandy*, p. 70).
41. Viollet-le-Duc probably exaggerated when he claimed it took one year. Even two years would have been fast; the construction might have lasted much longer than two years.
42. According to Viollet-le-Duc, the site lacked decorations, but Dan Snow claims that this was a Roman construction method for city walls and that Henry II used it to return to the 'power and grandeur of Rome' on the keep at Dover, while Edward I did the same at Caernarfon (Snow, *Battle Castles*, Kindle e-book location 1148).
43. The machicoulis (stone machicolations) at Château Gaillard are thought to be the first to appear in Western Europe and that they were inspired by Richard's Holy Land experiences. They are of the slot type and appear only on the keep. Wooden hoardings were used on the towers of the curtain walls.
44. Philip Warner in *Sieges of the Middle Ages* more aptly describes the curtain as consisting of convex buttresses about one meter apart giving the defenders a number of semicircular positions on the battlements that allowed coverage along the face of the wall.

45. According to some critics, allowing the enemy to attack from higher ground was a poor decision on Richard's part because it gave the enemy a superior position for observation. However, the weapons of the time were relatively short-ranged, which limited the enemy's advantage.

46. The term, derived from Old French, means 'to hit forward' or, in modern terms, 'advanced position'.

47. John was neither a fool nor an incompetent military leader. Unfortunately for him, his actions, such as campaigning in Brittany while Philippe II prepared to invade Normandy, sometimes gave that impression. His mistakes outweigh his successes.

48. Some had resorted to cannibalism and were so far gone that that the food the French gave them finished them off.

49. Part of the tower remains today. Some sources claim these towers also had mangonels on top to counter the enemy's siege engines, but most drawings of the towers show them all to be roofed and not making that a practical option, although they could have mounted ballistae.

50. No sources have an exact number for the garrison. Dan Snow in *Battle Castles* states there were 40 knights, plus sergeants, crossbowmen and others and estimates the full complement would have been about 300.

Chapter 7

1. William the Conqueror was not born in either of these.

2. See *Castle Builders* by Malcolm Hislop for other keeps with a similar interior.

3. In the nineteenth century, oubliettes were identified as dungeons where prisoners were put never to be seen again. In most cases, however, prisoners were kept at the highest level of a keep or tower. See Glossary.

4. As Philippe cast his eyes on Aquitaine, Alfonso VIII of Castile invaded Gascony claiming it by marriage and John watched his last French holdings slip from his grasp.

5. In 1215, Hugh became the castellan of Canterbury and Dover Castles.

6. Archbishop Hubert Walter's death that month resulted in a dispute to select his replacement. Pope Innocent III, against the wishes of John, picked Stephen Langton in 1207. He then issued an order of interdiction creating more problems for John.

7. Later, the English built Conway Castle on the estuary across from it.

8. Most sources call it 'powerful' but it seems Philippe II ordered Guillaume des Roches to build it late in the twelfth century and few details exist about it other than it withstood several sieges and was dismantled in the Wars of Religion and only a single tower remains.

9. Bouvines is an example of why major engagements were avoided unless one side was certain of victory. Of course, if victory was assured, the opponent would not fight. These battles most often were a roll of the dice and the winner, as in this case, could secure territory without long costly sieges. On the other hand, the loser often found this might conclude a conflict since great losses would leave one side without an army. Thus, risking a major field battle was seldom desirable.

10. The four keeps were somewhat similar in layout including forebuilding, four corner towers and a spine or cross wall dividing the keep resulting in two large rooms instead of one on each level. England has other somewhat similar impressive residential keeps.

11. William left his son Robert Curthose title to Normandy and Rufus, his favorite son, England.

12. Other castles involved included Tonbridge Castle that fell in two days and Pevensey Castle that held out for six weeks. Robert Curthose failed to come or send an army needed to support the revolt.

13. Boley Hill was on the south side of the town outside the old Roman city wall. The castle occupied the south-west corner of the remains of the old Roman wall and Roman Watling Street that lead to London passed through those Roman walls just north of the castle. The first Norman castle was on Boley Hill.

14. Corfe, built on a hill overlooking the town in a gap in a line of chalk hills was a formidable castle with a stone keep built by Henry I with three levels and no corner turrets. The castle withstood a siege by Stephen before Henry I initiated these impressive works which when complete included an inner bailey and three others with about ten curtain towers and two impressive gatehouses. In the seventeenth century Parliament had it demolished.

15. Shrewsbury was a motte and timber castle that finally collapsed by 1271 and was replaced by a stone castle. The timber donjon did not even have a palisade until 1229 so it is not possible to determine how strong a position this was although a town wall may have linked the tower with the Severn River securing one flank (Higham, *Timber Castles*, p. 138).

16. Newark was a wooden twelfth-century castle converted to stone later in the century when it acquired high walls and an impressive gatehouse. Henry had to lay siege to it for eight days to take it from one of John's knights.

17. The term 'men-at-arms' refers to knights and squires. Esquires or squires originally were shield bearers. They were often the sons of noblemen training to become knights. In most cases, archers, sergeants, hobilars who served as light cavalry and rode unprotected horses and others were not considered to be men-at-arms.

18. Berkhamsted, located NW of London, was a motte and bailey with a three storey stone keep. The motte was 12m (39.3ft) high and its enceinte included two water filled ditches. The enceinte enclose 4.5 ha (11 acres).

19. As a child, Simon V went with his father on the Albigensian Crusade. His father, Simon IV, died at Toulouse.

20. Burl, *God's Heretics*, Kindle e-book location 1115.

21. The name Albigensian was derived from the city of Albi where the Cathars had established their faith.

22. Panouillé, *Carcassonne*, pp. 11–15.

23. The types of siege engines are not identified but probably included perriers (stone-throwers with a man-powered sling), mangonels (beam-type stone throwers using a sling) or trebuchets (a large beam-type stone-thrower using a counterweight). Ballistas are mentioned, but these are giant crossbow-like machines and of little value against walls.

24. Many sources mention that the Cathar castles located in the mountains where they suffered from lack of water and depended on rain filling their cisterns. The same comment has been made about Carcassonne, although it was not in the mountains. At least one source claims there was no water shortage when the town surrendered.

25. It is not clear how many of the knights were serving feudal obligations and how many were there for forgiveness. Most French sources emphasize the forty-day service and

that was the length of a siege the defenders prepared for. In some cases knights and their retinues might leave on completion of service while others were just arriving. On the true crusades in the Holy Land feudal service did not come into play.

26. Tour Régine was built circa 1260 as the fourth castle.

27. There is disagreement on this subject. Burl, author of *God's Heretics*, uses sources that claim there were three trebuchets (only one large) and several mangonels. 'Bad Neighbour' seems to have been a common nickname for trebuchets. Prince Louis had a trebuchet of the same name at the siege of Dover.

28. Narbonne was under the Church. The legate Arnaud Amaury took revenge and excommunicated Simon de Montfort.

29. Few sources agree, but some concluded the city was surrounded by double walls; an old square enceinte based on the Roman walls and a newer round one, with a moat between them filled by water from the nearby Durançole and Sorgue rivers. This was largely destroyed after Louis VIII's siege of the city. The final set of medieval walls had twelve gates with square towers and drawbridges plus thirty-six more towers and fifty-six watchtowers (Source: Municipal Archives of Avignon: http://archives. avignon.fr).

30. Another son, also named Simon, claimed his English inheritance and joined and later revolted against King Henry III of England.

31. Seneschal in France often refers to the King's administrator for a city or a principal advisor.

32. For additional details, see Ornes, 'Report to Blanche of Castile on the siege of Carcassonne, 13 October 1240' in *Carcassonne: Le temps des sieges* by Jean-Pierre Panouille.

33. King Louis pardoned him in 1247 and together they went on a crusade to Egypt.

34. Sources vary as to whether the work was done in 1202 when a Cathar deacon requested it, in the 1230s or after the rebellion of 1240 began.

35. The French campsite was located near the modern-day parking lot for tourists and a short distance from the memorial to the Cathars.

36. There is some question regarding the range of the mangonels and trebuchets. Most experts agree that torsion-powered mangonels had a range of a little under 200m (219 yds) whereas counterweight trebuchets should have had a greater range. In both cases, the besiegers were only within range of the first barrier of wooden palisades below the castle and when they reached the Tour l'Est, they were probably within range of the next line of palisades.

37. The chroniclers do not agree on when or how the Tour de l'Est fell. In fact, there is little agreement about the months when these events took place or how long it took the besiegers to get their trebuchets in place. According to sources, the Gascons did not reach the Roc de la Tour until January.

Chapter 8

1. Robert brought 12 knights and 3,000 other men to defeat Prince Rhys at Herwenorgan. Robert, with his Welsh ally, then attacked Cardiff and this completed his conquest of Glamorgan. (Source: British History Online, 'The winning of Glamorgan: Documents', published Cardiff Records Committee, Cardiff, 1903, pp. 6–47.)

2. Dafydd is Welsh for David.

3. In England, Simon de Montfort, son of the elder Simon de Montfort who died in the Albigensian Crusade, had become Henry III's trusted friend and later turned

against him taking him and his son Edward I prisoner after the Battle of Lewes in 1264. Llywelyn signed a favourable treaty with Simon in 1265. However, that same year Edward and his father defeated and killed de Montfort at the Battle of Evesham.

4. William de Valence, a French nobleman and knight, became Earl of Pembroke for supporting the king in the Second Barons' War.

5. The Statute of Wales, also known as the Statute of Rhuddlan since it was issued from that castle, brought English Common Law to Wales.

6. The exact location of the first site of the castle is not known. It may have been on or near the site of a mound representing the old Roman fort north-west of the actual castle.

7. According to several historians, his idea for the lakes came from Kenilworth Castle's water defences.

8. The king put down the barons who had revolted and later the Despensers were allowed to return.

9. Builth was not finished and work stopped in 1282, Holt was turned over to a marcher lord in the 1280s and the motte-and-bailey castle at Aberystwyth (1277–89) was replaced with a concentric castle.

10. There is no consensus on the date of Master James' arrival, but according to one chronicler, it was in1278. Edward met Master James in Savoy while returning from a crusade in 1273 and was impressed with his work and brought him to England. It is possible he created the designs for the Welsh castles after the initial excavations were done. The castles he designed had two baileys, either side by side or in a concentric pattern (one inside the other) and a large gatehouse replaced the keep. His castles had high walls and projecting towers. These features were not found in all his castles maybe because their construction had started before he took over.

11. Avranches Tower of Dover Castle had unique firing positions similar to an experimental type added to the north wall that had a single embrasure that split into three loopholes on the exterior giving the archer a wider field of fire (for further details see: Friar, *Castles*, pp. 182–3).

Glossary

Allure (chemin de ronde in French and camino de ronda or adarve [from Arabic] in Spanish) – wall walk behind the parapet of a wall.

Arrow loop (archère in French, saetera in Spanish) – openings in walls or merlons for archers, see Loophole.

Ashlar – squared block of cut and shaped stone or freestone.

Atalaya (Sp.) – watchtower.

Bailey – enclosed courtyard or ward.

Bank – large mound behind the ditch of an Iron Age hillfort; palisades were often added to the inner bank.

Barbican (barbacane in French, barbacana in Spanish) – fortified outer gateway.

Barrel Vault – ceiling or roof consisting of cylindrical arches.

Bartizan – overhanging tower supported by corbelling or a buttress on a wall.

Bastide – (1) temporary fortification to support a larger complex; (2) thirteenth- and fourteenth-century fortified village and town in southern France called Villeneuve (new town) instead in northern France.

Bastille – isolated fort with tower placed in front of an entrance to an enceinte, not a barbican; generally, a temporary fort built by the besieger.

Rodemack, built between the twelfth and fourteenth centuries. Profile of walls at Porte de Sierck, which was reconstructed after being destroyed in 1944.

Bastion – tower-like structure with thick walls to resist artillery; usually not much higher than the walls; also any nondescript strongpoint of any type.

Batter – see Talus.

Battlement (almena in Spanish) – crenelated parapet at the top of a city or castle wall.

Beak or prow – angled projection forming a sharp sloping corner angle. Also, see plinth and talus.

Belfry – tall, mobile tower used in sieges.

Bergfried – freestanding fighting tower, usually associated with German fortifications.

Arrow and cannon loops: Top left: Najac – long slits most likely to provide light. Gisors: Wall tower with arrow loops – square holes for scaffolding. Middle: Arrow loops and a position for a light cannon. Bottom: Loops with circular openings for handguns. Bottom right: Cannon port in a tower.

Bartizans: Top left: An example of bartizans on Gravensteen Castle at Ghent. One is roofed, the other is not. The embrasures in this example are shuttered. They are supported on corbels and a wall buttress. Middle and bottom: These examples are atypical and very decorative. They are located at the Palace of the Popes at Avignon and are multi-level with arrow slits and larger openings.

Berm – (1) narrow path or flat area between a rampart and ditch; (2) raised bank of a canal or river.

Bretèche (also brattice in English) – machicolation covering only a door or window.

Castellum – diminutive form of the Latin castrum, replaced the original word in medieval Latin and gave rise to the terms castello (It.), castillo (Sp.), castle (Eng.), château (Fr.).

Castrum (pl. Castra) – Latin term for temporary and permanent fortified legionary camps or fort.

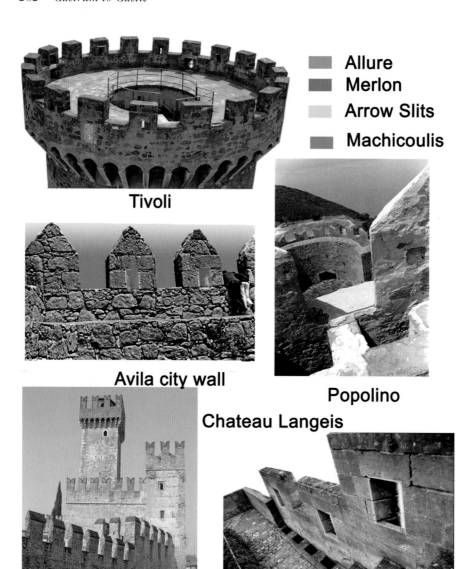

Battlements: Various types of merlons. Some had regional characteristics and others, like the swallowtail of the Ghibelline faction in Italy and the Guelph standard rectangular shape, indicated political affiliation.

Châtelet (gatehouse in English) – French term for small castle; usually gateways consisting of two connected towers with a drawbridge and portcullis, became a prominent feature during Hundred Years War and often took over the functions of the keep.

Chevauchée (O. Fr.) – raid during which plundering and pillaging are employed to weaken the enemy.

Drawbridges. Top left: Langeais has a typical drawbridge with two large beams attached to the bridge for lifting and lowering. When the bridge is raised, the beams go to a vertical position, filling the slots behind them in the wall. A third beam controls a small drawbridge for foot traffic. Top right: Similar to Montargis. Centre right: Similar drawbridge in the Verona city wall; the mechanism for operating the beams is located at the upper level. Heavy doors and one or more portcullis, which is also operated from the level above form the entrance complex. Some entrances include shooting positions in the sidewalls and murder holes in the ceiling to allow the defenders to fire on attackers trying to exit the passage, which may be blocked with doors and a portcullis. The bottom drawings show simpler types of bridges often found in outer works. The suspension method consists of a chain, usually attached to a winch, to raise and lower the gate or drawbridge.

Chemise – From the French 'shirt', wall surrounding the base close to its base; can be a shell keep surrounding a keep on a motte.

Cheval-de-frise (pl. Chevaux-de-frise) – originally, a tree trunk with projecting sharpened stakes. Later, wood and metal portable obstacles for blocking paths or confined areas; in modern times, wire replaced the sharpened stakes; also known as Frisian Horse and Spanish Rider.

Circumvallation – fortified line built around a fortification under siege and facing that position to keep the defenders from breaking out; see Contravallation.

Cistern – water reservoir to collect rainwater.

Citadel – strongpoint that may be considered a small fortress within a fortified place; usually within city walls or part of the walls.

Civitas (pl. civitates, Lat.) – township.

Contravallation – fortified line built around a line of circumvallation facing outward to prevent an enemy force from breaking through siege lines to rescue the defenders of a fortification.

Contrefort (Fr.) – buttress.

Coracha (Sp.) – wall extending from a fortified enclosure to protect access to a nearby point, such as a well.

Counterscarp (contrescarpe in French) – outer side of a moat or defensive ditch.

Crenel – opening in a wall of a building or a rampart, often found between merlons on ramparts.

Crenellations – battlements of a castle, fort or building consisting of alternating gaps (crenels) and merlons (q.v.).

Curtain or curtain wall – wall surrounding a castle, fort, fortress or city; often has corner or angle and interval towers.

Donjon (Fr.) – keep, may derive from a Celtic term meaning 'lord's tower'.

Drawbridge, pont-levis (Fr.), puente (Sp) – wood platform serving as a bridge and barrier.

Drum tower – circular tower.

Embrasure – opening in a wall, generally for weapons.

Enceinte – enclosing wall of a fortified site.

Escalade – scaling a cliff or a wall with ladders.

Échauguette – enclosed sentry box usually placed at the corner of a wall.

Fascine – bundle of brush and sticks used to protect troops digging trenches, defending trenches or to fill ditches in preparation of crossing during an assault.

Fausse braye (Fr.), falsa braga (Sp.) – low wall in front of the main wall serving as protection against artillery fire by covering the lower part of the main wall.

Forebuilding – extension or projection of a keep protecting the entrance, a stairway and entrance.

Fossa (Lat.) – defensive ditch.

Freestone – fine-grained stone that can be easily cut or shaped in any direction such as some types of limestone and sandstone; known as ashlar when cut.

Gabion – wicker basket filled with earth and/or stone.

Glacis – natural or artificial slope cleared of vegetation to allow clear fields of fire surrounding a fort or castle.

Groin vault – vault formed at the point where two barrel vaults intersect.

Hoardings, hourds (Fr.) – wooden projections with openings for dropping objects on the enemy below added to the battlements.

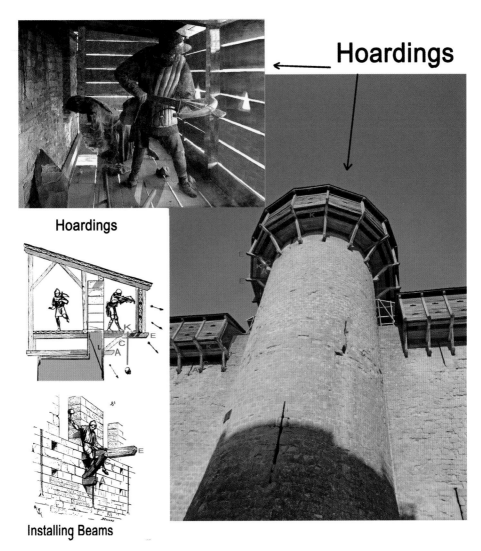

Hoardings

Hoardings

Installing Beams

Hoardings at Carcassonne. Diagram showing supports for hoardings and the initial installation process. (Photo courtesy of Rupert Harding)

Keep, donjon (Fr.), torre de homenaje or calahorra (Sp.), Bergfried (Ger.), maschio or mastio (It.) – main tower found in most early castles, could be the entire fortified position in some cases; usually served as a residence for a nobleman.

Loophole, meurtrière (Fr.) – shooting position in a wall for archers, a round opening was added or widened later to accommodate guns (see Oillet); called canonnière (Fr.), tronera (Sp.) when meant for a cannon.

Machicoulis (Fr.) – machicolations along a wall and/or tower, not to be confused with bretèche. Two types: slot formed by buttresses and corbelled by using corbells.

Machicolation – opening in a projecting stone battlement for dropping objects on attackers attempting to climb or destroy the walls.

Corbelled machicoulis: Top left: Interior and exterior view of machicoulis at Langeais showing the holes on the interior side and crenels and arrow loops in battlements. Bottom: Views of machicoulis in enclosed tower and walls in front of Langeais castle (floorboards covering the openings in centre photo). Top right: Machicoulis of the keep of Medina del Campo.

Mantlet – see Chemise.

Matacán (Sp.) – machicolation, bretèche or machicoulis.

Mine – tunnel dug beneath the wall of a fortification used that ended in a chamber where a fire was lit to collapse the wall; this technique was used since ancient times; later, explosives were used.

Moat, fossé (Fr.), fosa (Sp.) – broad ditch surrounding a fortification, often incapable of holding water.

Top: Rubble core of late thirteenth-century Denbigh castle wall in North Wales. (Photo courtesy of Bernard Lowry) *Bottom: Examples of markings left by masons.*

Murage – toll in towns under English control in the British Isles and English-occupied France for financing construction or repair of walls.

Mural tower – interval tower on a curtain wall.

Oilet or oillet – arrow loop with a circular sight hole at one end, mostly meant for artillery.

Oubliette (Fr.) – chamber at the bottom of a tower accessed through a trapdoor, may have given rise to a nineteenth-century myth that it as a prison; actually served as a storage area, a cesspool for the garderobes, some type of aeration system or an ice house.

Haupt Koenigsbourg

Wooden Wall Walk

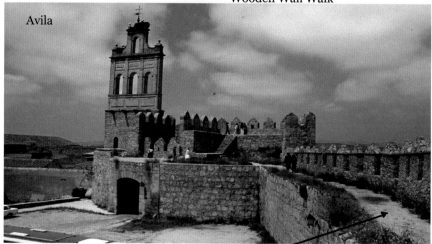

Avila

Walk Walk

Langeais

Wall walks. Top: Wooden wall walk supported by corbels behind the battlements. Middle and bottom: A more standard wall walk at the top of the curtain walls behind the battlements.

Oppidum (Lat.) – Roman walled provincial town.

Palisade – wooden fence, often made with timbers pointed at the top.

Plinth – see Talus.

Poliorcetics (Anc. Gr.) – art of siege warfare .

Portcullis, herse (Fr.), rastrillo (Sp.) – latticed grille of wood and/or metal lowered to close a gateway sometimes used in conjunction with doors and drawbridges.

Postern, poterne (Fr.) – small, often concealed doorway or gate; called sally port when large enough to allow troops through.

Praetorium (Lat.) – commanding officer's house in a Roman fort or fortress.

Principia (Lat.) – headquarters in a Roman fort or fortress.

Prow – see Beak.

Putlog holes – holes located in walls used to support scaffolding during construction, also used for the horizontal beams supporting hoardings, sometimes called sockets when meant for hoardings.

Quoin – corner or ashlar-lined corner.

Revetment – masonry facing or a retaining wall supporting a rampart.

Rib vaulting – intersection of two to three barrel vaults creating a ribbed vault,

Rubble – local stone of different sizes used in walls and various ways; the stones may be squared, laid out and held together with mortar or mixed haphazardly with cement or concrete to form the core of the wall.

Scarp, escarpe (Fr.), alambore (Sp.) – inside face of a moat or ditch.

Socket – in walls, refers to a usually square hole for the insertion of beams or joists for floors or hoardings.

Solar – room above ground level, great chamber or sitting room.

Spur – rectangular base forming a beak or plinth for a round tower; see Beak and prow.

Tabby – see Tapia.

Tapia (Sp.) – rammed earth or tabby; type of concrete commonly used for the walls of fortifications in Iberia and other regions; made of local raw materials such as earth, lime, chalk, gravel, clay and/or bone.

Talus, batter or plinth – outward slope that strengthens walls against siege machines; allows projectiles dropped from the top of the wall to roll towards the enemy.

Throat, gorge (Fr.) – rear of a fortification.

Turf-and-Timber – fortification consisting of an earthen rampart and a timber palisade; the earthen rampart generally consisted of dirt and rock excavated from the surrounding ditch. Turf consists of sod or sections of soil with grass placed on the earthen ramparts to prevent erosion of the site; it was intended to last for an indefinite period.

Tour (Fr.) – tower.

Turret – small tower on a larger tower or on battlements.

Vallum (Lat.) – earthen rampart or stone wall in Roman fortifications; ditch behind Hadrian's Wall where it includes the mounds on either side of the ditch.

Voussoir – wedge-shaped element used in building an arch or vault: each unit in an arch is a voussoir, the top one is the keystone.

Wall walk or rampart walk – walkway behind the battlements of a fort, fortress or castle; also called Allure.

Yett (Old Eng. and Scottish) – gate of wrought-iron bars forming a lattice; unlike the portcullis, it is hinged and opens like a door.

Bibliography

Alcock, Leslie. *Was this Camelot? Excavations at Cadbury Castle 1966-70*. New York: Stein & Day, 1972.

Altamira, Rafael. *Spain under the Visigoths*. Didactic Press, 2014 (ebook reprint of section from *History of Spain* published in 1911).

Anderson, William. *Castles of Europe: From Charlemagne to the Renaissance*. London: Ferndale Editions, 1980.

Andrews, Francis B. *The Mediaeval Builder and His Methods*. New York: Dorset Press, 1992.

Araguas, Philippe. 'Les châteaux des marches de Catalogne et Ribagorce (950-1100)', *Bulletin Monumental* Vol. 137, No. 3, 1979, pp. 205–24.

Ayton, Andrew and J.L. Price. *The Medieval Military Revolution*. New York: Barnes & Noble, 1995.

Bachrach, Bernard S. *Merovingian Military Organization 481-751*. Minneapolis: Univ. of Minnesota, 1972.

——. *Early Carolingian Warfare: Prelude to Empire*. Philadelphia: Univ. of Pennsylvania Press, 2001.

Beeler, John. *Warfare in Feudal Europe 730-1200*. Ithaca (NY): Cornell Univ. Press, 1971.

Bernage, Georges. *Le normandie et les Vikings*. Bayeux: Heimdal, 1992.

Bini, Monica, Alessandro Chelli, Anna Durante, Lucia Gervasini and Marta Pappalardo. 'Geoarchaelogical sea-level proxies from a silted up harbor: A case study of the Roman colony of Luni', *Quaternary International*, 2009, pp. 147–57.

Bishop, M.C. *Handbook to Roman Legionary Fortresses*. Barnsley: Pen & Sword, 2012.

Bisson, Thomas N. 'Feudalism in Twelfth-Century Catalonia', *Publications de' l'Ecole française de Rome*, Vol. 44, No. 1, 1980, pp. 173–92.

Bottomley, Frank. *The Castle Explorer's Guide*. New York: Avenel Books, 1979.

Bradley, Henry. *The Story of the Goths*. Perennial Press, 2016 (reprint of 1887 ed.).

Bradbury, Jim. *The Medieval Siege*. Woodbridge: Boydell Press, 1992.

——. *Philip Augustus: King of France 1180-1223*. New York: Routledge, 1998.

——. *The Routledge Companion to Medieval Warfare*. New York: Routledge, 2004.

Breeze, David J. *The Frontiers of Imperial Rome*. Barnsley: Pen & Sword, 2011.

Brown, R. Allen. *Rochester Castle*. London: HMSO, 1969.

——, *Dover Castle*. London: HMSO, 1979.

——. *Castles from the Air*. Cambridge: Cambridge University Press, 1989.

——, et. al. *Castles: A History and Guide*. Poole: Blandford Press, 1980.

Bruand, Yves. 'Le château de Gisors (Principales campagnes de construction)', *Bulletin Monumental de Société Française d'Archéologie*, tome 116, n. 4, 1958, pp. 243–65.

Burl, Aubrey. *God's Heretics: The Albigensian Crusade*. Stroud: The History Press, 2013 (ebook, hardcover 2002).

Burr, William Hurbert. *Ancient and Modern Engineering and the Isthmian Canal*. New York: John Wiley & Sons, 1902.

Bury, J.B. *Cambridge Medieval History* Vol. II. New York: Macmillan Co., 1913.

——. *History of the Later Roman Empire* (2 vols). New York: Dover Edition, 1958.

Butler, R.M. 'The Roman Walls of Le Mans', *Journal of Roman Studies* 48, 1958, pp. 33–9. Doi: 10.2307/298210

Campbell, Duncan. *Greek and Roman Siege Machinery 399* BC-AD *363*. Oxford: Osprey, 2003.

——. *Siege Warfare in the Roman World 146* BC-AD *378*. Oxford: Osprey, 2005.

——. *Roman Legionary Fortresses 27* BC-AD *378*. Oxford: Osprey, 2006.

——. *Roman Auxiliary Forts 27* BC-AD *378*. Oxford: Osprey, 2009.

Cantor, Norman (ed.). *The Encyclopedia of the Middle Ages*. New York: Viking. 1999.

Carey, Brian. *Warfare in the Medieval World*. Barnsley: Pen & Sword, 2006.

'CATHARES: Les forteresses de l'Hérésie', *Pyrénées Magazine*. Milan Presse, 2002.

Chadych, Danielle. *Paris: The Story of the Great City*. London: Andre Deutsch Ltd., 2014.

Chant, Christopher. *Castles*. Edison (NJ): Chartwell Books, 2008.

Chapman, Charles E. *A History of Spain founded on the Historia de Espana y de la civilizacion espanola of Rafael Altamira*. New York: Macmillan Company, 1918 (ebook reprint).

Chatelain, André. *Chateaux Forts images de pierre des guerres medievales*. Paris: Rempart 1983.

——. *Architecutre Militaire Medievale: principes elementaires*. Paris: Rempart, 1970.

Christie, Neil and Hajnalka Herold. *Fortified Settlements in Early Medieval Europe: Defended Communities of the 8th and 10th Centuries*. Oxford: Oxbow Books, 2016.

Cirelli, Enrico. 'Ravenna – Rise of a Late Antique Capital', *Debating Urbanism Within and Beyond the Walls* AD *300 -700*. Leicester Archaeology Monograph 17. Univ. of Leicester: 15 Nov. 2008

Connolly, Peter. *Greece and Rome at War*. London: Macdonald Phoebus, 1981.

Couvin, André. *Découvrir la France Cathare*. France: Nouvelles Editions Marabout, 1978.

Cowper, Marcus. *Cathar Castles: Fortresses of the Albigensian Crusade 1209-1300*. Oxford: Osprey, 2006.

Creveld, Martin van. *Technology and War*. New York: The Free Press, 1989.

Dass, Nirmal (ed., trans.). *Viking Attacks on Paris: The Bella parisiacae urbis of Abbo of Saint-Germain-des-Prés*. Paris: Peeters, 2007.

Davis, Philip. 'English Licences to Crenellate: 1199-1567' (PDF), *The Castle Studies Group Journal* 20, 2006–2007, pp. 226–45.

Delbrück, Hans. *History of the Art of War: The Barbarian Invasions*. Lincoln (Neb.): Univ. of Nebraska Press, 1980.

——. *History of the Art of War: Medieval Warfare*. Lincoln (Neb.) Univ of Nebraska Press, 1980.

Dennis, George T. (trans.). *Maurice's Strategikon*. Philadelphia: Univ. of Penn., 1984.

Dept. of the Environment. *Tower of London*. London: HMSO, 1967.

Devèze, Lily. *The City of Carcassonne*. France: J. Bardou, n.d.

DeVries, Kelly, et al. *Battles of the Medieval World. 1000-1500*. New York: Barnes & Noble, 2006.

Donnelly, Mark P. and Daniel Diehl. *Siege: Castles at War*. Dallas: Taylor Publishing, 1998.

Edwards, Owen. *A Short History of Wales*. London: T. Fisher Unwin Ltd., 1922 (reprint of 1906) (2016 ebook).

Elton, Hugh. *Warfare in Roman Europe* AD *350-425*. Oxford: Oxford Univ. Press, 1997.

Embleton, Ronald and Frank Graham. *Hadrian's Wall in the Days of the Romans*. New York: Barnes & Noble, 1984.

Enaud, François. *The Château of Vincennes*. Paris: Caisse Nationale des Monuments Historiques, 1965.

Erlande-Brandenburg, Alain. *Cathedrals and Castles: Building in the Middle Ages*. New York: Harry N. Abrams Publishers, 1993.

Faucon, Regis and Yves Lescroart. *Manor Houses in Normandy*. Paris: Ullmann, 1995,

Fazzini, Paolo and Marina Maffei. 'The disappearance of the city of Luni', *Journal of Cultural Heritage*, 2000, pp. 247–60.

Ferrill, Arther. *The Fall of the Roman Empire: The Military Explanation*. London: Thames & Hudson, 1986.

Fields, Nic. *Hadrian's Wall* AD *122-410*. Oxford: Osprey, 2003.

——. *Rome's Northern Frontier* AD *70-235* Oxford: Osprey, 2005.

——. *Rome's Saxon Shore* Oxford: Osprey, 2006.

——. *The Walls of Rome*. Oxford: Osprey, 2008.

Friar, Stephen. *The Sutton Companion to Castles*. Stroud: Sutton, 2007.

Gies, Joseph & Frances. *Life in a Medieval Castle*. New York: Harper & Row, 1979.

Goodall, John. *The English Castle 1066-1650*. New Haven: Yale Univ. Press, 2011.

Grabois, Aryeh. *The Illustrated Encyclopedia of Medieval Civilization*. New York: Octopus, 1980.

Grant, Michael. *The Army of the Caesars*. New York: Scribners and Sons, 1974.

——. *The Roman Emperors*. New York: Barnes & Noble, 1985.

Gravett, Christopher. *Medieval Siege Warfare*. Oxford: Osprey, 1996.

——. *Norman Stone Castles (1) Europe 1066-1216*. Oxford: Osprey, 2003.

——. *Norman Stone Castles (2) Europe 950-1204*. Oxford: Osprey, 2004.

Gregorovius, Ferdinand and Annie Hamilton (trans.). *History of the City of Rome in the Middle Ages* Vol. IV, Part I. London: George Bell & Sons, 1896.

Gregory of Tours and Lewis Thorpe (trans.). *The History of the Franks*. New York: Penguin Books, 1974.

Griffith, Paddy. *The Viking Art of War*. London: Greenhill Books, 1995.

Guadalupi, Gianni and Gabriele Reina. *Castles of the World*. New York: Metro Books, 2013.

Hackett, John (ed.). *Warfare in the Ancient World*. New York: Facts on File, 1989.

Halle, Guy le. *Précis de la fortification*. Paris: PCV Editions, 1983.

Halsall, Guy. *Warfare and Society in the Barbarian West 450-900*. New York: Routledge, 2008.

Haywood, John. *Historical Atlas of the Vikings*. London: Penguin, 1995.

Heath, Ian. *Armies of the Dark Ages 600-1066*. England: Wargames Research Group, 1976.

——. *Armies of the Middle Ages*, Vol. 1. England: Wargames Research Group, 1982.

Higham, Robert and Philip Barker. *Timber Castles*. Mechanicsburg (PA): Stackpole, 1995.

Hill, Brian E. *Charles the Bald's 'Edict of Pîtres' (864): A Translation and Commentary*. University of Minnesota: MA Thesis, 2013.

Hishop, Malcolm. *How to Read Castles*. London: Bloomsbury Publishing, 2013.

——. *Castle Builders*. Barnsley: Pen & Sword, 2016.

Hodgkin, Thomas. *Italy and Her Invaders: The imperial restoration, 535-553*. Oxford: Henry Frowde, 1895.

Hooper, Nicholas and Matthew Bennett. *Cambridge Illustrated Atlas: Warfare, The Middle Ages 768-1487*. New York: Cambridge Univ. Press, 1996.

Hughes, Ian. *Belsarius: The Last Roman General*. Barnsley: Pen & Sword, 2014.

Jefferson, Samuel. *The History and Antiquities of Carlisle*. London: Whittaker & Co., 1838.

Johnson, Stephen. *Late Roman Fortifications*. Totowa (NJ): Barnes & Noble, 1983.

Jones, Dan. *The Plantagenets*. New York: Viking. 2012.

Jones, Gwyn. *A History of the Vikings*. New York: Oxford Univ. Press, 1968.

Jotischky, Andrew and Caroline Hull. *The Penguin Historical Atlas of the Medieval World*. London: Penguin Books, 2005.

Kaufmann, J.E. and H.W. *The Medieval Fortress*. Mechanicsburg (PA): Combined Publishing, 2001.

Keen, Maurice (ed.). *Medieval Warfare: A History.* New York: Oxford Univ. Press, 1999.

Konstam, Angus. *British Forts in the Age of Arthur.* Oxford: Osprey, 2008.

LaMonte, John L. *The World of the Middle Ages: A Reorientation of Medieval History.* New York: Appleton-Century-Crofts, 1949.

Lavelle, Ryan. *Fortifications in Wessex c. 800-1066.* Oxford: Osprey, 2003.

Le Bohec, Yann. *The Imperial Roman Army.* New York: Hippocrene Books, 1994.

Le Goff, Jacques and Julia Barrow (trans.). *Medieval Civilization 400-1500.* New York: Basil Blackwell Ltd. 1988.

Lebedel, Claude. *La tragédie des Cathares.* Rennes: Editions Ouest-France, 1998.

Lee, Sidney (ed.). *Dictionary of National Biography.* London: Smith, Elder, & Co, 1896 (multi-volume).

Lepage, Jean-Denis. *The Fortifications of Paris: An Illustrated History.* Jefferson (NC): McFarland & Co., 2006.

Lewis, Archibald Ross. *The Development of Southern French and Catalan Society 718-1050.* Austin: Univ. of Texas Press (The Library of Iberian Resources Online), 1965.

Line, Philip. *The Vikings and Their Enemies.* New York: Skyhorse Publishing 2015.

Marcellinus, Ammianus and Charles Yonge (trans.). *The Later Roman Empire* AD *354-378.* Didactic Press, 2014.

Marren, Peter. *Battles of the Dark Ages: British Battlefields* AD *410 to 1065.* Barnsley: Pen & Sword, 2006.

Matteini, Nevio. *The Republic of San Marino.* San Marino: Azienda Tipografica Editoriale, 1981.

Mawer, Allen and William Corbett. *Cambridge Medieval History (Book XII).* E-book. Perennial Press, 2016 (reprint).

McLynn, Frank. *Richard and John: Kings at War.* Cambridge (MA): Da Capo, 2008.

Mesqui, Jean. *Les châteaux forts: De la guerre à la paix.* Italy: Decouvertes Gallimard Architecture, 1995.

——. *Château Forts et fortifications en France.* Paris: Flammarion, 1997.

Miller, William. 'The Republic of San Marino', *American Historical Review.* Vol. VI, No. 4, July 1901, pp. 633–49.

Milner, N.P. (trans.). *Vegetius: Epitome of Military Science.* Liverpool: Liverpool University Press, 1993.

Mommsen, Theodor. *The Provinces of the Roman Empire: The European Provinces.* Chicago: Univ. of Chicago Press, 1968.

Nicholson, Helen. *Medieval Warfare: Theory and Practice of War in Europe 300-1500.* New York: Palgrave Macmillan, 2005.

Nicolle, David. *Medieval Warfare Source Book* (Vols 1 and 2). London: Arms & Armour, 1995.

——. *Medieval Siege Weapons (1): Western Europe* AD *585-1385.* Oxford: Osprey, 2002.

Nobile, Marco. *Bracciano: The Odescalchi Castle and its History.* Terni: Plurgraf, 1990.

Norman, Vesey. *Medieval Soldier.* Barnsley: Pen & Sword, 2010.

Nossov, Konstantin. *Ancient and Medieval Siege Weapons.* Guilford (Ct): The Lyons Press, 2005.

Official Guide to Windsor Castle. London: HMSO, 1980 (reprint of 1949 ed).

Oldenbourg, Zoe. *Massacre at Montségur: History of the Albigensian Crusade.* London: Phoenix, 2006 (reprint of 1961 version).

Oman, Charles. *A History of the Art of War in the Middle Ages* (Vols 1 and 2). London: Greenhill, 1924.

——. *Castles.* New York: Beekman House, 1978.

——. *The Dark Ages 476-918* AD. Pyrrhus Press, 2014 (e-book reprint of 1893 ed.)

Ordericus Vitalis and Thomas Forester (trans.). *The Ecclesiastical History of England and Normandy* (Vols I, II & II). London: Harry Bohn, 1854.

D'Orsi, Mario. *Castel Sant'Angelo* (guide book). Rome: National Military and Art Museum, 1968.

Panouille, Jean-Pierre. *Carcassonne: Le temps des sièges (Patrimoine au présent)*. Paris: Presses du CNRS, 1992.

———. *Carcassonne: History and Architecture*. Rennes: Editions Ouest-France, 1999.

Parker, Henry Michael D. *The Roman Legions*. New York: Dorset Press, 1992 (reprint of 1928 ed.).

Paris, Mathew, and Rev. J.A. Giles (Trans.). *English History From to 1235-1273* (3 vols). London: Henry G. Bohn, 1854. Digitalized: https://archive.org/stream/matthewparisseng01pari#page/n5/mode/2up

Paris, Mathew, and H.R. Luard (ed.) *Chronica Majora*. London: Longman & Co., 1876. Digitalized https://archive.org/stream/matthiparisien03pari#page/n9/mode/2up

Parment, Roger. *The Castle of Robert the Devil*. Rouen: Imp. A Vallée, n.d.

Paulus, Diaconus and William D. Foulke (trans.). *History of the Langobards*. Philadelphia: Univ. of Penn., 1974 (reprint of 1907 edition).

Peping, Eugène. *Chinon son château ses églises*. Paris: J. Lanore, n.d.

Pérez Garcia, Victor Lluis. 'Late Roman and Visigothic Fortifications in Conventus Tarraconensis (Hispania): The Organization of Border Defence', *Aqvila Legionis*. Madrid: Signifer, 2012, pp. 165–202

Phillips, Alan. *Castles and Fortifications of Wales*. Stroud: Amberley Publishing, 2013 (ebook).

Platt, Colin. *The Castle in Medieval England & Wales*. New York: Barnes & Noble, 1996.

Previté-Orton, C.W. *The Shorter Cambridge Medieval History, Volume 1, The Later Roman Empire to the Twelfth Century*. Cambridge: 1979 (reprint of 1952 ed.).

Procter, Colonel George. *The History of Italy, From the Fall of the Western Empire to the commencement of the Wars of the French Republic*. London: Whittaker & Co. 1844.

Prokopios and H.B. Dewing (trans.). *The Wars of Justinian*. Indianapolis: Hackett Publishing Co., 2014.

Purton, Peter. *A History of the Early Medieval Siege c. 450 – 1200*. Woodbridge: Boydell Press, 2010.

Quehen, René. *Peyrepertuse et San-Jordy: Guide du Visiteur*. Toulouse: La PHIM, 1979.

Raffa, Enzio. *San Gimignano: The Town with Beautiful Towers* (guidebook). Italy: Brunello Granelli's Edition, n.d.

Rees, William. *Caerphilly Castle and its place in the Annals of Glamorgan*. Cambridge: D. Brown & Sons, 1974 (reprint of 1937 ed.).

———. *Cardiff Castle: Illustrated Handbook*. London: Cardiff Parks Dept, n.d.

Richmond, Ian A. *The City Wall of Imperial Rome*. Yardley (PA): Westholme, 2013 (e-book reprint of 1931 ed.).

Rigold, S.E. *Portchester Castle*. London: HMSO, 1965.

Robinson, James Harvey. *Readings in European History* (vol 1). Boston: Ginn & Co., 1904.

Roquebert, Michel and Christian Soula. *Citadelles du Vertiges*. Toulouse: Edouard Privat, 1972.

Rowling, Marjorie. *Everyday Life in Medieval Times*. New York: Dorset Press, 1968.

Saalman, Howard. *Medieval Cities*. New York: George Braziller, 1968.

Sancha, Sheila. *The Castle Story*. New York: Penguin Books, 1979.

Santosusso, Antonio. *Barbarians, Marauders and Infidels*. Cambridge: Westview, 2004.

Sarantis, Alexander and Neil Christie. *War and Warfare in Late Antiquity*. Leiden (Netherlands) Brill, 2013.

Savage, Anne (trans.). *The Anglo Saxon Chronicles*. New York: St. Martin's, 1983.

Sawyer, Peter. *Kings and Vikings*. New York: Methuen & Co. Ltd, 1982.

——. *The Oxford Illustrated History of the Vikings*. New York: Oxford Univ. Press, 1997.

Scholz, Bernhard Walter (trans.). *Carolingian Chronicles: Royal Frankish Annals and Nithard's Histories*. Ann Arbor: Univ. of Michigan Press, 1970.

Sciotti, Lamberto and Adriana Nastri. *Sermoneta*. Italy: EuroStampa, 1989.

Scudamore, Cyril. *Normandy*. London: Methuen & Co., 1906.

Sergeant, Lewis. *The Franks*. New York: Waxkeep Publishing, 2014 (reprint of 1898 ed.).

Sibly, W.A. (trans.) and M.D. Sibly (trans). *The Chronicle of William of Puylaurens*. Woodbridge (UK): Boydell, 2003. ('The Siege of Toulouse in 1217-18, according to The Chronicle of William of Puylaurens'. De Rem Militari (Society for Medieval Military History) posted 24 March 2014.) http://deremilitari.org/2014/03/the-siege-of-toulouse-in-1217-18-according-to-the-chronicle-of-william-of-puylaurens/

Snow, Dan. *Battle Castles: 500 Years of Knights and Siege Warfare*. London: Harper Press, 2012.

Stubbs, William. *Chronica magistri Rogeri de Houedene*. London: Longmans, 1868 (www.archive.org/details/chronicamagistri).

Syndicat d'Initiative Fougères. *Notice sur le Chateau de Fougères*. Fougères: La Chronique de Fougères, nd.

Tacitus and W. Hamilton Fyfe (trans.). *The Histories*. Oxford: Clarendon Press, 1912.

Toy, Sidney. *Castles: Their Construction and History*. New York: Dover Publications, 1985 (reprint of 1939 ed.).

Tracy, James D. (ed.). *City Walls: The Urban Enceinte in Global Perspective*. New York: Cambridge University Press, 2000.

Turk, Sofia. 'The defensive system of the late Roman *limes* between Germania Secunda and Britannia'. Masters Thesis: Universita Ca Foscari Venezia, 2012.

Viollet-le-Duc, Eugène-Emmanuel. *Dictionnaire raisonné de l'architecture française du XI au XVI siècle*. Paris: Edition Bance – Morel of 1854 to 1868 (https://fr.wikisource.org/wiki/Dictionnaire_raisonné_de_l'architecture_française_du_XIe_au_XVIe_siècle).

Viollet-le-Duc, E.E. and M. Macdermott (trans.). *An Essay on the Military Architecture of the Middle Ages*. London: J.H. and J. Parker, 1860.

——. *Castles and Warfare in the Middle Ages*. Mineola (NY): Dover Publications, 2005 (reprint of 1860 ed.).

——. *Military Architecture*. London: Greenhill, 1990.

Ward, John. *The Roman Fort of Gellygaer in the Country of Glamorgan*. London: Bemrose & Sons, 1903.

Warner, Philip. *Sieges of the Middle Ages*. London: G. Bell and Sons, 1968.

——. *The Medieval Castle*. New York: Barnes & Noble 1993 (reprint of 1971 ed.).

Warry, John. *Warfare in the Classical World*. New York: St. Martin's Press, 1980.

Webster, Graham. *The Roman Imperial Army*. Totowa (NJ): Barnes & Noble Books, 1985.

Wenzler, Claude. *Architecture du Château Fort*. Rennes: Editions Ouest-France, 1997.

Williams, Geoffrey. *The Iron Age Hill Forts of England: A Visitor's Guide*. Great Britain: Images Malvern, 1993.

Wilson, Roger. *Roman Forts: An Illustrated Introduction to the Garrison Posts of Roman Britain*. London: Bergstrom & Boyle, 1980.

Wood, Michael. *In Search of the Dark Ages*. New York: Facts on File, 1987.

Woodward, B.B. and William Cates. *Encyclopaedia of Chronology*. London: Longmans, Green and Co., 1872.

Zosimus (translated by anonymous). *New History*. London: Oxford, 1814.

Index

Page numbers in *italics* refer to illustrations.